CHINA PAINT & OVERGLAZE

by Paul Lewing

CHINA PAINT & OVERGLAZE

by Paul Lewing

Published by

The American Ceramic Society
735 Ceramic Place, Suite 100
Westerville, Ohio 43081

www.ceramics.org

The American Ceramic Society

735 Ceramic Place, Suite 100

Westerville, Ohio 43081

© 2007 by The American Ceramic Society

All rights reserved.

11 10 09 08 07   5 4 3 2 1

ISBN: 1-57498-269-9

Graphic Design and Production : Melissa Bury, Bury Design, Westerville, Ohio
Editor/Project Manager: Bill Jones

Cover: (top) "Grapes" by F.B. Aulich. Photo courtesy of Betty Burbank. (center) "Life Science" by Kurt Weiser, (bottom) "Shipwreck" by Paul Lewing.

Frontispiece: "Lily in Wedgwood Style" by Marcia Stivelman

Printed in China

Dedication

China painting is to women what poker is to men.
—Carrie Scott Harrison, New York Tribune, November 13, 1888

For Rudy, my teacher.
For Dave, my hero.
For Ruth, my true love.

Acknowledgments

Hundreds of people have contributed facts, tips, and contacts to the compilation of this book, and I wish I had space to thank each of them individually. However, a few individuals and organizations deserve special recognition.

Barbara Henderson got me started. Suzanne Hieb (Willoughby's Colors & Supplies), Jeanne Valentine (*The China Decorator*), Melody and Jeanette Gulikson (Colorific Porcelain), Arbra Corriea (Sonie Ames' daughter), and Rosemarie Radmaker all knew far more than they thought they did. The Seattle Public Library was absolutely indispensable throughout the process.

Gene Patterson, Barbara Henderson, John Hesselberth, Edouard Bastarache, Monona Rossol, Marci Blattenberger, Erik "The Lab Rat" Wagg, and Jon Singer reviewed parts of the text. Any mistakes that remain are entirely mine.

Pictures for the history chapters came from Seattle Art Museum, the Art Gallery of Greater Victoria, the President Benjamin Harrison House (Jennifer Capps, Curator), World Organization of China Painters Museum (Mary Early, Curator), Judy Chicago and her Through the Flower Foundation, and Frank Lloyd Gallery. Collectors who generously agreed to the publication of images include Cherryl Meggs, Jean and Roger Helm, Betty Burbank, Marci Blattenberger, John Baymore, Sam and Dianne Scott, and Ann Cline.

It has been my privilege to be part of two remarkable online communities, Clayart and Porcelain Painters International Online. Someone in these forums knows the answer to every question, and I relied heavily on that. Special thanks go to their respective moderators, Mel Jacobson (Clayart) and Marci Blattenberger and Betty Gerstner (PPIO).

All of the artists who sent pictures of their work for the book deserve my gratitude for making this however good a book it is. But those five who agreed to be interviewed for the profiles have earned special mention: Russell Coates, Barbara Jensen, Celeste McCall, Kurt Weiser, and André van de Putte.

I'm grateful to the American Ceramic Society for asking me to do this book, to Bill Jones for being my editor, and to Melissa Bury for her outstanding design work.

Without Marci Blattenberger's expertise, support, and contacts, this would be a far poorer book. The astounding generosity of Mel Jacobson, through the ACerS Clayart Fund and the Clay It Forward program brought tears to my eyes. Without him, there would be almost no pictures in the first history chapter.

My wife Ruth has lived through every moment of triumph, disappointment, anger and glee that this project has generated in three and a half years. I can never thank her enough for her patience and understanding.

The one person who deserves to be most singled out for gratitude is my proofreader and unofficial editor. I would never have agreed to start this project without the help of my very close friend Fred Sweet.

Contents

Preface

I came to china painting from the world of studio ceramics, but I was a painter first. I started painting with oils when I was eight, and sold my first painting at ten. Throwing on the wheel seduced me away from painting, but not for long. My pots soon became as much about painting as pottery could be. When I quit throwing to concentrate on tile murals in 1986, china paint attracted me with its brilliant color, fine detail, and quick firings.

I have never had any lessons in china painting, so I have always done a lot of things "wrong," especially in my commitment to water-soluble mediums. In writing this book, I have tried to cover the traditional methods and materials completely, while also detailing how I do things more unconventionally. I don't pretend to be an expert in the use of the more esoteric overglaze techniques, but I hope I've covered the basics well enough to get you started. I also hope I've encouraged artists to try overglazing and china painting in new ways. I believe the question should never be, "Will this work?" but rather, "How can I make this work?"

Those readers who are used to decorating with underglazes and glazes will need to embrace several new concepts to use china paints effectively. Once you get these, the medium becomes a real treat to use.

First, think of it as paint, not as glaze. Any effect you can achieve with any form of paint (oil, water, acrylic, or latex), or any kind of ink, you can achieve with china paint. You can have any shade, hue, or tone you desire, and you can tell before it's fired exactly what color it's going to be, with very few exceptions.

Second, it doesn't have to be finished in one firing. Many effects can only be developed slowly. There's no limit to how many times you can refire a china-painted piece. This medium, and this book, is based on the concept that the glaze firing is only an intermediate step in the creative process.

Third, you can wipe it off as easily as you can put it on. Once you get used to painting on a hard, slick surface, you'll find you can do things you can't do with any other medium.

This book differs from most books on china painting in that there are no studies to copy, and no lessons on color theory or design. I don't intend to tell anyone how or what to paint. What I have included, in as great a depth as I can manage, is a comprehensive telling of overglazing's long and fascinating history, and a serious study of the ceramic chemistry, with particular emphasis on color development and safety/durability issues.

The medium is ripe for another renaissance. It needs the raucous energy and freewheeling experimentation of the typical studio clay artist combined with the discipline, control, and technical mastery of the typical china painter. It needs new imagery, applied to new forms, with new techniques and materials.

Sadly, potters and china painters have had almost no contact since they both lost their factory jobs during the Industrial Revolution. While the two subcultures are very different, they have a lot to offer each other. It has been my privilege to be part of both families, and my greatest hope for this book is to be a bridge between the two.

Happy painting!
Paul Lewing
Seattle, Washington

Introduction

A Few Words About Words

Lots of people talk about forming and decorating clay, and they all use the same words. However, different groups mean completely different things by them. For instance, each group (potters, china painters, art historians, and the tile and dinnerware industries) has its own concept of what porcelain is, or what the difference between china paint and overglaze enamel is. Before we start talking about these, we need to be clear about what we mean.

Porcelain

Marco Polo may have been the first person to refer to the white pots from China as *porcellana,* the Italian name for a translucent white seashell[1]. Or he may have just been the first to write it down. Regardless, in his day there was only one substance of its kind, and only one group of people anywhere who knew how to make it. There hasn't been that kind of agreement since.

The American Ceramic Society's *Ceramic Glossary* (1984) defines porcelain as "a glazed or unglazed vitreous whiteware used for technical purposes." Frank and Janet Hamer's *Potter's Dictionary of Materials and Techniques* (1997) says it's "a vitrified, white and translucent ware…fired at 2380°F (1300°C, or Orton cone 10) plus."

This is what potters mean by the word "porcelain." It has to be white; it has to be high-fired; and it has to be translucent.

China painters refer to three kinds of porcelain: hard-paste, bone china, and soft-paste. Hard-paste is fired to 2300–2372°F (1260–1300°C);

Bridget Chérie Harper, "Predator," china paint on porcelain, 14½" x 8" x 5", 2002. *Photo: Tony Aquilino.*

1

Cindy Kolodziejski, "Pearl Necklace," earthenware, china paint, 17″ x 6″ x 5″, 1999. Courtesy of Frank Lloyd Gallery. *Photo: Anthony Cuñha.*

bone china to 2156–2192°F (1180–1200°C); and soft-paste to 1832–2012°F (1000–1100°C). This means hard-paste would be fired to Orton cone 10-12, bone china to Orton cone 5–7, and soft-paste to Orton cone 06–01. Today's studio potters would consider hard-paste to be true porcelain, but are reluctant to call any clay fired to cone 6 or below porcelain, and would never refer to bone

china as porcelain. All three substances are white, but soft-paste porcelain is not usually translucent.

Art historians tend to refer to all three varieties as porcelain, without distinction. Occasionally, they might make a distinction between porcelain and bone china, but not between hard-paste and soft-paste. If they make a distinction as to clay body, it is often a trade name, such as Parian porcelain.

The tile manufacturers' trade group in the US, the Tile Council of America, also has a definition of porcelain. It requires only that the absorbency rate be lower than 0.5%. In effect, this demands firing to a high temperature, but no specific cone number is standard. Note that there is no mention of color or translucency. One of their most popular products these days is porcelain tile that mimics stone of all kinds. Consequently, there are tiles referred to as "porcelain" which have the same color and opacity as granite, marble, sandstone, slate, or travertine. No potter or china painter would consider any of these to be porcelain, although they would admit that porcelain could be colored intentionally.

Most people, regardless of their field of expertise, will acknowledge that the essential clay in porcelain is kaolin, but, in some fields, there may even be some confusion about this term. The main test used by mineralogists to distinguish one clay mineral from another is X-ray-diffraction. This test detects no difference between kaolin, ball clay, and fire clay, recognizing all three as b-axis-disordered kaolinite. Potters know there are huge differences.

Ceramic

If it's not porcelain, then it's ceramic. This is true in the lexicons of china painters and tile manufacturers, but not in those of potters and art historians. However, I have seen china painting texts that refer to everything other than porcelain as "pottery," including building facades. Neither potters nor art historians would ever use that terminology. To

them, "pottery" is invariably vessel-related.

To art historians, and even more so to potters, the definition of the word "ceramic" has more nuances than that. The Hamers define "ceramics" as "clay products made permanent by heat." The American Ceramic Society, serving ceramic engineers and materials scientists as well as clay artists, has an even broader definition. For them, any material that is neither organic nor metallic is ceramic. Until recently, they also defined "ceramic" as clay-based, but today's high-tech ceramic materials often have no clay at all involved in their manufacture.

To potters, if it's not porcelain, then it must be some other kind of clay, all of which is ceramics. Consequently, they refer to non-porcelain work as stoneware, earthenware, terra cotta, and so on.

Art historians also are usually more specific when describing clay. They will sometimes describe clay bodies that are similar to porcelain as "proto-porcelain" or "porcellanous stoneware." Or they will sometimes use trade names like "Creamware," "Parian porcelain," or "Jasperware."

In the tile industry, tile that is not porcelain is ceramic tile. By this they mean that it does not meet the industry standard for "impervious," i.e., that its absorbency rate is more than 0.5%. I have even heard tile showrooms refer to this more porous tile, whether glazed or not, as "bisque."

China

Because it was invented in China, all vitreous whiteware came to be known in Europe as "china," regardless of its form or function. Today, both potters and china painters mean fine white tableware when they refer to china. Whether the material is soft porcelain, hard porcelain, or bone china, the defining quality of "china" is its use in the serving of food. Neither of these groups would call sculpture made of the same materials china.

The tile industry never uses the term "china" for any of its products. However, manufactured

Linda Lighton, "Diva I," clay, glaze, china paint, lusters, 19" x 10" x 7". *Photo: E. G. Schempf.*

sinks are designated as either porcelain or "vitreous china." This term refers to a clay body, which is slightly coarser than porcelain, and not nearly as white. Potters might call this clay body white stoneware or porcellanous clay.

One unfortunate result of the word's usage in reference to overglazing is that a library or internet search for "china paint" will yield masses of infor-

Richard Milette (Canada) "Teapot," ceramic, decals, lusters, 6¾" high, 1992. *Photo: Raymonde Bergeron.*

mation about wall coating materials in East Asia, and very little about ceramic overglazes.

Bisque

To china painters, "bisque" means unglazed fired clay. It may be fired to the maturing temperature of the clay, or not. Glenn Nelson's *Ceramics; A Potter's Handbook* also defines bisque as "unglazed ware."

Art historians use the word to mean the same thing. For instance, I have seen references to "a porcelain sculpture on a bisque base." The piece in question was obviously all one piece, but only part of it was glazed.

Many clay artists, particularly British artists, use the term interchangeably with "biscuit," although Hamer and Hamer make a distinction. They also define "bisque" as "unglazed fired pottery," but go on to state that "bisc" and "biscuit" are "used to imply the industrial method of a high temperature firing of the unglazed ware to be followed by a lower temperature glaze firing." However, they state, in regard to the term "biscuit," "individual potters imply the use of a temperature lower than the following glaze firing." In America, this is most potters' definition of the word "bisque," while "biscuit" is almost never used in any ceramic context.

Another group of people who use the term

Paula Collins, "Oval Grape Tile," 18" x 13".

"bisque" to mean something entirely different are chefs, but that's a different kettle of soup.

China Paint/Overglaze Enamel

The term "china paint" seems to have first come into general use in the early 20th century, when the decorating of ceramic objects became a hugely popular individual pastime, independent of factory production. It was not until its revival in popularity in the 1950's and 1960's that "china paint" became the more common terminology.

Until that time, the term "overglaze enamel" usually described all forms of colors melting at approximately Orton cone 018–015, and fired onto an already fired glaze. For art-historians, this is still the most prevalent usage.

Today, some make a distinction between china paint, which they define as being translucent, and overglaze enamel, which is opaque. Amaco's® product called Versacolor™ is an example of an overglaze enamel by this definition.

But china painters use the term "enamel" today to mean something slightly different. What they buy from china paint suppliers as "enamel" is a more refractory, opaque product that is applied very thickly, resulting in a raised surface. As late as 1915, *Keramic Studio* magazine was referring to this thicker material as "raised enamel," while referring to all other forms of overglaze color as "flat enamel."

"China paint" and "overglaze enamel" are not the only terms used to describe this substance, however. "Mineral paints," "mineral colors," "vitrifiable colors," "polychrome enamels," and "vitreous enamels" are all terms I have seen in art history books. I have, in fact, seen pictures of pieces from the same factory and time period, which were virtually indistinguishable in appearance, designated by two or three of these terms on the same page. "Polychrome" is a particularly nebulous term,

which means only "having many colors." It does nothing to describe material or technique.

"Onglaze decoration" is another term that is sometimes used to describe china painting, but more often it refers to the process of painting on an unfired glaze layer, as in the majolica technique. Others may use the term "inglaze decoration" to describe this process, particularly at higher temperatures. When viewing pictures of painted work, it is sometimes almost impossible to tell which definition the author is using.

Sometimes the issue is even more confused, as when Taxile Doat often uses the words "enamel' and "glaze" interchangeably, even when referring to high-fired work.

Many artists who work in this medium prefer not to be called "china painters" at all, but rather "porcelain artists." This is a result of their desire to be seen as fine artists, rather than mere decorators. To potters, the term "porcelain artist" would invariably evoke the image of someone who formed their artwork from porcelain, regardless of how it was finished.

What I Mean by the Words

In this book, I intend to use the terms "china paint," "overglaze," and "overglaze enamel" interchangeably, except in those sections where I am referring specifically to distinct products now on the market. In those instances, I will use the terms as those who market and work with them do.

Being a former potter, I will use the words "porcelain," "china" and "ceramic" as potters do. The word "bisque" will refer to unglazed fired clay of any kind, regardless of whether the firing was to The maturing point of the clay or lower.

Throughout this book, I will cover only those materials and processes that are fired to a temperature below Orton cone 014.

We spend our days looking for the secret of life. Well, the secret of life is art.
I find it harder and harder to live up to my blue china.

—Oscar Wilde

The History of Porcelain and Overglaze Decoration

1000 AD TO THE INDUSTRIAL REVOLUTION

China

Imagine that first porcelain pot. Imagine the potter taking that first porcelain pot out of his kiln, warm after the kiln has cooled for days. It has finally worked—after years, generations even—of prospecting, mining, grinding, mixing, processing, forming—years of testing firing methods, clay formulations and glazes, resulting only in piles of landfill.

But this time there's no cracking, no slumping, and no bloating. This time the potter has a kiln load of pots made of an entirely new substance. They glow when the light hits them, they're watertight, and they ring when they're tapped. And they're WHITE!

This happened some time during the Sòng Dynasty in northern China, about 1000 AD, just before the imperial court was forced to flee south ahead of Genghis Khan's army of Mongol saddle bums. Porcelain production started again during the Southern Sòng Dynasty between 1127 and 1279, but its greatest development began in the early Ming Dynasty, after the porcelain factories at Jingdezhen in Kiangsi Province became an official enterprise of the emperors in the 14th century.

Porcelain has been produced in volume at Jingdezhen since the 11th century, after the requisite materials, kaolin (a white plastic clay) and *petuntse* (a feldspathic material similar to Cornwall Stone), were discovered nearby.

A couple of other technological developments had to be achieved before pure white high-temperature porcelain was possible. First was the invention of the climbing kiln. This was a long chamber built on a slope, which essentially turned the whole kiln into a chimney and created enough draft to achieve temperatures above 2300°F (1260°C). This high heat was enough to melt any wood ash that accumulated on the pots during firing into a hard glossy sheen, which provided the starting point for glaze development. But this material was also limiting, in that it coated everything it contacted with a runny green-brown effect. To protect clear glazes from the fly ash and aid in stacking, *saggars* (closed fire clay boxes) were invented.

But no culture has ever been able to leave an undecorated surface alone for long, so potters began to paint on their porcelain. Their most notable achievement was painting in blue using cobalt oxide under a clear glaze, first with imported cobalt from the Middle East, then with domestic supplies. When the Fuliang factory was established in 1278 at Jiangzuo Yuan, not only was the cobalt from the Middle East, but many of the decorators as well. Certain of the designs and compositions are markedly Islamic in feel. However, throughout its history, China has periodically closed its borders to foreign trade, and from 1368 to 1398, this was the case. When the borders reopened in 1403, imported cobalt became available again. In the meantime, Chinese artisans had developed their own sources, as well as their own techniques and aesthetics.

The best pure white porcelain was made during the reign of Yung Lo (1403–1424) and the classic period of blue and white underglaze painting was during the reign of Hsuan Te (1426–1435). After the Wan Li period of the Ming Dynasty (1522–1619), the cobalt was smelted rather than simply washed, resulting in an even purer blue underglaze.

Middle Eastern cobalt was preferable to Chinese because it was lower in manganese, and was therefore a truer, less purple, blue. It was imported in a form known as *smalt*, a frit made by melting silica, potash and cobalt oxide, which was then ground to a fine powder. The source material for the cobalt was smaltite, a mineral compound of cobalt, nickel and arsenic, primarily from the Badakshan area of Afghanistan. Cobalt had been used as a colorant for glass as early as 1500 BC in the Amarna region of Egypt. Chinese potters were also using two other metal oxides as underglaze painting media, iron and copper, both of which had disadvantages.

The color from iron oxide is very temperamental in its response to thickness of application and atmosphere. Not only does the color vary according to the degree of oxidation or reduction, but so does its fluxing power. In reduction, the iron becomes a flux and blurs into the clear glaze. Variations in the chemistry of the glaze itself also affect the color.

Copper is even more problematic. While iron varies from dark red to black, copper goes from red in reduction to green in oxidation, sometimes in different places on the same piece. It also varies with thickness, and has the added problem of volatility, which sometimes makes it disappear altogether.

Cobalt, though it is unaffected by atmosphere differences, and its variation with thickness is controllable and even usable, also has its limitation. It can only make shades of blue.

The high heat and reducing atmosphere of the wood-fired kilns destroyed a lot of colors, so potters turned to the use of overglaze enamels, which were fired onto the surface of the shiny clear glaze

in a later, lower temperature firing. However, the idea of a subsequent lower firing to achieve bright color was not a new idea. A similar technique was already in use on metal and glass, and that was probably where potters got the idea.

There is also some evidence that potters knew how to make high-fired clay before they worked out glazes that would mature in the same firing. For a time, they made pots of porcelain, fired them unglazed to vitrification, and then refired them at a lower temperature with the lead glazes they had been using on their earthenware. It is possible that the formulations for overglaze colors were based on these lead glazes, modified to melt at even lower temperatures. There are a few examples of overglaze enamel on stoneware in China as early as the 12th century.

About 1200 AD the first overglazes began to appear on porcelain, with red being first, then yellow and green. Iron red overglaze was really developed during the ban on foreign trade from 1368–1398. The reigns of Chia Ching and Wan Li (1522–1619) are considered the height of the *ducai*, or "joined" style, so named because of the incorporation of underglaze, glaze, and overglaze. Some sources differentiate between the ducai style and the slightly later and more elaborate "five-color" style. The five colors were the white of the body with clear glaze, the underglaze cobalt blue, and the red, yellow, and green overglazes.

When the Ming Dynasty ended in 1644, there was another period of political instability, which lasted several years and cut off the enormous Chinese export trade with Europe, the Middle East, and the rest of Asia. This was to have a huge effect on the history of porcelain and overglaze manufacture. The Portuguese had had a trading colony in Macao since 1557, and the Dutch began trading out of Batavia (Jakarta) in Indonesia in 1602. Between then and 1682, the Dutch East India Company carried over 16 million pieces of Chinese porcelain to Europe.

Sending porcelain to Europe on camels and horses over the Silk Road was inefficient, costly, and risky. But transporting it in sailing ships was an entirely different matter. Breakage was minimal once it was stowed in the holds, and its weight became an asset rather than a liability. Since it was not damaged by bilge water, it became the perfect heavy, high-profit ballast for a cargo of lightweight and delicate silk, sandalwood, spices, and lacquer wares. Jingdezhen became the largest industrial complex in the world, with thousands of kilns and hundreds of thousands of workers.

After the start of the Qing Dynasty in 1662, production of enameled porcelain resumed and new styles of decoration evolved. There was less reliance on underglaze blue as the basis for drawing, and more emphasis on areas of colored overglaze grounds setting off panels of enameled painting. Also, by this time a more complete palette of overglaze colors had been developed.

By the end of the Ming Dynasty, the output of private kilns had outstripped that of the imperial ones. However, overglaze enameling remained mostly an enterprise of the imperial court. During the reign of Kiangsi (1662–1722) a small amount of ware was made in Jingdezhen and taken to court painters in the Forbidden City in Beijing to be overglazed. It was there that contact with glass and metal artists inspired ceramic artists to develop new colors and styles. Most of the overglazes on the vast quantities of export porcelain were manufactured in Beijing and sent to Jingdezhen for application.

One style of overglaze enameling has come to be known as *famille verte*, in which shades of green enamel colored with copper oxide predominate. This was sometimes done against a black enamel background and referred to as *famille noire*. Slightly later, most notably during the reigns of Yung Cheng (1723–1735) and Ch'ien Lung (1736–1795), another color scheme known as *famille rose* predominated. This palette, which

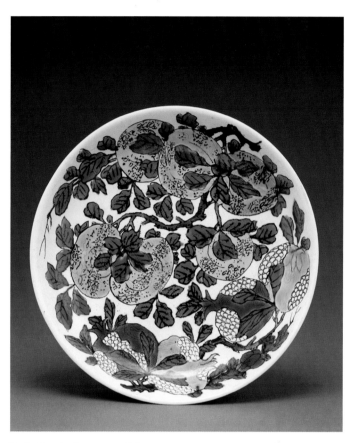

Dish, Jingdezhen ware, Ch'ing Dynasty, Kiangsi reign mark (c. 1680-88). Porcelain with incised, famille verte enameled decoration, 1¾" x 9¾." Seattle Art Museum, Eugene Fuller Memorial Collection. *Photo: Paul Macapia.*

incorporated new gold-based rose, opaque arsenic white, and lead/tin yellow, first appeared in Jingdezhen in 1720.

The changes in the chemical makeup of the enamels (see Chapter 7, "The Chemistry of China Paint") allowed stylistic changes as well. While the transparent famille verte colors had to rely on black outlining and stippling to model and accentuate form, the opaque famille rose palette could use color gradation and crisp highlights.

By this time, the interchange of styles, images, and colors between Asia and Europe was so intense

Dish, Export ware, Jingdezhen. Qing Dynasty, Yung Cheng period (1723–35). Porcelain with famille rose overglaze enamels, 1½" x 7¾." Seattle Art Museum, gift of Mrs. Thomas D. Stimson. *Photo: Paul Macapia.*

that these Chinese decorating styles are characterized by names given them by French collectors.

Much of what we know about porcelain production in Jingdezhen at this time comes from two letters written by a Jesuit missionary in 1712 and 1722. Père d'Entrecolles wrote in great detail to his superiors in France about the processes involved, but he knew nothing of ceramics. Had his keen observations been combined with even rudimentary knowledge, his letters might have provided more than tantalizing hints to European researchers. Even so, his descriptions of production methods were to have great influence on later European manufacturing.

After this period of the early Qing Dynasty, porcelain and overglaze enamel production in China only repeated and copied itself, and the cutting edge of innovation moved elsewhere.

The Middle East

Before the arrival of European sailing ships in Asia, there was so much interchange of ideas, materials, techniques and workers between China and the Middle East that is impossible to know exactly when or where the idea of refiring a ceramic object to achieve a bright color originated. Chinese potters knew how to make lead glazes of the same three colors as the first enamels, and were firing them to temperatures only slightly higher than overglazes. Middle Eastern craftsmen were accomplished metal enamelists and glass painters well before they began doing the same techniques on ceramic ware. It appears that Persian and Chinese potters discovered the principle of overglazing independently at about the same time.

Earthenware pots with overglaze enamel, from about the same era as the earliest Chinese overglazes (late 12th century), were made at Rayy and Sultanabad in Persia. Two kinds are known, one on a white glaze and the other in black, red, and white enamel on a blue background.

These were the best of the region's potters at this time, the Seljuks, who conquered Turkey in 1071. Their clay body was not porcelain, but a fritted body made of lead, soda, and lime. In addition to red, black, and gold overglaze, they used blue and turquoise underglaze. Their overglaze work, called Mina'i ware, was stylistically based on miniature paintings of humans and animals. The Seljuks also produced tiles with reduction luster glazes and overglazes of silver and copper oxides.

After the 14th century the most highly developed ceramic work was made in Turkey, in Kutahya and Iznik. It reached its peak during the reign of Suleyman the Magnificent (1520–1566) particularly with the potter Sah Kulu. The style faded in the 17th century and was almost gone by the 18th century, but it has been revived recently. It incorporates almost indistinguishable colors of overglaze and underglaze.

Japan

In the late 15th century, no one in Japan knew how to make porcelain, although they had seen and collected Chinese porcelains for almost two hundred years. The Shogun Hideyoshi Toyotomi, like many of the Japanese military and political leaders of his time, was an avid fancier of pottery.

So he launched the so-called Pottery Wars against Korea, with the express aim of capturing Korean potters and bringing them back to Japan to teach Japanese potters how to make porcelain. One of these Korean potters, Ri Sampei, found appropriate clay near Arita in Hizen Province in 1616. The earliest porcelain produced in Japan was from the nearby Karatsu kiln site. Between 1633 and 1639, Japanese imperial edicts banning trade with China and limiting contact with European and Southeast Asian outlets gave a huge impetus to the domestic Japanese porcelain industry.

Sambei Kanegae, as he came to be known, knew how to make porcelain, but he didn't know about overglaze. The Koreans had learned about porcelain from the Chinese, but did not use overglazes.

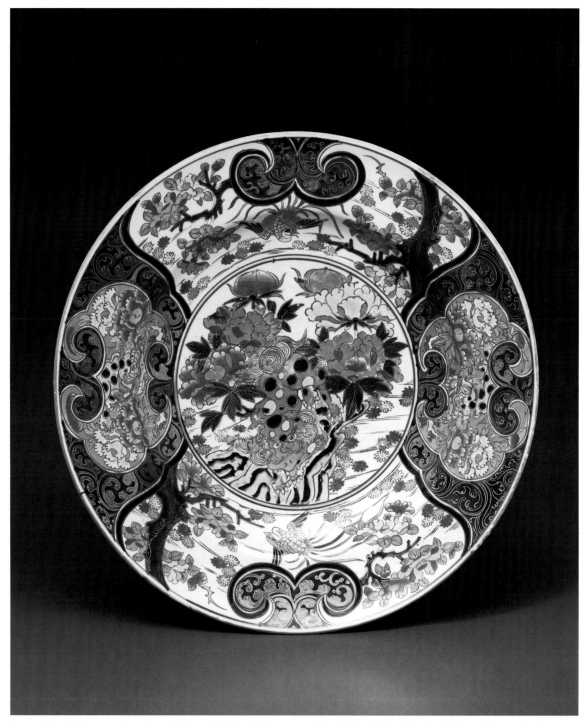

Large plate, Arita ware, Imari type, Edo period, late 17th century. Porcelain with underglaze blue and overglaze enamel, 3⅜" x 21¼." Seattle Art Museum, Floyd A. Naramore Memorial Purchase Fund & by exchange. *Photo: Paul Macapia.*

Barber Bowl, Imari. Porcelain with overglaze enamel, 2½" X 10⅜", late 17th century. Gift of Miss C. F. Hodgens. *Courtesy of Art Gallery of Greater Victoria, BC, Canada.*

Vietnamese and Thai potters had also learned how to make porcelain, but did only a little very simple overglazing.

A ceramics dealer, Tokuzaemon Tojima, in effect became an industrial spy, and learned how to make overglazes from Chou Chen-Kuan, a Chinese potter in Nagasaki. He then passed the secret on to Kakiemon Sakaida. In 1644, Kakiemon produced the first Japanese overglazed porcelain in his own unique style. Soon several other kilns and styles developed, most of them in the Arita area. Kakiemon ware featured red, green and blue overglaze used sparingly in an elegant pictorial style that became very popular in Europe. Its red was of a unique warm shade.

Between 1640 and 1650, most of the Arita kilns went from a Korean to a Chinese style of production, with more division of labor, and the quality of the ware improved markedly. In the 1670's, the Kakiemon factory developed a much finer and whiter porcelain body, which they formed with jigger wheels (a combination of throwing and molding).

Imari ware, named after the port from which it was shipped, was exported in huge quantities, especially through the Dutch East India Company. It had an underglaze blue and overglaze red and gold palette, with very little white clay left undecorated. Its red was a more vermilion shade, and the pots often depicted European subjects in enclosed panels. Later it evolved into a more densely patterned look, with less emphasis on representation. These pots were often made to order for Europeans, and the potters' lack of contact with Westerners frequently led to charming inaccuracies in the figures.

Kutani ware was produced near Arita, in Kaga, for 40 to 50 years starting in about 1655. It then went through a hiatus of about 50 years before production began again. The later work never attained the bold and daring pictorial style of Ko (Old) Kutani, though. It used only green, indigo, yellow, and purple overglaze, with very little or no red. One unique feature of Kutani ware was that no two pieces were alike.

The Nabeshima clan controlled the area around Arita, and established their own kiln at Iwaya Kawachi about 1630. They moved production to Nangawara near Arita about 1660, and moved again in 1675 to Okawachi Mountain in Imari. Nabeshima ware's high point was reached between approximately 1688 and 1736, and was a Nabeshima clan monopolistic enterprise that was never exported. The ware was often highly patterned, reminiscent of fabric designs, particularly Yuzen silks. Even when pictorial it typically had unusual cropped compositions, which were uniquely Japanese. The Nabeshima decorators used only gold, green, yellow, and a very restrained red.

Another style that started about this time was Satsuma ware, but its only overglaze decoration was in gold. Most of these factories are still producing today, making ware that has changed very little since its inception.

Soon after Kakiemon began producing overglazed porcelain near Arita, Ninsei Nonomura opened his studio in Kyoto, producing what was known as Omuro ware. Ninsei is an example of the individual studio potter whose name has always been associated with his work in the same way a painter's would be. This was never the case for potters in either China or Europe, although a few decorators were recognized by name in Europe. This tradition was to have great influence on the Mingei Movement in Japan and the Arts and Crafts Movement in Europe and America in the 19th and 20th centuries.

By the 18th century, the secret of porcelain formulation had gotten out and it was being made at Tobe, Sue, Komine, Ito, and other kilns. During the Bunka Era (1804–1818) manufacture started in Seto, which eventually overtook Arita in volume.

Rectangular Dish, Ko-Kutani. Porcelain with overglaze enamels, 7¼" x 4⅛". Gift of James & Joanna Davidson. *Courtesy of Art Gallery of Greater Victoria, BC, Canada.*

Kutani/Kaga Dish, Kutani. Porcelain with underglaze blue and overglaze enamels, 2⅓" diam. Gift of James & Joanna Davidson. *Courtesy of Art Gallery of Greater Victoria, BC, Canada.*

Kutani/Kaga Dish, Kutani. Porcelain with underglaze blue and overglaze enamels. Side view.

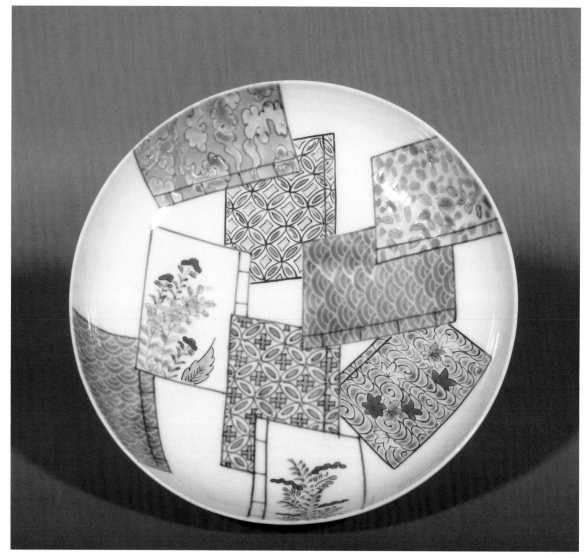

Dish, Nabeshima. Porcelain with underglaze blue and overglaze enamels, 7" diam. Gift of James & Joanna Davidson. *Courtesy of Art Gallery of Greater Victoria, BC, Canada.*

The desire among Japanese elites for personal collections of overglazed porcelain with a more Japanese esthetic was a huge impetus for the establishment of these factories, but world politics and economics were important too. It's no coincidence that this period corresponds with the period of uncertainty between the Ming and Ch'ing Dynasties in China, from 1644 to 1662. By this time porcelain was much admired and collected in Europe, and though European and Middle Eastern potters knew how to paint on unfired tin-glazed earthenware in the manner known as majolica, it would be another fifty years before true porcelain was made in Europe.

European ships had been docking in China for almost two hundred years, and by 1650 the Dutch, French, Portuguese, English, and Italians all had trading companies operating throughout Asia, dealing in all sorts of products. Porcelain was one of the most valuable commodities on the world market at that time, and the Japanese jumped at the opportunity to add it to their export trade, although between 1641 and 1854, only the Dutch had direct access to Japan.

Japanese decorators made very few technical innovations, but their esthetic influence was enormous worldwide. Their work had been popular in Europe in the 17th and 18th centuries, but after Commodore Matthew C. Perry forced the Japanese emperor to open their markets in 1854, Japanese products of all kinds began reaching the world in huge quantities. The International Exhibition in London in 1874 and the 1876 Centennial Exhibition in Philadelphia introduced Japanese goods to the common people of Europe and the United States. The huge displays of Japanese decorated porcelain were one of the main factors in the booming popularity of china painting in the U.S. in the late 19th century. Mary Louise McLaughlin, a catalyst in that movement, raved about Japanese design in her 1884 book, *Suggestions to China Painters.*

The stylistic elements that were so distinctive were asymmetrical compositions, the relationships of painted to patterned areas, and the integration of areas of flat color with intricate detail in patterns.

Germany

Friedrich Augustus II, Elector of Saxony and King of Poland, was another powerful admirer of porcelain. Following the fashion first started by the aristocrats at the French court under Louis XIV, he had amassed a huge collection by the year 1700. He was such a devoted collector that in 1717 he traded an entire regiment of 600 dragoons to the King of Prussia for 151 pieces of Chinese porcelain, which included 18 huge vases. He regretted this later, when these cavalrymen, known as the Porcelain Soldiers for as long as there was a Prussian Army, were part of a Prussian force that invaded Saxony.

He became one of the first to indulge in the fad of entire rooms made of porcelain, with floors, walls and ceilings all painted and embellished, custom made to fit the space. When he died in 1733, his so-called Japanese Palace housed his collection of 40,000 pieces. The porcelain collection was only one attraction of the glittering Dresden court, which included the silversmith Johann Jakob Irminger, the lacquerer Martin Schnell, and as Kapellmeister, Johann Sebastian Bach.

For almost two hundred years, Chinese porcelain had been arriving in Europe in quantity, and potters had been trying to duplicate it. From Middle Eastern potters they had learned the methods of painting mineral oxides on an unfired glaze, made white and opaque by the addition of tin oxide, and a very sophisticated genre of majolica ware had developed, especially in Italy. There were instances in which overglazes had been used on this earthenware, but when brilliant color was possible in a single firing, overglazing was unnecessary. As early as 1620, German potters used overglazes to decorate their dark salt-glazed stoneware as well, especially on beer steins.

Still, no one in Europe knew how to make true porcelain. The Medicis in Italy had come the closest, and had made some soft-paste porcelain as early as 1575, but it wasn't very good quality and it wasn't commercially successful. There had also been a little made in France, but that came to nothing as well.

It wasn't until 1708, when Augustus the Strong, as he was known, arrested Johann Friedrich Böttger and had him brought to court in Dresden, that things changed. Böttger was an alchemist who was not having much luck turning base metals into gold, so Augustus set him to trying to manufacture porcelain, the second most expensive commodity in the world. This research led Böttger to mix and heat up many combinations of minerals and in 1709, working with the physicist Ehrenfried Walther von Tschirnhaus, he made the first viable hard-paste porcelain in Europe with clay he found near Meissen. The following year Augustus had a factory built in the Albrechtsburg castle in Meissen, and porcelain was in production, nearly 800 years after the Chinese had first made it.

Three variations on porcelain were eventually developed in Europe: hard-paste, fired to 2300–2370°F (1260–1300°C); soft-paste, fired to 1832–2010°F (1000–1100°C); and bone china, fired to 2155–2190°F (1180–1200°C). In potter's terms, hard-paste would be fired to Orton cone 10–12, bone china to Orton cone 5–7, and soft-paste to Orton cone 06–01. Today's studio potters would consider hard-paste to be true porcelain, but are reluctant to call any clay fired to cone 6 or below porcelain, and would never refer to bone china as porcelain.

All of these variations are made by mixing a white china clay (kaolin) with a flux to lower the vitrification temperature. The fluxing mineral is usually a feldspathic mineral like Chinese petuntse or English Cornwall Stone (china stone). These also add silica, the most important glass-former in glazes, which helps make the ware translucent. Sometimes the flux is something like soapstone or talc, which results in a body much like today's talc/ ball clay white low-fire clays. In bone china, the flux is bone ash (tricalcium phosphate) resulting from calcining (burning or roasting) cattle bones, added to the body in amounts sometimes equaling the clay content.

European alchemists had been misled by porcelain's translucence to believe that it was more chemically akin to glass, so their success at making soft-paste porcelain was obtained by mixing the kaolin with chalk, lime, and ground glass or frit. These frits varied from location to location, but they were concocted from combinations of sand, alum, sea salt, gypsum, soda, nitrate, and soapstone.

Böttger's great realization was that, rather than adding glass to the clay, the secret lay in adding more heat and turning the clay itself into something more closely resembling glass. His first true porcelain was a mixture of one part kaolin with seven to nine parts alabaster. But within ten years after the Meissen factory went into production, they were mixing the kaolin with feldspar and silica, and the product was essentially identical to the Chinese material. Their original work with the alabaster had a slight yellowish tinge, but this new formulation had the bluish tint they admired in Chinese pots.

The kaolin was churned with running water, decanted, and run through a filter press. The alabaster was then mixed in, it was filter pressed again, and left for eight weeks. It was then kneaded and pressed again, and was ready to be worked. The pots were dried up to three months, during which time they shrank 24–28%. A bisque firing to about 1472°F (800°C) got them ready to be glazed with a mixture of clay and alabaster, then they were fired to 2642°F (1450°C), at which point they were ready for painting.

Böttger made advances in fired gold and silver, and developed a pink luster, but his only inventions in the field of enamel colors were a deep green and a dark red. Böttger managed the Meissen factory until his death in 1719, when the painter Johann Gregorius Höroldt and the modeler Johann Joachim Kändler succeeded him.

Höroldt first came to Meissen in 1717 from Vienna, where he was a well-known painter of chinoiserie murals. He was a brilliant decorator and became a brilliant enamel chemist, but was a harsh and tyrannical manager. Samuel Stöltzel and David Kohler had also been working at the

Sugar bowl with stand, Johann Ehrenfried Stadler, Meissen, c. 1726-28, hard-paste porcelain with enamels and opal luster, (bowl) 4⅝" x 5¼" x 4", (stand) 7" in diameter. Seattle Art Museum, gift of Martha & Henry Isaacson. *Photo: Paul Macapia.*

problem of new colors since Böttger's death, but it wasn't until Höroldt got access to Kohler's note-books upon Kohler's death in 1723 that he was able to come into his own. Between 1723 and 1733 he developed sixteen new colors. He also invented the muffle kiln, which protected the ware from the flames without the use of saggars. Essentially, a muffle is a large permanent saggar, around which the flame passes. Until the invention of the electric kiln in the 20th century, almost all overglazes were fired in muffle kilns.

Kändler had been a sculptor's apprentice before coming to Meissen in 1731. He was hired after several other sculptors had been unable to realize Augustus's dream of a porcelain menagerie. He eventually did produce this remarkable life-size clay zoo, which was enameled in lifelike colors.

Another astounding feat of Kändler's was the production of the legendary Swan Service, made between 1737 and 1742 for Prime Minister and Meissen Director Count Heinrich von Brühl. This dinnerware service eventually grew to about

2200 pieces, all with color and many with modeled figures. Its style of relatively sparse decoration came about largely because Kändler and Höroldt were feuding at this time, and Höroldt refused to let his staff work much on the project. But the set proved to be a trendsetter, and taste moved away from Höroldt's signature style of elaborately detailed court scenes and fantasy landscapes in cartouches set off by gilding and surrounded by areas of colored ground.

Kändler's other accomplishment was his invention of a new art genre, the figurine. He was an imaginative and prolific sculptor, who turned out elaborate tableaus for Augustus's lavish entertainments. They featured hundreds of figures, many of them portraits or caricatures of court personalities.

It was inevitable that the secrets of porcelain making and enameling would get out. Augustus' preoccupation with several wars and innumerable mistresses made his payments to the factory's suppliers and workers sporadic. Working conditions were horrific, the pay was low, and Höroldt was a tyrant. The owner of the kaolin mine began selling the clay to other aspiring factories, although he had a contract that forbade it. And workers left, taking parts of the secret with them, even though it was akin to treason.

One of these was Johann Georg Heintze, Höroldt's first apprentice. He fled, was captured and imprisoned (where he was forced to paint porcelain with no pay), escaped and fled again. He went first to Breslau, then to Vienna, then Berlin. Most of the decorators' names are unknown and their painting unattributed, but Heintze's fondness for inserting an obelisk into any landscape painting lets us track his progress through the new porcelain factories of Europe.

Another practice of Meissen which allowed the secret to get out was its selling of substandard ware "in the white"- glazed but undecorated. Meissen workers painted at home for extra money, and

free-lance artists, called *hausmalers,* set up kilns of their own. Many of these were alchemists and they developed a lot of enamel colors.

Other centers of porcelain manufacture soon opened all across Europe, in such places as Höchst, Frankenthal, and Nymphenburg in Germany, and in Doccia, Italy. The first factory after Meissen to be built was the Du Paquier factory in Vienna, Austria, set up in 1719 by Meissen Kiln Master Samuel Stöltzel, who was bribed away from Dresden. Porcelain also was later produced in huge quantities in Holland, in all of the Scandinavian countries, and in Russia, almost always as an enterprise of a noble or royal family.

For instance, when Augustus' granddaughter, Maria Amalia Christina, married Charles III, King of Naples, in 1738, she is said to have given him seventeen separate sets of Meissen china. Charles was himself a great fancier of porcelain and had built his own soft-paste factory at Capodimonte, which operated from 1743 to 1759. At that point Charles III became King of Spain and moved the factory, with all its workers, their families, and tons of material, to a new factory at Buen Retiro, near Madrid, which operated until 1808. Another of Augustus' daughters married the Dauphin of France, who owned the Vincennes factory, and yet another married Maximillian III Joseph, Elector of Bavaria, and owner of the Nymphenburg plant.

France

In 1726 the earliest production of soft-paste porcelain began in France at Chantilly in a workshop established under the auspices of Louis Henri de Bourbon, the Prince de Condé. But another French brand name, that of the great factory of Sèvres, was to become the most respected in Europe. It was established in Chateau de Vincennes near Paris in 1753, then moved and went into full production at Sèvres in 1756. From the beginning, it was completely under the control of the king of France, Louis XV, and all its output belonged to him. Its

"Ruth," Royal Vienna, 18th century. Collection of Betty Burbank, editor of *The China Decorator*. *Photo: Betty Burbank.*

"Rinaldo & Armida," Dresden, 8½", 18th century. Collection of Betty Burbank, editor of *The China Decorator. Photo: Betty Burbank.*

other great backer was Madame de Pompadour, the favorite mistress of the king. She was a great promoter of French arts and culture, and to this day, any line of china paints will include at least one color with her name on it, usually a dark, rich iron red.

Sèvres also had begun its production making soft-paste porcelain, but in 1768, it switched entirely to hard-paste. Some sources say the formula was purchased from Peter Anton Hammong, one of the many disaffected workers who fled Meissen. This followed the discovery of kaolin near Limoges in that year. A manufacturer of faience already in existence there converted to porcelain in the 1770's, and was absorbed into Sèvres in 1784.

Before long, a distinct Sèvres style had developed. Forms were ostentatious and gaudy, as befitted the world's most culturally influential monarch, and featured lots of intricate flourishes, scrollwork, and gilding. Backgrounds of brightly

"Venus, von Grazien Umgeben," Dresden, 8½", 18th century. Collection of Betty Burbank, editor of *The China Decorator. Photo: Betty Burbank.*

Pair of miniature orange tubs, Pierre-Antoine Méreaud, Vincennes or Sèvres, 1756-57. Soft-paste porcelain with enamel colors and gilding, 3⅝" x 2¾." Seattle Art Museum, funds from estate of Mary Arrington Small & Decorative Arts Council. *Photo: Paul Macapia.*

colored grounds set off decoration depicting flowers, birds, and genre scenes.

One specialty of the Sèvres artists was realistic porcelain flowers, mounted on wires. Madame de Pompadour delighted in receiving Louis XV on a winter day in front of a realistic, scented porcelain bower.

The years after the French Revolution were hard ones for the Sèvres name, as they were for any royal enterprise. In 1793, the factory became state property, and in 1800 it began its greatest period of creativity and stability with the appointment of a new director.

Alexandre Brongniart was a geologist, mineralogist, botanist, and zoologist, with no ceramic experience when he took over the reins, but he adapted to it brilliantly. He became the father of modern ceramic chemistry, and he made innovations during his tenure, not just in the fields of clay and glaze chemistry, but also in firing techniques, marketing procedures, and factory management. He must also have been an adroit politician since his directorship, which lasted till his death in 1847, included the Consulate; the rise, fall, and return of Napoleon Bonaparte; and the Restoration of Louis XVIII. The enterprise was on a good enough footing at his death to survive the onset of the Second Republic in 1848, and beyond.

To this day, slipcasters use Brongniart's Formula

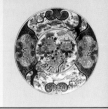

to convert slip measure to dry weight, a critical determination for the density of casting slip. He converted the factory entirely to hard-paste porcelain and developed new clay bodies and glazes. Queen Marie Amelie was a fan of deep, rich colors, and Brongniart developed many for her.

Even after Brongniart's days, the spirit of innovation persisted. Sèvres established the world's first museum of ceramics. The firemen there used something like a pyrometric cone before anyone else, and were the first to fire small kilns reliably in either reduction or oxidation, helping to create the demand in the mid-1880's for copper red, celadon, and matte glazes. In 1884, the glaze chemists developed the first zinc macrocrystalline glazes. The painters, as early as 1757, were the first to use rose and purple overglazes based on gold as a colorant, and are said to have been the first to use a color wheel. Another of their achievements in the late 19th century was a new method of overglazing called *grand feu*, done at a much higher temperature than traditional overglazing.

The clay technicians developed what they called *grès cérame*, which today we might call white stoneware. They also perfected underglazes and colored porcelain bodies, as well as the style of painting under the glaze with thick colored slips known as *pâte-sur-pâte*.

Until 1895, ninety percent of the designs for Sèvres shapes and images came from artists working in the factory, but any French citizen could submit designs, for which they were paid a 25% royalty. Renowned French artists such as Jean Fragonard were also invited to work on porcelain, starting a tradition of artists working in both china painting and more conventional mediums. One such artist was Pierre-Auguste Renoir, who began an apprenticeship at age 13 in the Lévy Frère porcelain factory in Paris. From 1854 until the factory's bankruptcy in 1858, he painted fans, lampshades and blinds. At the Paris Exposition in 1900, the Sèvres display astounded the world with its huge variety of designs and techniques, many of them from artists outside the factory.

In 1903, a store opened in Paris to sell to the general public. From 1870 until then, all the work had been sold to museums, or through the company's own showrooms. Before that, the entire output had been the property of the monarchy. And in the early 1900's the Ministry of Education opened the world's first School of Ceramics at Sèvres. Another astounding management decision taken about this time decreed that every ten years, the factory would publish all of its new technical information.

Though other porcelain factories opened in such places as Bayeaux and Vierzon, Sèvres was, and remains, the world's most respected porcelain brand name.

England

Porcelain production had always been an enterprise of emperors, kings and noble families, both in Asia and on the Continent. This fashion never caught on with the English gentry, so entrepreneurs like Wedgwood and Spode stepped in. Consequently, English ceramic work was never as elaborate in form or as extravagant in decoration as Continental wares. By the 1770's English manufacturers were pioneering the use of printing and transfer techniques to apply their overglazes, lessening the need for individual painters. This practice meshed well with the increasingly mechanized processes of the impending Industrial Revolution.

In England, the first soft-paste porcelain was not produced until 1744 at the Bow factory. Another enterprise began in the Chelsea section of London in 1745, but it went out of business in 1784.

The most important contributions to the history of clay and overglazes by British potters were two unique clay types, bone china and creamware.

In 1749, Edward Heylyn and Thomas Frye, of Bow, patented a process for making bone ash by

Teapot and cover, Chelsea, 1750–53, soft-paste porcelain with enamel colors, 4½" high. Seattle Art Museum, gift of Martha & Henry Isaacson. *Photo: Paul Macapia.*

calcining (burning) cattle bones. This was used as the flux with kaolin to make a translucent white clay body. Josiah Spode modified and improved the process and by 1800, all British factories were producing bone china, though hardly anyone else in the world used it.

Creamware is a white earthenware glazed with a clear lead glaze that is decorated with overglaze enamels. A slightly-later variation known as pearlware is the same clay tinted very slightly blue with cobalt. The English emphasis on ware for the masses made creamware, with its lower cost and less demanding techniques, an attractive alternative to porcelain. English creamware is much less

ostentatious in form and less opulent in decoration than most European porcelain as well.

By the time Josiah Wedgwood opened his factory in 1759, he already had several competitors. He was a fifth-generation potter whose family had been in the business for over a hundred years. Two of his uncles had a good reputation for their salt glazed ware. Josiah was apprenticed to his older brother Thomas as a thrower, at the age of nine.

The pottery he established became the most renowned in England. One reason for its reputation was Wedgwood's practice of never letting a piece that was less than perfect leave the workrooms. Smallpox had crippled him as a child, and one of

his legs was amputated. He would stalk the factory floor inspecting all aspects of production, and if he saw a piece that was not up to the Wedgwood standard, he would smash it with his crutch.

The letters of Père d'Entrecolles from Jingdezhen are said to have been his model for the division of labor and assembly line methods of Wedgwood's manufacturing.

Legendary as it is, the Wedgwood line's importance lies not in porcelain or overglaze decoration, but in other forms of clay work. However, some other English workers did make innovations in overglaze decoration. William Billingsley, a painter at the pottery in Swansea, developed the technique of painting flowers with china paint and wiping out highlights to achieve a very naturalistic look. And in 1757, the Worcester factory became the first to use printing on a large scale, and developed a method of transferring a copperplate engraving onto pottery in black overglaze.

Differences in taste, style, forms, materials, and forming methods provide interesting contrasts between Asian and European porcelain shapes and decoration.

Asian potters were far more skilled at throwing on the wheel than their European counterparts, and their clay bodies were much more suitable for use on the wheel. Press molding was much more prevalent in Europe, since soft-paste porcelain is very hard to throw with any size or grace, and bone china is worse. Bone china is the epitome of what potters call "short" clay—nonplastic and prone to cracking when distorted.

In Asia, forms were laid up in molds made of wood, their shapes often inspired by wooden and lacquerware objects. However, in Europe the mold material was either plaster or iron. And the European forms themselves were often inspired by metalwork, since the royalty was devoted to elaborate metal utensils. By the time porcelain manu-

facture began in Europe, the prevalent esthetic was for shapes featuring discrete panels painted in great detail, which were surrounded by areas of solid color ground and framed by elaborate gold scrollwork frames. This suited the tastes, the techniques, and the materials of the Europeans very well.

It's hard to know exactly when and where new colors and shades of overglaze were developed, since there was so much interchange among producers worldwide. It's not surprising that many of the colors were discovered in Europe, since alchemists there had been working not only with gold itself, but with all the elements they knew, in their centuries-long quest to synthesize gold. Regardless of where they were invented, almost all the colors and shades of overglaze and china paint that are known today were in use by the end of the 18th century.

United States

Porcelain production was late getting started in the United States. This was partly due to lack of suitable clay, as the great kaolin deposits in Florida were not discovered until the 20th century. And partly it was due to lack of demand. Americans' egalitarian outlook led to less ostentatious display among wealthier families, and their preference, then, as now, was for European luxury goods.

Several porcelain workshops were opened in the 1820's and 1830's, all in the area around Philadelphia and New Jersey, but none stayed in business for more than a few years. The earliest to survive for a while was Tucker Porcelain. By the late 19th century, Ott & Brewer of Trenton, New Jersey, was the best-known manufacturer, putting out a variety of eggshell porcelain they called "Beleek." They used this name partly to trade on the well-known Irish porcelain of that name, but also because most of the workers were Irish immigrants who had worked there.

. . . from being considered conspicuous, or in the minority, the exceptional one now is he or she who does not at least make an effort to paint on china.

—*Nicola di Rienzi Monaches*

The History of Porcelain and Overglaze Decoration

INDUSTRIAL REVOLUTION TO THE PRESENT

James Watt's improvements to the steam engine, starting with the condenser in 1765, are generally acknowledged as the starting point of the Industrial Revolution. But the Industrial Revolution was more a process than an event, which in some ways could still be said to be going on. What characterized the Industrial Revolution was the new relation of labor to capital, changes in the management of industry, and improvements in factory production. This involved increased specialization of labor, more mechanization, and the standardization of materials and processes.

The textile industry in England was the first to see huge changes. Henry Cort's invention of the grooved rolling mill in 1783 meant that steel shapes were standardized, making it easier to build the machines that would make the products.

Changes in the Ceramics Industry

As mechanized mixers, blungers, and filter presses made the work of processing clay much easier, the big change in overglaze decoration came in the form of printing. It was no longer necessary to hand paint every image on every pot. A design could be drawn once on paper, in any traditional two-dimensional art medium, and transferred to the pots by laborers totally unskilled in painting. The original artist no longer needed any expertise in overglazing.

The first ceramic transfers were done in the Doccia factory in Italy in 1737, and by the end of the 18th century, transfer printing of engravings was common. An engraved copper plate was inked and wiped with oil, and then printed onto a flexible glue or gelatin material shaped to fit the pot. This was then laid on a sandbag-like form that conformed to the pot's shape, and dry color was dusted on. The overglaze powder stuck to the oil and was blown off the unoiled areas, then the pot was pressed onto the form.

John Sadler and Guy Green, two printers in Liverpool, England, are generally credited as the first to print designs on tile, although they may not have been. In 1751 John Brooks, an Irish engraver working in London, applied for, but was not granted, a patent for his method of printing on china and enamel. Sadler and Green astounded the industry in 1756 by printing more than 1200 tiles in six hours, a feat that would have needed a hundred painters to duplicate. At first they used wood blocks, but they soon switched to copper plate engravings. They were wildly successful, producing not only their own tiles and pottery, but also selling transfer prints to other manufacturers. Wedgwood was one of their largest customers, and used Sadler and Green prints for their very popular line of creamware.

In the beginning, Sadler and Green printed only the outlines of their designs in black, which the factory's relatively unskilled painters then filled in by hand. Later, the designs were printed in multiple colors. After the 1840's, the printing of multi-color engraving, registered on dots in the design, was common. The invention of lithography in 1797 gave printers yet another option.

Harry Baker of Hanley patented a transfer process in 1781 that was similar to today's decals. It used a two-layer material. The image was printed onto paper, which was then covered with a varnish. The color, with the varnish, was then floated off the paper, and applied to the pot. The varnish burned off in the firing.

Yutensai Miyassaki is credited with the first use of silk screening, in Japan, some time in the early 18th century. He adapted the process from stencil painting. By the early 1900's, most overglaze decoration patterns originated as silk screens.

In terms of the standardization of processes and materials that the Industrial Revolution brought about, no one in the history of ceramics has made more important contributions than Hermann Seger, the Director of Research at the Berlin Royal Porcelain Factory.

Seger is known for four major innovations. His Seger Rules for overcoming crazing and his Seger Analysis (or rational analysis as it came to be known), which describes the makeup of a clay body, are of little concern to a china painter. The Seger Formula, or unity formula, his method of analyzing fired glazes, is still the best way to understand the chemistry of glazes. This is a mathematical method for converting a recipe of raw ingredients to an analysis of a molecule of fired glaze (see Chapter 7, "The Chemistry of China Paint").

Seger's fourth innovation, the invention of the pyrometric cone, is the most helpful to china painters. The potters at Sèvres were using something like a pyrometric cone about 1880, and Chinese potters may have been using something similar as early as 1280. But Hermann Seger standardized the formulas for cones and determined end points for each cone number in 1885. His system for numbering the cones is determined by the chemical composition of the cone material itself, based on his unity formula. This helps to explain why the progression of cone end point temperatures is so apparently incongruous.

In the early 20th century, Professor Edward Orton, Jr. of The Ohio State University in Columbus, Ohio, developed another line of pyrometric cones based on the same concept, but his temperature numbers differ slightly from Seger's. His Standard Pyrometric Cone Company has been called The Orton Foundation since his death in 1932.

Before cones, potters relied on their ability to judge kiln temperature by the color in the chamber, and by the use of draw trials (small rings of clay, glazed and decorated just like the ware). These were placed just inside a peephole and snagged out with a wire hook to see if the glaze or enamel had properly melted.

Cones are actually more accurate in testing glaze behavior than pyrometers, because they measure not just the degree of temperature, but heat work, which is a function of both time and temperature. Their use allowed a level of consistency in firing a particular kiln that had never been possible before, and allowed a fireman to know that a new kiln was firing just as a familiar kiln had.

China Painting by Individuals

Huge numbers of overglaze decorators, many of them women, were put out of work by changes in the industry. As today's cutting-edge technology often becomes tomorrow's hobby, so it was for recreational china painting, particularly in the United States.

In the latter half of the 19th century, industrial dinnerware and tile manufacturing, hand decoration of china, and pottery forming by individuals separated into three distinct subcultures. Aside from the introduction of a few new colors, virtually nothing has taken place in the world of industrial production since 1890 that concerns the subject of this book, while for the most part, studio potters have chosen other decorating options, which we will get to later.

On the other hand, china painting by individuals became one of the world's most popular

This 11" plate, manufactured by Limoges and signed "A. Broussillon," is typical of the enormous output of hobby and semi-professional painters of this era. It has been in the author's family since 1893, and was probably painted in Darke County, Ohio.

recreational activities, for both men and women. Changes in technology helped make this possible, as did the proliferation of schools, magazines, organizations, and exhibitions. By 1907, Nicola di Rienzi Monachesi was able to write, "the disciples of this charming art number many thousands. It is a favorite employment with the old, the young, the rich, and the poor, irrespective of sex; the idle enjoy it, and the busiest manage to find time to indulge in this fascinating occupation." Estimates of the total number of china painters in the U.S. during the 1890's range from 4500 to 25,000, with the latter probably closer to the true number.

In 1882 Paris-based Lacroix began marketing china paints to individuals in small quantities. By 1899, the June issue of *Keramic Studio* magazine listed ten available brands.

Kilns were evolving as well. No longer was it necessary to fire in a kiln fueled with wood, coal, or charcoal. Small wood and coal-fired kilns do not work efficiently, and charcoal needed to be raked out and replenished during the firing. Many a lady was killed or burned badly when her flowing dress caught fire during this operation. All three fuels were dirty, dangerous, and hard work.

In the 1880's and 1890's, small kilns fueled with

Ad for Ideal Kilns, from *Keramic Studio*, Vol. XV, #10, February 1914, p. 178.

natural gas, kerosene, and "manufactured gas" began appearing. These were often made of cast iron and lined with firebrick. They made it possible for a school art department, a community center, or even an individual to have a kiln that would fire consistently and easily, in a small space.

The earliest mention in the ceramic literature of an electric kiln was in 1901, but they did not come into general use until several decades later. The earliest popular ones were large, required 3-phase wiring, and often had walls nine inches thick. They heated and cooled very slowly, but they required even less firing expertise than gas kilns, and had the added advantage of always firing in oxidation.

China painting's popularity waned during the two World Wars and the Depression, but the 1950's saw a huge resurgence. New houses were built with lots of electric power, women had leisure time again, and a new type of kiln was introduced. The top-loading octagonal or round kiln with 2½-inch thick walls, which ran on household current, made it feasible for an individual artist

to own a kiln. The introduction of an automatic shutoff device made the kiln more reliable, and the addition of an override timer made it even more so. In the 1990's, kiln controllers run by a computer added another degree of assurance, and enabled an artist to regulate a kiln on any specialized firing schedule automatically.

Adelaide Alsop Robineau and *Keramic Studio*

In 1909, British-born Taxile Doat came to the United States from France, where he had been the Director of the Sèvres plant, and began teaching ceramics at the University City Pottery at St. Louis University. This was part of the American Women's University, which grew to have branches all over the country. Doat was not known as a china painter himself, but in his program, as in most other ceramics schools of the time, he taught overglazing along with underglazing, glazing, and all the forming and firing techniques. His real contribution to the field of china painting was his tutelage of Adelaide Alsop Robineau.

Robineau had been a china decorator in New York prior to studying in St. Louis, but worked very little with that medium after she began making her own pots. Her "Scarab Vase" is probably the single best-known ceramic piece made anywhere in the world between 1900 and 1950.

Her most lasting contribution to the art of china painting was her magazine, *Keramic Studio*, first published in May of 1899. She and her husband, Samuel Edward Robineau (later with the help of George H. Clark) put the magazine together in their home in Syracuse, New York, and in 1912 established the Four Winds Pottery School there on what would become Robineau Road.

The first issue began with her reasons for starting the publication. "This magazine is the outgrowth of an increasing demand for practical designs and instructions for students of keramics. Now that the decoration of china is no longer a

Faculty of the first Four Winds Pottery Summer School, 1912. Left to right, Miss Jessie M. Bard, Miss Bertha Riblet, Mrs. Kathryn E. Cherry, Mrs. A. A. Robineau, Mr. Dawson Watson. From *Keramic Studio*, Vol. XIV #6, October 1912, p. 116.

fad, but a serious study, a profession, or means of livelihood to thousands outside of potteries, something more is required of decorators than the stereotyped spray of flowers and the inevitable butterfly." Robineau edited the magazine until her death in 1924. It was renamed *Design* and continued under that name until April of 1930. Virtually every well-known clay or overglaze artist contributed articles and designs to the magazine, including Taxile Doat, Mary Chase Perry, Charles Fergus Binns, and Franz Bischoff.

Keramic Studio provided the model for all china painting magazines since. It included in every issue patterns to copy; gallery and show news; editorials about the art; articles about historical, artistic, and technical subjects; and the doings of various organizations. After the first few issues, they published the answers to correspondents' questions, and a few years later, began to include the questions as well, which was much more helpful. Later they also published ads for schools, books, and products.

The organization whose proceedings *Keramic Studio* covered was the National League of Mineral Painters, which began in 1892 with chapters in New York, Chicago, Boston, Milwaukee, Brooklyn, Detroit, Jersey City, Louisville, Bridgeport, Columbus, Providence, and Denver. Its third president, Laura Howe (Mrs. Worth) Osgood, wrote in the debut issue of *Keramic Studio*, "Believing that a higher place for keramics could only be won through artists imbued with a love of country, and realizing that it is a patriotic obligation as well as privilege to arouse and foster the national element, these loyal promoters succeeded in combining … into a federation known as the NLMP." This thread of patriotism runs strongly throughout American china painting. Mrs. Robineau often enjoined her readers to use American porcelain and colors. In October of 1914, she encouraged them to buy American Beleek china from New Jersey, now that European china was unavailable because of "this useless and stupid war."

In addition to printing the "Club News" section, each issue also included "In the Shops," a review of shows and new products, and "In the Studios," which detailed the doings of prominent china painters. The November 1900 issue contains this historic item: "A State School of Keramics has been established at Alfred, New York, under the direction of Mr. Charles F. Binns, late of the Trenton Potteries and formerly of the Royal Worcester Porcelain Works, England. This is the second school of its kind in the United States, and should be of great benefit to students of Keramics. The *K. S.* will try to give further details later."

The American Style of China Painting

In the last quarter of the 19th century, several European immigrants to the United States began painting porcelain in a more naturalistic style, with shaded backgrounds and washes of color that became known as the American Style in the U.S., or the "soft technique" in Europe. This was in contrast to the more stylized Meissen style, which almost never featured shaded backgrounds. The most prominent artists of the genre were Franz Bischoff, Franz Bertram Aulich, and George Leykauf. The three were all from Germany, and all lived for a time in the Detroit, Michigan, area, where they were well acquainted and cordial with each other.

Franz Bischoff was probably the best-known porcelain painter of his day. After his arrival in New York in 1885, he worked as a decorator of china lamp shades before starting his own school there. At the invitation of a patroness, he moved to Dearborn, Michigan, started another Bischoff School of Ceramic Art, and stayed until 1908. By then he was frustrated with the difficulty of finding models for his signature rose paintings, and a trip to California won him over. He moved to South Pasadena and established a huge Italian Renaissance-style house, garden, and studio along Arroyo Seco, which became a tourist attraction. He was equally accomplished in oils and watercolors, like many porcelain artists then and now. His oils of the California landscape are well known, but as a china painter, he became known as "The King of Roses." His style of rendering roses, with no outlines and a few white highlights, is still the predominant one today. Like many of his contemporaries, he marketed his own line of overglazes, and is credited with developing the grayish pink gold-based color, Ashes of Roses.

Bischoff was noted for the unusual organization of his palette, and for his dexterity with a brush. Writing in the *Art Amateur* in April 1895, S. J. Knight reported, "He will fill his brush with some warm, clear color, and by a peculiar movement of the wrist, pressing on the brush and wriggling it …he will sweep around the petals of a rose, and leave a background which has a firm, clear line next to the flower, and as the color is gradually exhausted from his brush, fades away to nothing. A petal of a rose will be put in with a solid, circular sweep; then a dab from his finger, and presto! it is beautifully modeled."

Bischoff seldom used a pad, but modeled his forms with the ball of his thumb, and used his fingers and fingernails to create highlights. He was also fond of introducing raised paste and rococo scrolls into his work, which he felt "helped me out of many a tight place." He usually selected the very plainest of china to work on, and fired most pieces three times, the first fire being the highest.

Franz Bischoff, "Roses," plaque, 18," diam. 1904. Painting is from the book *Paintings on Porcelain Featuring Franz Bischoff* published by Ann Cline Studio. (See "Resources' for more titles) *Photo: Ann Cline.*

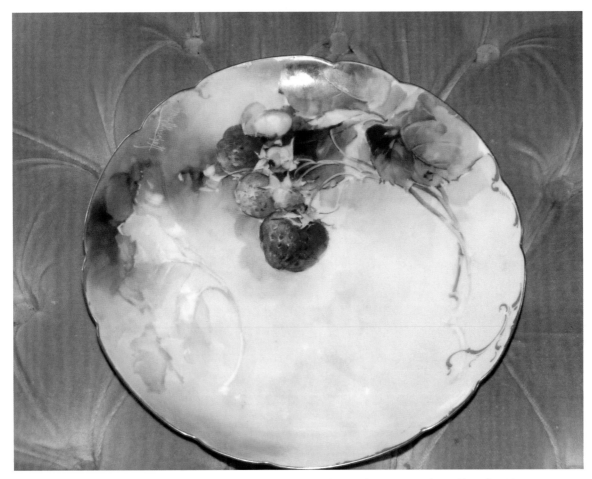

Franz Bischoff, "Strawberries," Limoges plate, 9" diam. Collection of Cherryl M. Meggs. *Photo: Cherryl M. Meggs.*

Franz Bertram Aulich was born in 1856 in Silesia and studied art in Dresden and Berlin. He came to the U.S. in 1893 and opened a studio in Chicago's Auditorium Building, the site of numerous china painting studios. He was a popular teacher, and was a good friend of Bischoff's. He was particularly noted for his paintings of grapes and roses, and worked in a style reminiscent of Berlin.

Aulich's and Bischoff's painting styles differed in one important aspect. Aulich tended to begin with strong colors, and tone them down with overlays of gray, in a very naturalistic style. Bischoff, a more impressionistic painter, usually started with an initial layer of grays and added stronger colors. He once wrote, "You will become an artist only when you learn the importance of gray."

George Leykauf was perhaps most instrumental in developing the softer and more naturalistic American Style. He had apprenticed at Meissen and was Taskmaster in charge of the Decorating Department when he emigrated in 1876. Like many his contemporaries, he was known for his paintings of flowers and grapes, which often included a spider web, but his images of shells and seaweed were also famous. His use of gray and

Continued on page 37

The China Painter in the White House
Carrie Scott Harrison

First Lady Carrie Scott Harrison, 1889. *Photo: President Benjamin Harrison Home.*

Caroline Scott Harrison would have been well known even if she had not been a china painter. She was the wife of President Benjamin Harrison, the first First Lady with a college degree, and the first President General of the Daughters of the American Revolution.

When the Harrisons moved into the White House after his election in 1888, Carrie Harrison organized classes there for the wives and daughters of legislators and cabinet members, and persuaded her painting teacher, Paul Putzki, to move to Washington, D.C., to teach them. She set up her kiln at the home of Mrs. John Wight in Kendall Green.

Putzki had been trained in Dresden, worked for a while as a decorator in a factory in East Liverpool, Ohio, and taught in both New York City and Chicago. A wealthy woman from Richmond,

Indiana, persuaded him to teach a class there once a week, where Mrs. Harrison became his student. He was once described in a newspaper as "a young looking man with pleasant manners, a handsome face, frenzied brown hair, and other characteristics of the German artist."

Carrie Harrison painted numerous porcelain pieces while in the White House as souvenirs for her friends, firing some in her own kiln, but most in Putzki's. Many a baby boy whose parents named him after the President received a milk set painted

Carrie Scott Harrison. Pierced flower plate.
Photo: President Benjamin Harrison Home.

Paul Putzki. Plate with violets, 8½" diam.
Photo: President Benjamin Harrison Home.

Harrison White House China.
*Photo: President
Benjamin Harrison Home.*

by the First Lady, who always included a four-leaf clover in her decoration, as a wish for good luck and as a signature. Though she worked in watercolor and embroidery as well, china decoration was her favorite "because there is an element of chance in it. No matter how carefully one has painted a piece, there is always a doubt as to how it will look when it comes out of the furnace, and this adds an excitement to the pleasure of creating the beautiful."

She collected all the remnants of dinnerware from previous presidential administrations and displayed them in the China Room. In 1891, she designed the Harrison White House china set. Her initial sketches were modeled on the Lincoln set, which had been painted in 1865 by Edward Lycett, an Englishman living in New York.

Mrs. Harrison's dinnerware had a border design of corn, because "corn is indigenous to the North American soil. I think they will be right pretty." Paul Putzki rendered the final designs, based on her sketches. It was not a full service, but four sizes of plates in two variations of her design. To this would be added after-dinner coffee cups and saucers that unfortunately did not arrive until shortly after her death in October of 1892. The dinnerware was produced by Haviland China in France, even though President Harrison was a fierce promoter of American products. The set was reordered by the William McKinley and Theodore Roosevelt administrations and is still used occasionally. It was a great favorite of Jackie Kennedy.

Teaching at the White House was a good career move for Putzki, who continued to teach after Mrs. Harrison's death. The March 1903 issue of *Keramic Studio* contained ads for his schools in New York and Baltimore, and he was often interviewed in local newspapers when he traveled.

Most of the information and all of the pictures in this feature are courtesy of The President Benjamin Harrison Home, 1230 North Delaware St, Indianapolis, IN 46202 (www.surf-ici.com/harrison) and its curator, Jennifer E. Capps.

subdued coloring was quite distinctive, and he also had the distinction of never having repeated an image. Also like many of his contemporaries, he worked in another medium as well. In his case it was silk, in the form of scarves and the linings of women's coats. His punch bowl won first prize at the World Columbian Exposition in 1893, and the top prize at the Brussels World's Fair in 1897. Much of the gold scrolling on Leykauf's work is said to have been done by his nieces, Tillie and Julie.

Paul de Longpré was an immigrant from France. His career was remarkably similar to Bischoff's, although he was self-taught. He also came to New York, and in 1899, moved to Southern California for the flowers. He bought a lavish Moorish-style home, studio, showroom, and garden as well. In his case, it was located near the corner of Cahuenga Avenue and Hollywood Boulevard in Hollywood.

Edward Lycett was a bit older than the previous group of artists, and came to the U.S. in 1861 from Newcastle-under-Lyme, England. He painted the china for the Civil War gunboat *Monitor*, and designed a set of dinnerware for the Lincoln White House. Mrs. Lincoln requested the very popular magenta color for the borders, but had to settle for lilac, as Lycett's kiln would not fire the magenta properly.

Very little is known about the work of "Wagner." Some sources say that this was an individual artist, others that it was the name of a studio. It is possible that the artist is Celeste Wagner, an Austrian-born portraitist and Bischoff's teacher, or it may be the name of a Viennese studio. There is even disagreement as to whether the work was produced in the U.S. or Vienna. What is certain is that the name is attached to some exquisite portraits and figure studies, many depicting classical, allegorical, or Biblical subjects.

Mary Louise McLaughlin's enthusiastic writing about the Japanese porcelain painting she had seen

Franz Bertram Aulich, "Morning Glories" platter.
Collection of Jean & Roger Helm. *Photo: Jean Helm.*

Franz Bertram Aulich, "Grapes," coupe plate, 16," 1902.
Collection of Betty Burbank, editor of *The China Decorator*.
Photo: Betty Burbank.

George Leykauf, "Geraniums" plate, 14" diam., 1904. Collection of World Organization of China Painters Museum. *Photo: Mary Early.*

at the 1876 Centennial Exhibition in Philadelphia was instrumental in popularizing the art. This appeared in her seminal 1884 book, *Suggestions for the China Painter.* McLaughlin was a member of the group of society ladies in Cincinnati, Ohio, who are said to have organized the first classes in china painting in America. She was also instrumental in starting Rookwood Pottery, but left the establishment because of disagreements with its owner, Maria Longworth Nichols.

Susan Frackelton's book *Tried by Fire: A Work on China-Painting* (D. Appleton: New York, 1886) was perhaps as influential as McLaughlin's. Frackelton, a potter, china painter, teacher and entrepreneur from Milwaukee, Wisconsin, invented gas-fired home kilns, and helped create the National League of Mineral Painters. While she and McLaughlin agreed that nature was the preferred subject for the decoration of china, Frackelton espoused a naturalistic approach, while McLaughlin was a devotee of "conventionalized" design.

Bessie Bennett taught at the Art Institute of Chicago, along with Abbie Pope Walker, and often judged *Keramic Studio's* regular design competitions. Chicago was home to a large number of overglaze artists and teachers. Many of their studios were concentrated in the Auditorium Building and the adjoining Auditorium Tower. F. B. Aulich was the most prominent, but D. M. Campana, Helen Hastings, Evelyn Beachy, Ione L. Wheeler, Gertrude E. Estabrooks, Mrs. A.A. Frazee, Anna Armstrong Green, and Marguerite M. Yeoman all taught out of their studios there. The Marshall

Wagner, Royal Vienna plate with raised paste, 10½″ diam. Collection of Cherryl M. Meggs.
Photo: Cherryl M. Meggs.

Field Building housed another concentration of studios, including those of Mabel C. Dibble, Helen M. Topping, Helen G. Halsey, Jeanne M. Stewart (whose exquisite floral studies are still available to-day) and Blanche van Court Schneider, who later moved to the Auditorium Building.

Wilder Austin Pickard started Pickard China in Edgerton, Wisconsin in 1893. The company moved to Chicago in 1897 and is still in business today, although the company moved to Antioch, Illinois, in the late 1930's. In 1937, the company developed its own clay bodies and glazes, and quit using imported (primarily Limoges) ware. Their wares are characterized by rich color and a lavish use of gold, and many contemporary china paint-ers like to paint in the "Pickard style." Another of their significant contributions to the field of china painting was their employment of a large contingent of decorators, some of whom went on to become well known as independent artists. Two of the well-known decorators who stayed with the company were Jeremiah Vokral and Wilder Pickard's wife, Emma.

Venetian-born Dominick M. Campana joined the company as a decorator in 1900 and left two years later to establish his own studio, teach class-es, and write several classic textbooks including *The Teacher of China Painting* (1908). He founded a china paint and supply company that still bears his name today.

Another Pickard decorator who became well known as an independent artist was Emil Aulich, cousin (some sources say brother) of F. B. Aulich, with a very similar style.

Jeanne M. Stewart, "Grapes" study, from *Keramic Studio*, Vol. XV #10, February 1914, p. 163.

Maude Mason, another prominent teacher, marketed her own lines of both porcelain shapes and overglaze colors from her studio at 48 East 26th Street in New York City, which she shared with her sister Elizabeth. Kathryn A. Cherry of Brooklyn, New York, who taught with Robineau at the Four Winds Pottery School, also marketed a line of colors under her own name. Prior to her move to New York she had been a prominent china painter in St. Louis, and taught at the American Women's University in University City, Missouri.

Dorothea Warren O'Hara released *The Art of Enameling on Porcelain* in 1912. This appears to be the publication that defined what china painters now refer to as "enamel"—the thick, opaque material that stands up in a raised mound on the surface of the glaze. Today, her distinctive style of "conventional" design, primarily on American Beleek china, looks more typical of 1953 than of 1913.

Henrietta Barclay Paist taught classes in her St. Paul, Minnesota studio. She was also a frequent contributor to, and Assistant Editor of, *Keramic Studio*.

The work of all the prominent china painters of the day appeared frequently in the pages of *Keramic Studio*, both in the form of photographs of ceramic work and, more frequently, as watercolor studies. Anna B. Leonard of New York was one of these artists, who also assisted in the production of the magazine. Other artists whose work and studies appeared frequently were Sarah Wood Safford and Leta Horlocker (both of New York), Alice Willits Donaldson, Jessie M. Bard, and Catherine Klein.

The Decline and Revival of China Painting

China painting continued to be incredibly popular all over the world until World War I (1914–1919) put an end to almost all leisure activity. There was some renewed interest in the 1920's, but the faster pace of life and the rigid, mechanical nature of the popular Art Deco style did not lend themselves well to the painstaking technique and romantic subject matter typical of china painting. The Great Depression (1930–1941) and World War II (1939–1945) not only made painting on china seem ridiculously frivolous, but also obliterated women's leisure time and extra money, requiring them to enter the labor market in order for them and their countries to survive.

The mid-50's saw a huge revival of interest in china painting, along with all other hobbies and

Ann Cline, Cream & Sugar in a Pickard style, with black pen work on gold, 6" high.

leisure activities. By that time, men had come home from the war, and women had quit their jobs to raise the children who were now going off to school during the day. They were living in new houses that were big enough to have room for a studio in a spare bedroom or a part of the garage or basement.

What enabled china painting to regain its place as a very popular hobby was the introduction of the top-loading octagonal electric kiln, and very soon after that, the automatic shutoff device. No longer was it necessary to fire one's work at a school or community center, nor was it necessary to know much about firing. The new kilns ran on the same kind of wiring that was being installed for new appliances such as dishwashers, clothes washers and dryers, and stoves, so it was unnecessary to have 3-phase wiring, as the older, more massive, electric kilns did.

As Europe recovered from the war, colors and china began to reappear, particularly from Dresden, Germany, where china painting and porcelain had first appeared in Europe. The original Meissen factory had miraculously survived the firebombing there, and was back in business. A few companies began to manufacture china paint colors in the United States as well, including L. Reusche, Fry's, Chapman & Bailey and Willoughby's.

As early as the 1890's, artists such as F. B. Aulich marketed lines of colors under their own names. Virtually none of these artists actually manufactured the paints themselves, and this is still true today. Typically, an artist will buy large quantities of colors from one or more manufacturers, packaging it into smaller vials with their own labels attached. Sometimes, two or more colors may be combined to get a special tint, or the colors may be renamed. Often they are merely repackaged.

One artist whose career followed a typical path was Sonie Ames. She had always been interested in art as a child in Utah, and had admired a painted plate her mother had gotten as a gift. After working in an airplane manufacturing plant in California during the war, she began to paint china in 1950, studying with a local artist in Long

Emil Aulich, "Grapes" tankard, 13" high. Collection of Jean & Roger Helm. *Photo: Jean Helm.*

Individual china painters became well known for their work, particularly as a new, softer, style of painting became more prevalent. Many of these artists supplemented their reputations and their incomes by selling books of their most popular studies, and by marketing their own lines of colors. This business model is still a typical one today, as artists who are known for portraits, for example, will put out a line of their favorite portrait colors. Air travel made it feasible for a prominent teacher to hold classes and seminars all over the country.

Dorothea Warren O'Hara, Lenox cracker jar. From *Keramic Studio*, Vol. XIV #10, February 1913, p. 205.

Beach, California, until she could take lessons from Jean Sadler. Sadler, one of the first traveling teachers, was well known at the time for her pale pinks and dull reds.

Ames began exhibiting about 1954, and teaching in 1956, becoming widely admired for her very soft style of painting roses. In the early 1960's, Sonie began to market her own line of colors after her main supplier became unreliable. She continued to buy one color (a shell pink) from this supplier, but most of her other colors were bought from L. Reusche or Chapman & Bailey. In addition to supplies and her book, *Roses and the Fine Art of China Painting*, her line included about 65 tints, only one of which (Apple Blossom Pink) she actually mixed herself. Eventually, she moved to Oregon and continued to paint and market her colors and studies until her death in 1992.

Ann Cline, Jayne Houston and Joyce Berlew followed much the same career path as Sonie Ames, establishing prominent supply businesses and lines of paints carrying their names in the 1960's and 1970's.

Other prominent china painters of the day included Marcella Fagan, Hazelle Gibbons, Helen Karr, Annette Krum, Ann Krummel, Jane Marcks, Ruth F. Venable (who studied with Bischoff and Aulich), and Rosemarie Radmaker.

Contemporary
Magazines & Organizations

Keramic Studio was not the only magazine for china painters in 1900, nor was it even the first. Luella E. Braunmiller wrote *Lessons for the China Painter* in 1882, and first published *The China Decorator* in New York in 1887. The magazine continued into the 1900's.

In 1956, Nettie Pillet began publishing a newsletter in Los Angeles, which grew into today's magazine *The China Decorator,* named in honor of the earlier publication. Since 1962, several members of the Burbank family have published it,

Sonie Ames, "Roses," framed coupe plate, 13" diam. Collection of Jean & Roger Helm. *Photo: Jean Helm*

Jean Sadler, "Poppies," plate, 12" diam.

with its offices now in Shingle Springs, California. The magazine is much like an updated version of *Keramic Studio*, with studies, news of seminars, ads for suppliers, and articles on the history and techniques of china painting. *The China Decorator* also maintains an outstanding library and book dealership.

In 1962, a group of china painters in Dallas, Texas, led by Lucretia Donnell, formed the International Porcelain Artists and Teachers Association (IPAT). Originally open to teachers only, it now accepts non-teachers as well. The

Jane Marcks, "Portrait of a Young Girl," 8" x 10." Collection of World Organization of China Painters Museum.
Photo: Mary Early.

group currently has about 3000 members in 50 countries. They publish *Porcelain Artist* magazine, with headquarters and a small museum in Grapevine, Texas, and administer a teacher certification program.

The same year that the IPAT was created, Pauline Salyer began publishing *The China Painter,* and organized a statewide association of china painters. Five years later, she both published her first book, *The Great Artists of China Decoration*, and established the World Organization of China Painters (WOCP). In 1983, she authored the book, *Oriental Porcelain Painting*. The WOCP headquarters are still located in Ms. Salyer's hometown of Oklahoma City, Oklahoma. The organization's 7000 members belong to state, county, regional, or national clubs, or they may be part of the organization's association of individual teachers, artists, and dealers.

In 1984, WOCP purchased the property that currently houses its corporate headquarters, magazine production and museum, whose collection is comprised of "pieces which represent honors achieved in this art field, by persons who have made, and continue to make, outstanding contributions to porcelain art." The two most popular areas are the Reception Room, which displays porcelain art by many noted artists, and the State Room, which houses changing displays of painting from state and national organizations. Other collections are housed in rooms with particular themes, such as the Victorian Room, the Oriental Room, the Holiday Room, and the Blue Room (antique porcelain). Antique china paints and supplies are displayed in the Library, along with an extensive collection of books, videos, and instructional patterns, studies, and lessons, and the Gift Shop carries china and supplies donated by members. The World Organization of China Painters organizes regular regional, national, and international exhibitions and conventions, as does the IPAT.

Pauline Salyer, "European Style Flowers," tureen, 11" high x 14" wide, 1985. Collection of World Organization of China Painters Museum. *Photo: Mary Early.*

San Do, "Portrait of Pauline Salyer," framed tile, 8" x 10," 1991. Collection of World Organization of China Painters Museum. *Photo: Mary Early.*

Mariela Vilasmil (Venezuela), "Native Child," 16" diam. 2004. Collection of World Organization of China Painters Museum. *Photo: Mary Early.*

Mika Nakashima (Japan), "Japanese Lady," 12" diam. 1989. Collection of World Organization of China Painters Museum. *Photo: Mary Early.*

Judy Chicago's "The Dinner Party"

One of the most ambitious and significant art pieces of the 1970's, in any medium, was the multimedia installation piece called "The Dinner Party," by Judy Chicago. This triangular piece, 48 feet on a side, took the shape of a table with 39 place settings, each with its own plate, goblet, flatware, and embroidered runner. In addition, it included woven tapestries and linen tablecloths, and was set on a floor of handmade porcelain tiles. This massive piece, completed in 1979, consumed Judy Chicago and scores of volunteers, almost all of whom were women, for five years.

The theme of The Dinner Party," a reinterpretation of "The Last Supper," was the place of women, and women's work and art, in Western civilization. Each of the 39 place settings depicted a female mythological or historical figure of significance. In addition, the names of 999 additional women of achievement were fired, in gold and iridescent luster, onto more than 2300 12-inch triangular porcelain tiles to form the "Heritage Floor."

The focal point of each place setting was a 14-inch porcelain plate decorated with china paint in a design originated by Chicago. The plates began as slabs, and were then formed into plates on a jigger machine by the project's ceramic advisor, Leonard Skuro. More slabs were attached to the surface of the plate, then it was bisqued, glaze fired, and china painted. At least five firings were needed for each plate, and losses were initially devastatingly high.

China paint and embroidery were, to Chicago, the two art forms that most perfectly symbolized the place of women in art and society. Both skills were usually passed down from one individual to another; both involved patient, painstaking work; both were usually done in a domestic setting and resulted in objects intended for the home; and both were largely ignored by the larger art world.

China painting had struck Chicago as the quintessential women's art medium in 1971, and

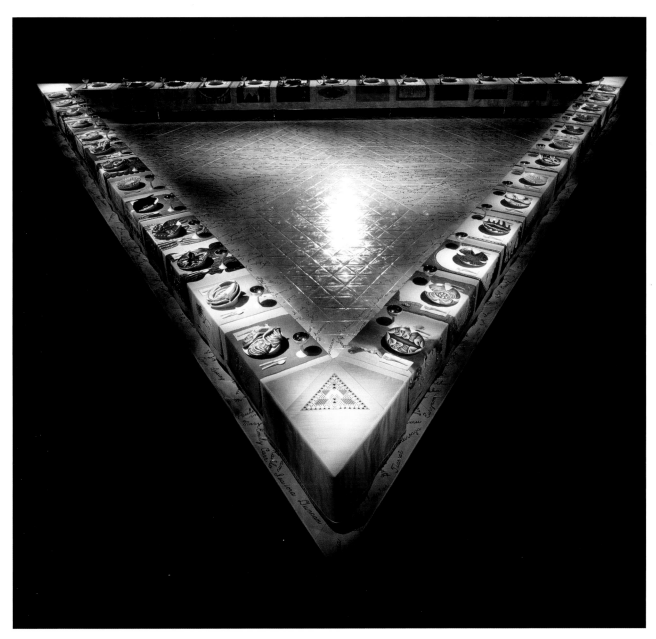

Judy Chicago, "The Dinner Party," overall view, 48' on a side, 1979. Courtesy of Through the Flower and Judy Chicago. *Photo: Donald Woodman.*

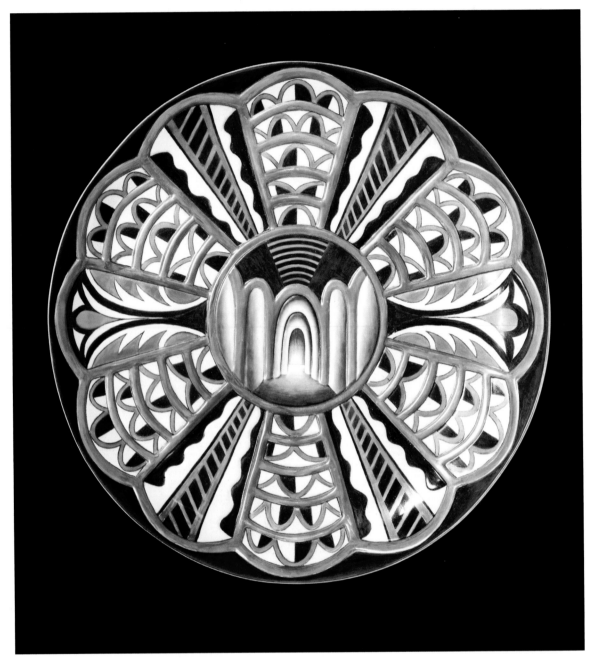

Judy Chicago, "Isabella d'Este," plate, 14" diam. Isabella d'Este helped support the Urbino majolica factory. Courtesy of Through the Flower and Judy Chicago. *Photo: Donald Woodman.*

she had begun taking lessons with Miriam "Mim" Halpern in the Los Angeles area in 1972. She began to paint and exhibit her china painted work in art galleries, and it was at one of these openings, at the Ann Hughes Gallery in Portland, Oregon, that she met Rosemarie Radmaker, a local porcelain artist.

Radmaker was very excited to see china painting shown in a traditional art venue, and eventually became the technical advisor to the china painters working on "The Dinner Party," making numerous trips to Chicago's Santa Monica studio. Her participation was emblematic of women's careers, in that she, as a widow, would not have been able to offer her services had her mother not been able to tend her children.

Judy Chicago, "Primordial Goddess," plate, 14" diam. Courtesy of Through the Flower and Judy Chicago. *Photo: Donald Woodman.*

Rosemarie Radmaker, "Roses" plate. Courtesy of Through the Flower and Judy Chicago. *Photo: Donald Woodman.*

National Porcelain Art Month

One of the most notable milestones in the history of American china painting occurred in 1980, when the 96th Congress of the United States issued a Joint Resolution, signed by President Jimmy Carter, declaring July of that year to be National Porcelain Art Month. One of the clauses in the resolution states that " throughout history, the art of porcelain painting… has been recognized as a fine art by all of the world's great civilizations…."

Ninety-sixth Congress of the United States of America

AT THE SECOND SESSION

Begun and held at the City of Washington on Thursday, the third day of January, one thousand nine hundred and eighty

Joint Resolution

Designating July 1980 as "National Porcelain Art Month".

Whereas the art of painting on porcelain requires great skill, intensive training, and great artistic ability, and produces works of beauty; and

Whereas throughout history, the art of porcelain painting has provided a medium for the preservation of history and culture, and further, has been recognized as a fine art by all of the world's great civilization; and

Whereas growing thousands of American artists have studied, explored, and enhanced the historic skills of porcelain painting, adding immeasurably to the cultural enrichment of our Nation; and

Whereas the efforts of these artists bring rich beauty and expanded dimensions to our national culture for the benefit and enrichment of the lives of all citizens: Now, therefore, be it

Resolved by the Senate and House of Representatives of the United States of America in Congress assembled, That July 1980 is designated as "National Porcelain Art Month", and the President is authorized and requested to issue a proclamation calling upon the people of the United States to observe such month with appropriate ceremonies and activities.

Speaker of the House of Representatives.

APPROVED

JUL - 2 1980

President of the Senate Pro Tempore.

Jimmy Carter

Proclamation by U.S. Congress, signed by President Jimmy Carter, declaring July 1980, National Porcelain Art Month.

China Painting on the Internet

Numerous suppliers, magazines, organizations, and individual artists have established their own web sites, many of whom are listed in the Resources section of this book. There are, in addition, several important sites that serve as electronic meeting places and information clearing houses.

The most important of these is Porcelain Painters International Online (PPIO, at *www.porcelainpainters.com* or *www.ppio.com*), which began in May of 1997. Marci Blattenberger and Betty Gerstner have compiled links to suppliers, schools, and artists, as well as a teachers' database and numerous articles, studies, and lessons about all aspects of china painting. PPIO's most important contribution to the field, however, is its moderated electronic mailing list. The list currently has over 1000 subscribers in 32 countries, who share information, stories, and support around the world.

The China Painting List *(www.china-painting-list.com)* owned by R. Janette Graham in Brisbane, Queensland, Australia, is another huge collection of links to painters' personal and business sites, as well as the sites of museums, dealers, schools, and publications around the world.

Studio Clay Artists

Almost every technological revolution spawns nostalgia for the way things were before, and the Industrial Revolution was no exception. From the first, some lamented the loss of the human touch in soulless mechanical processes. By the end of the 19th century what came to be known as the Arts and Crafts Movement was well established, spurred on by the writings of William Morris and others.

This movement hearkened back to a simpler time when everyday objects were produced by hand, in small workshops, by individuals or small groups, under the supervision of one master. Ideally, all steps of the process would be done by this individual or small group. This was a model

Forms and Imagery
Kurt Weiser

Like many potters, Kurt Weiser originally wanted to be a painter, in his case Salvador Dali. However, a required ceramics course at Interlochen High School in his native Interlochen, Michigan, hooked him on clay. With an undergraduate degree from Kansas City Art Institute and two years of teaching behind him, he returned to Michigan to get his MFA from the University of Michigan at Ann Arbor. From 1975 to 1989, he was the Director and Resident Artist at the Archie Bray Foundation in Helena, Montana. Since then, he has taught at Arizona State University in Tempe.

After building a new studio in Tempe, he found he could not continue with the style of work he had been making in Montana. During a trip to Thailand with a friend, he filled several sketchbooks with drawings, having no plans for them at all. An invitation to a large teapot show led him to transfer these drawings onto those forms, using a sgraffito technique through black slip. He soon decided to do the drawings in color and, disliking the feel of underglazes, turned to china painting on the advice of a friend.

Kurt admits to having had the typical potter's prejudice against china paints. He had been aware

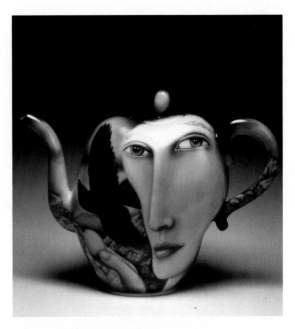

"Life Science," teapot, 10" x 12."

"Orbit," jar, 17" x 14," 2002. Front view.

"Bug Lesson," jar, 18" x 12," 1995.

"Bug Lesson," detail.

of historical and contemporary overglazing, but only vaguely. "I was a conformist. I wanted to do cone10 reduction in the Mingei style."

He ordered some china paints from Rynne China Company and began to paint. To this day, he has never had a formal lesson in china painting. At first, he added his son's acrylic painting medium to his china paints. However, this dried in minutes. A search for a better painting medium led him to the studio of Jerry Bolton in Mesa, Arizona, where he bought a lifetime supply of her medium mixture, the only china painting medium he's ever tried.

Mrs. Bolton told him that he was the only man who ever came into her shop with a question other than "Where's my wife?"

Kurt slipcasts his porcelain forms and fires them to cone 10. He then sprays on a cone 5 clear glaze and refires them. His forms for china painting are simple and clean, with rounded profiles that do not dictate imagery. Most are based on classical forms and snuff bottles (a genre Kurt has always loved), although greatly enlarged, as if seen in a fun-house mirror. Many have been drastically flattened, allowing two distinct sides for complementary images. Originally,

"Sleeper," jar, 18" x 12," 1994. Front view.

"Sleeper," jar, 18" x 12," 1994. Back view.

the forms were based on drawings from his sketchbooks, in which he would draw the outlines of pots and fill them in with imagery.

Kurt's current work is a series of globes and other closed forms, completely covered with painting. They require bisquing in a large bowl of grog to prevent warping, and elaborate support systems to enable handling and firing. Each form gets its own porcelain stand, which Kurt epoxies to the piece for the glaze firing, and again for each china paint firing.

Most of Kurt's paintings are fired three times, the first two firings to cone 019, the last to cone 018. This is the reverse of most china painters' practice of firing to progressively lower temperatures. He

avoids gold-based colors, finding them too shiny for his taste, and he uses only a few of the cadmium reds. He has never used a mixing medium, preferring to work directly with a painting medium.

He used to make detailed drawings for each piece, but now simply begins painting, adding imagery based on what he's already done. He relies on his imagination and a large file of pictures he's collected over the years. His son maintains that he starts by painting a leaf, and continues to draw vegetation until he knows what he wants to do. Kurt says, "I used to make art "on purpose," about form and materials. Now I don't question what I'm painting. I've learned to just get out of my own way."

Hamada Shoji (Japan), *Tokkuri* (sake bottle), stoneware, glaze, wood-fired (oxidation), red and green overglaze enamels, fired in small wood-fired muffle kiln, 6" x 4," c. 1955-60. Private Collection.

from medieval and Renaissance times, and it appealed strongly to the romantic sensibilities of the day. Not only did they yearn for an earlier time, they most often took as their models everyday and peasant ware, rather than the products of imperial and court patronage. A similar phenomenon was taking place in Japan, known as the Mingei Movement. It also exalted the work of medieval Japanese and Korean potters, whose pots were prized for the tea ceremony. These pots were the ceramic opposite of the enameled ware produced for the Nabeshima clan and other elites.

This was never the model for china painters. Theirs had always been a specialized profession, and they had never made the objects they decorated. If they had not actually worked in a large

Howard Kottler, "Look Alikes," plate with commercial decals, 10⅜" diam. 1972.
Collection of Sam & Dianne Scott. *Photo: Sam Scott.*

factory, they had at least produced their ware to others' specifications, at home or in small family workshops. They had almost never designed the patterns themselves, they were used to copying the motifs assigned to them, and their wares were never intended for casual everyday use. The best-known china painters were painters first and foremost; porcelain was only one of the surfaces they painted on.

For potters and tile makers it was different, and the differences led virtually all of them to make choices other than overglazing. For one thing, they now had an enormous range of clays, glaze formulas and techniques, kiln types and decorating methods. Even those clay artists who viewed their work as a painting medium had many options, from underglazing to colored glazes to majolica, and more. After World War II, those who wanted bright colors and ease of application, without the necessity of studying glaze chemistry, had a huge range of commercially available glazes and underglazes in the cone 06–04 range.

Another reason that potters tend not to use china paint is that most are either what the British potter Michael Cardew referred to as "mud and water men," or they love fire and flames. It's rare to

Richard Shaw, "Paintbox with Balboa Watercolors," glazed porcelain with overglaze decals, 4¾" x 13" x 9½," 2003. Courtesy of Frank Lloyd Gallery. *Photo: Anthony Cuñha.*

find a potter who has all the skills to design, throw or cast his clay forms, develop suitable glazes, fire the work competently, and then decorate it with a medium that feels as different from clay and raw glaze as china paint does.

Thomas Minton published his first book of tile patterns showing his newly perfected encaustic technique in 1835. This added another option to the already bewildering variety of decorative and forming techniques for tile artists in the Victorian era. Well over 100 brands of tile were being manufactured in England at that time, and almost none of them were hand-painted with overglazes. The best-known tile designer of his day, William de Morgan, chose Turkish Iznik designs as his inspi-

ration, working with ceramic colorants on a raw glaze in the majolica style.

China painting would seem a more logical choice for tile artists than for potters. Indeed, many tile artists, especially those who come to it from a painting background in another medium, do choose china paint. Despite the advantages of china paint as a tile-decorating medium (particularly the fact that, on commercial ceramic tiles, the adjacent undecorated field tile will always match the painted tile), more tile artists opt for some other decorating process.

Leach, Hamada, Voulkos, and Autio

Bernard Leach was unquestionably the most influential potter of the 20th century, worldwide.

Ralph Bacerra, "Untitled Lidded Vessel," earthenware, 32" x 18½" x 16," 2001. Courtesy of Frank Lloyd Gallery. *Photo: Anthony Cuñha.*

Ron Nagle, "Shades of Sade," porcelain with overglaze, 5⅞" x 4" x 2¼," 2002. Courtesy of Frank Lloyd Gallery. *Photo: Don Tuttle.*

Though British, he grew up in Japan, and was equally at home in either country. Not only did he become the model for a generation of potters throughout the English-speaking world through his example and his writing, he was almost as much the voice of the Mingei in Japan as its most prominent writer, Yanagi Soetsu, author of *The Unknown Craftsman.*

Together with Hamada Shoji, Leach provided the example of a small workshop in which the master designed and did at least some work on almost every piece that came through the studio. Leach and Hamada both trained their own sons as potters, as well as apprentices. Their work grew out of peasant traditions in Japan and England, and their choice of kiln technology was, for the most part, high-temperature reduction firing. The mystique of cone 10 reduction for functional pottery persists among potters to this day.

Hamada, however, did do some overglazing, unlike virtually all of his contemporaries. He went to Okinawa for a few weeks every year to make pots from the local clay, specifically to overglaze. Later he built a special enameling kiln at his compound in Mashiko and overglazed some of the ware he made there.

He used only green, amber, and a Kutani red, sometimes in abstract patterns but often in his signature sugar cane motif. Hamada ground his colors with a mortar and pestle, using tea as a medium. His kiln was constructed as two updraft bottle kilns sharing a common wall, although he only used one chamber. It was fueled with pine wood, and used a large bisque bowl as a door.

In the mid-1950's, two charismatic young World War II veterans, Peter Voulkos and Rudy Autio, began making ceramic work that embodied the ideals of Abstract Expressionism at the Archie Bray Foundation in Helena, Montana, and the world of studio pottery has never been the same.

Voulkos' work was never about painting at all, and while Autio's later evolved into a very graphic style, neither ever used overglazes. Their overwhelming influence on the next generation of clay artists only served to drive those artists farther from the use of china paint.

Funk Art and Beyond

Around Davis, California, in the 1960's and early 1970's, a number of clay artists led by Robert Arneson, David Gilhooly, Clayton Bailey, and others, began making sculptural objects that were narrative, witty, and provocative. The style became known as the Funk Movement, and was limited almost entirely to the West Coast of the United States.

In an earlier time, their sculpture, which owed a lot to Käendler's Meissen figurines and his famous porcelain zoo, would have been colored with overglaze enamels. But the ease of use and the wide range of bright colors of glazes and underglazes in the low-fire range, found in hobby greenware shops, led the Funk artists more to that option. A few of these artists did use china paints, but primarily as accents of color, or for touching up faults from higher temperature firings.

However, another product of the greenware supply shops did appeal to the Funk artists. An enormous range of images was available in the form of ceramic decals, both custom made and through catalogs.

The best-known user of commercial decals was Howard Kottler of Seattle, Washington. He used them on commercially made white china plates, as well as on his own sculpture. His best-known work featured witty collages of cut-up and altered decals, often on political themes. The fact that he made neither the form nor the decoration himself provoked endless debates on the difference between art and craft in the "Letters" column of *Ceramics Monthly* magazine.

Another artist of this genre who uses decals, both commercial and homemade, is Richard Shaw. His *trompe-l'oeil* sculpture, while mostly low-fire glazed and underglazed, is often embellished with china painting as well.

Ralph Bacerra's pots, while not exactly in the Funk mode, are definitely California in feeling. Their bright colors and eye-catching patterns are some of the few examples of china painting in the world of studio pottery and clay academia. Bacerra handbuilds elaborate forms, then embellishes their surfaces with intricate patterns in layers of underglaze engobes, transparent glaze, overglaze colors, and gold luster.

Ron Nagle's small sculpture and cup forms are handbuilt porcelain, with glazes. Nagle then applies china paint to intensify and deepen the color of the surfaces.

Educational Systems

One of the main differences between the potters' subculture and the china painters' is how they each acquire their skills and techniques, and how mastery is recognized.

In the late 19th and early 20th centuries, overglaze decoration was taught in art school ceramics departments, along with throwing, mold making, glazing, underglazing, firing, and all the other ceramic skills. This is no longer the case, as china paint has fallen completely out of fashion among academic clay artists.

Most prominent clay artists today are academically trained, and have earned a Bachelor's degree, if not a Master's. As a result, most of these artists have some training in other art disciplines, as well as art history.

A few potters have received their training in an apprenticeship setting, but community recreation centers provide schooling for most potters and clay artists who are not trained in academia. Many of these artists are exposed to a variety of techniques and technologies, such as raku, highfire reduction, midrange and lowfire oxidation, and occasionally wood, salt, or other firing, but almost never to overglaze painting.

Regardless of their systematic training, clay artists almost all patronize a well-developed network of specialized workshops and short classes led by prominent artists. These are often held in the same schools and art centers as their regular classes, but also in a number of well-known centers, which offer almost nothing but workshops, primarily in the summer. Many of these nonprofit workshop centers offer college credit. It is rare to find a clay artist whose life and work has not been drastically changed by an intensive workshop experience. It is also rare to see a workshop in china painting offered by one of these centers, and rarer still to see it as part of a college or art center curriculum.

Because of this deficiency, china painters usually get their education in a much less structured or formal way. Almost all have learned their craft in classes taught and organized by individuals, who usually teach in their own shops or homes. Often the teacher is also a distributor of supplies and equipment, and some also offer classes in the molding and glazing of greenware. Some teachers have an IPAT Certificate of Mastery, and though the tests for this certification are extensive and rigorous, it is not an academic degree.

Many students of china painting already have some experience in oil painting or watercolor. Some have an art degree, and most select the class closest to their homes.

A number of well-established schools offer intensive classes in china painting, ranging in length from a few days to two weeks, although the option of college credit is rare. There is also a well-developed system of seminars and short classes for china painters, taught by well-known artists, who almost always focus on specific techniques for painting a particular subject. Local china painting clubs (often affiliated with the World Organization of China Painters) provide an important setting for sharing techniques and information, as well as the venue for seminars by guest artists.

While both china painters and potters are incredibly generous with technical information, the form that information takes is often quite different between the two groups. When asked a question such as, "How did you get that effect?" a china painter's answer usually will include the names of products. A potter's answer is more likely to come in the form of a recipe, with the assumption that the questioner will make the necessary product himself. It is very rare for a ceramics instructor to sell any kind of supplies to students, while this is common practice among china painters. Two factors account for this difference: china painters use most materials in very small quantities, and ceramics instructors are usually paid far better.

There is another difference between the two groups that is obvious within minutes to anyone who encounters a group of china painters or potters. China painters are, with exceedingly few exceptions at any level, women. And while the majority of students in ceramics classes are women, most of the best-known clay artists, until quite recently, have been men.

Love your palette as your house.

—Anonymous, *The Class Room #1, 1909*

Tools and Equipment

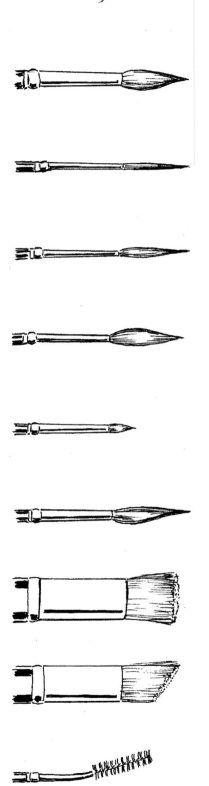

Almost any of the supplies for other forms of painting, and many of those for ceramics or printmaking, are useful for china painting. Most novice china painters have had some experience with at least one other form of art, and will have many of the necessary tools already on hand.

Brushes

My brother the musician always says there's nothing to playing the piano; you just hit the right key at the right time. I reply that there's also nothing to drawing; you just make the right mark in the right place. And very often in art, that "right mark" is best made with a brush. When choosing brushes, remember that the only thing that matters is the finished art. Your hand and eye determine where the "right place" is, but the brushes make that "right mark," and thus, are your most important tools.

Artist's brushes are designated as watercolor or oil painting brushes, softer ones generally being for watercolor and stiffer ones for oil. Watercolor brushes generally work well for china painting, particularly if water is used as the medium. Oil-based china paint is a bit thicker and stickier, so many china painters, including myself, prefer a slightly stiffer brush. Size, shape, and hair type are the variables that affect the cost and function of a brush.

Shapes

A brush's designation is determined by the shape of its ferrule (the metal or plastic piece that holds bristles to handle) and its end profile. Some common round-ferruled shapes are rounds, liners, riggers, scrollers, scripts, and stencils.

A good watercolor round is the one indispensable brush. Most china painters prefer them in sizes 4 to 6. The very tiny ones are superfluous if you have a larger one with a very good point.

Liners are long and thin, and *riggers* (so named because they're good for drawing the rigging of ships) are longer still. They make long, thin, even lines. The point of a liner may be round or it may

Brush shapes with round ferrules. Top to bottom: round, liner, scroller, script, cat's tongue, cut liner, stencil, deerfoot, whirley.

CHINA PAINT & OVERGLAZE

Paul Lewing, "Verses," china paint on porcelain tile, each 12" x 8," 2005. Text was printed full-size, transferred to the tile using graphite paper, and lettered with a #2 script brush.

be angled, in which case it is called a *cut liner*. A more exaggerated version of this shape may be made with a flat ferrule and be called a *sword liner*, specifically designed for banding.

Scrollers are slightly thicker in the body, but also have a long thin point. They are used when a line with a small amount of variation in width is needed. They are also the brush of choice for raised paste and enamel work.

Scripts are similar to liners, but with fatter bodies. If only the point is used, they make lines similar to liners, but if you press down slightly, they will produce a wider line. As the name implies, they are used for italic script.

Stencil brushes are flat on the ends, and are used to fill stencils with even areas of color. They can also be used to remove brush strokes laid down with another brush, producing a stippled pattern. Water-based china paint blotted with a dry stencil brush will have a finer grain pattern than that made with a wet brush. Very tiny stencil brushes can be hard to find, but you can make your own by clipping the end off an old round. When a stencil brush's end is cut at an angle, it is referred to as a *deerfoot stippler*. Some brush suppliers make a variation on the stencil brush shape, with shorter, softer bristles, called a *pouncer*.

A **cat's tongue** brush has a thick body, and a short, sharp point. A flat-ferruled version of this shape is often called a *berry brush*, and is specifically designed for painting many tiny shapes, such as the individual seeds of blackberries.

Mops may be round or flat, but often have no ferrule. They hold large quantities of liquid and

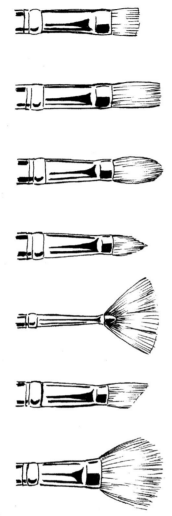

Brush shapes with flat ferrules. Top to bottom: flat, bright, filbert, fitch, fan, angled, mop.

flat side down, or the point will split or "quack" into a shape resembling a duck's open bill. Many quill brushes are sold without a handle, requiring the artist to move points from one handle to another, which often splits the quill. They should be soaked in warm water to soften them and pushed gently onto the handle. If they do split, you may slip a short piece of heat-shrink tubing over the quill and heat it gently with a match.

The common flat-ferruled shapes are brights, flats (also known as shaders), filberts, and fitches.

Brights are the most versatile flat-ferruled brushes. They are slightly longer than they are wide. *Flats* are similar, but their length and width are the same. Both are used to fill in broad areas and washes of color, and both are made with either square or angled tips. Flats and brights make a broad, straight-sided, square-ended mark when they're moved up or down, and a thin mark when moved sideways. Moving them in a circular motion produces a C-shaped mark.

Paul Lewing, "Psalm 121:1,2," 40" x 52." First Presbyterian Church, Seattle, WA. Lettering done with a #8 bright.

dispense it a little at a time. Mops are also used dry to pick up powdered color when laying a dry ground.

Most of the above brush shapes are made with either metal or quill ferrules. Many china painters prefer quill brushes to metal ferrules because they are more flexible and "spring" better. Quill brushes also differ from ferruled brushes in that they are not perfectly round, and must be held with the

Filberts have a rounded profile and make an oval mark. *Fitches* taper to a chisel point and make a teardrop shape, useful for drawing foliage. Fitches and filberts are typically not moved sideways, but only up and down, although the straight side of a fitch can be used like the square end of a flat.

Fans also have a flat ferrule, but the bristles are splayed into a wide rounded end. They are useful for making streaky marks, and are often used dry to blend areas of different colors while the paint is still wet. Clipping some of the bristles can result in very interesting marks.

Flats and *rounds* are the most versatile shapes. A selection of these and a good liner or rigger will cover most painting situations. Many china painters use no more than a small round, a liner, and a large and small shader, either square or angled. In traditional china painting the "American style", featuring soft naturalistic effects, is usually painted using square shaders, while the more rigid and brighter "Dresden style" employs more rounds and liners.

Whirleys (or spooleys) and *spatter* brushes are unlike the above shapes, and are made up of stiff bristles protruding from a central shaft. A whirley's bristles are very stiff and short, and are designed to be dragged through a wet stroke to simulate hair. Spatter brushes have longer bristles, as well as a piece of wire or wood along one side. When the brush is rotated against the wire, droplets of paint are flung onto the work.

Bristles

The best watercolor brushes are Kolinsky sable, renowned for strength, springiness, and fine point. Next best are red sable, not as springy as Kolinsky, but about half the price. Sabeline is a fine ox hair dyed to resemble sable, and is cheaper but not as good. The cheapest watercolor brushes are squirrel, sheep, or goat hair. Squirrel hair is very fine and limp.

The best oil painting brushes are hog bristle and very stiff. Hog bristle brushes are generally too stiff for most china painters' taste. A softer oil brush might be mongoose, and an ox hair brush will be softer yet. "Camel hair" is a trade name applied to any number of hairs, none of which come from camels.

The wide variety of synthetic bristles has an enormous range of stiffness, price, and holding capacity. It is often difficult to compare brands of brushes, because so many different bristles are simply labeled "synthetic." Nylon bristles, which do not taper, are very resilient and easy to clean.

Price

This is a tricky issue for ceramists because biqueware and raw glaze abrade brushes quickly. A fine brush that would last a watercolorist a lifetime may lose its point in a year or two of oxide decoration. China painting is not nearly as hard on brushes, as the smooth glazed surface is not as abrasive. For banding or laying on flat areas of glaze, an expensive brush may be wasted. Sometimes though, only a very good brush will make the mark you need, consistently and repeatedly.

With brushes, price is a very good indication of quality, so remember that your brushes are your most important tools. It's often tempting to save a little money by getting the next-best bristles, or a slightly smaller size, but all that matters in making art is what it looks like. Skimping is foolish if the art doesn't look right.

Care

Never dip a dry brush into colors, either water- or oil-based. The brush will not load completely if the bristles are not wetted first. Dip the brush into water or other medium and dry it slightly on a rag.

Brushes should be rinsed after use as dried china paint will abrade the bristles. Soap or solvent is not necessary with water-based china paints, but might be with gum-filled commercial products.

Oil-based mediums should be rinsed out in clean turpentine or paint thinner. Some china painters also rinse their brushes in alcohol at the end of each session. Avoid strong solvents such as lacquer thinner, shellac remover, or acetone, as they will weaken the glue which holds the hairs in place. If you work with both oil and water mediums, use a separate set of brushes for each.

Never rest a brush on its bristles. A brush left to dry that way becomes useless. Brushes which have the bristles glued into the handle, like sumi brushes, should not be left to dry with the tips up. Sumi brushes often have a silk loop on the end of the handle, used to hang the brush point down. Don't let your brushes dry on a heating element or in a blast of hot air. This will dry out the natural oils and make the brush less flexible.

Use a palette knife to mix colors, not a brush. I must admit I am consistently guilty of this sin, and my brushes pay the price for it.

If you transport your brushes, protect the tips. You can buy a specially made brush case, but a length of plastic pipe or even a cardboard box will work as well. I roll mine in a woven bamboo place mat, which allows them to dry, as well as protects them. Specially made brush boxes are available, with springs fixed inside, to hold brushes in place.

Testing Brushes

Evaluating brushes is very difficult, but some art supply stores will provide plain water and paper. New brushes often have a protective plastic sleeve over the bristles. If you remove this, be very careful if you put it back on, as it's easy to bend a few hairs back and damage them. Sharp-pointed brushes usually have a stiff sizing in them to protect the point. Soak this out in water before testing them.

Drop a dry unsized brush on its tip to assess springiness. Wet it and see if it comes to a point naturally. Make strokes up, down, and in a circle, to see the differences in the mark. Push the brush

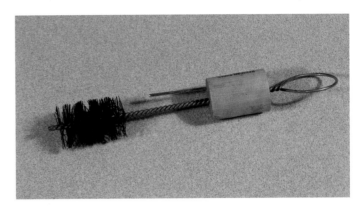

A spatter brush.

straight down to see what mark that makes. Vary the pressure from light to hard to light again, to see if the point returns. Keep doing this until the brush is dry to test its capacity.

Brush Strokes

A brush's size, shape, and type of bristle all contribute to the mark it will produce, but the art is in the stroke. While there are an infinite variety of combinations and permutations, all brush marks are the result of a few basic motions. Try all these motions with every one of your brushes. Try them with the brush well loaded, and almost empty. Use a very fluid medium and a sticky one, on both vertical and horizontal surfaces. Notice how a soft or a stiff brush, or a short or long handle, feels. Just lightly touch the surface, and continue to press until the ferrule touches the work.

The easiest stroke might be called a "pecking" stroke. Just touch a loaded brush tip straight down on the surface. A flat brush produces a line; a round one, a dot. Notice how clean or frayed the mark is. Continue this until the brush is empty, noting how well the tip springs back, how the color flows, and how much the brush will hold.

Make a "comma" stroke by moving this dot stroke to the side. Push down, ease up, move the tip, and lift up. A good brush will make a clean

Sam Scott, Vase, porcelain, 14" tall, black matte glaze, spattered red china paint. *Photo: Dana Drake*

mark throughout the stroke, with no stray hairs dragging alongside.

A "C" or "S" stroke is made by moving the brush tip sideways and in a half-circle. A flat-ferruled brush will leave a thick or thin trail according to the angle it's traveling. Notice how thin a line you can make when traveling sideways. Test your control of pressure by making this stroke with a round or a liner. If you can maintain an even pressure when changing directions, you will leave a line of even width.

You should also be able to make a line of even width with a flat or bright, using a straight stroke. This is the stroke you will use most often, to fill in areas of color. It's most often made by pulling the brush toward yourself, but practice making it in all directions.

Try using more than one color on your brush. To load a round brush with two colors, fill it normally, blot off the tip, and load the tip with a contrasting color. Using a flat brush, load each side with a different color. For an even gradation, mix the two colors next to each other on a palette, and drag the brush back and forth between them until they blend. Now practice all the above strokes.

An interesting practice exercise is to load two colors on a flat or bright, and make a straight stroke in which you vary the pressure on one edge, but not the other. This produces a mark that is straight on one side and wavy on the other. Interesting leaves and vegetation can be depicted this way. Flip the brush over and draw the other side of the leaf, to shade on the opposite side.

Oriental Brushes

Hake brushes are sheep or goat hair, with a handle of flat wood or multiple bamboo stems. They are wonderful for applying slips or oxide washes, but are too soft for most china painters' tastes, particularly for oil-based mediums.

Oriental **sumi** (sometimes written as *sumi-e* or *fude*) brushes are the most sensitive and expressive marking instruments ever devised. Their use is a completely separate discipline from Western painting, calling for a different attitude toward making marks, and even a different grip. Whereas the Western idea is to keep working on an area until you get it right, the sumi concept is to visualize a stroke so well before it's made that it's perfect the first time. In sumi painting, there is no erasing, and no covering up.

The best sumi brushes are wolf hair, but sable and Kolinsky brushes are also very good. The test in which you drop a dry brush on its tip to see how high it will bounce is particularly indicative of the quality of sumi brushes. A really good wolf hair sumi brush will bounce more than half the height of the drop.

The most important difference between sumi painting and Western painting is in how the brush is gripped. Western brushes are usually held like a pencil, or sometimes on the thumb and the tips of all four fingers.

To grip a sumi brush in the proper position, extend your hand, with the open palm up. Place the brush between the middle and ring finger, just ahead of the last knuckle, with about an inch of the handle below your fingers, and the tip down. Now close your hand, so that the tip of your thumb touches the tip of your index finger. The brush should be vertical, with two of your fingers on each side of the handle. Do not close your hand tight, but let the brush lay naturally in your hand.

To demonstrate the difference this makes, first hold your brush like a pencil. Move it up and down, back and forth, and around in a circle, going as far as you can with each motion. Then roll the brush in a spinning motion as far as you can, with the tip stationary. Now hold the brush in the position for sumi painting, and make the same motions. You will notice that you have almost double the range of motion. This may seem awkward at first, but with practice, you will be

CHINA PAINT & OVERGLAZE

Brushstrokes made with a round-ferruled brush.

Brushstrokes made with a flat-ferruled brush.

able to make much more controlled and expressive marks, particularly those long, thin marks that vary from thick to thin. And for long strokes, this grip makes for a much more fluid use of hand, wrist, and arm.

In traditional sumi painting with black ink only, shaded strokes are made by grinding a hard ink stick on an ink stone, which has a well in one end. The ink becomes very dark on the stone, and lighter where it is diluted with water in the well. Typically the brush is loaded with pale ink from the well, the tip is wrung out, and only the tip reloaded with dark ink. Colored shaded strokes are made with different colors of ink on different areas of the brush. My teacher would go so far as to load the reservoir of the brush with one color, and the tip with another. Then she would use another brush to apply a third color to one

side of the brush, and a fourth to the other. It was astounding to watch her produce a four-color mark by varying pressure and rolling the brush, in a long, graceful stroke.

All of these same techniques are possible for china painting. It may even be easier to paint in this style on a non-porous surface, because brush speed is not so critical. The paint needs to be quite fluid, whether water- or oil-based. It is even possible to use colors from different china paint color groups on the same stroke, as the colors do not really mix.

Of the four basic strokes used in sumi painting, the most common is a tapered stroke, rounded where the brush first meets the surface, and pointed on the tip. A bamboo leaf is a perfect example of this stroke. It's made with a quick flick into the surface. The harder you press, the fatter the mark.

Try making it short and thick, and then long and tapered. Make it in all directions. Try slightly flattening the tip of the brush to open it before you stroke, to make a frayed mark. This stroke calls for a decisive, confident motion.

In the second basic stroke, the brush tip never leaves the surface, traveling all the time. Pressing harder or softer makes thicker or thinner lines. These marks look like grass stems, and are the real tests of a good sumi brush. The best brushes will make an incredibly long line, and spring back to a fine point until the brush is completely dry. The motion for this stroke is languid and relaxed.

The third basic stroke is thick on both ends and thin in the middle. It's made by pressing down at first, picking the tip up a bit, running to the end of the stroke, pressing down again, and then lifting up off the surface. The stems of bamboo, and the branches of trees, are made this way. Practice making a mark that is equally thick on both sides of the thin part, rather than one that has all the thickness to one side. This is done by pressing straight down, rather than putting the tip down, then drawing it toward yourself and back. The trick with this stroke is in a smooth transition from slow to fast progress, and from hard to light pressure, without being jerky.

The fourth, and hardest, stroke makes a round mark by putting the brush down and spinning it in place. It can be made in several ways, depending on where you want the dark part of the mark.

Load a brush with light color, tip it with dark, press the tip straight down, and twirl the brush in place. This will make a mark that is only slightly darker on the outside than in the center. Now load the brush the same, hold it at an angle to the surface, touch the tip down, and rotate the brush around its point, keeping the handle at the same angle to the surface all the way around. This motion, usually done counterclockwise by right-handed artists, makes a circular mark, dark in the center. Another variation is to load and spin the

Left: hake brush. Middle: seven different sumi brushes. Right: bamboo hake.

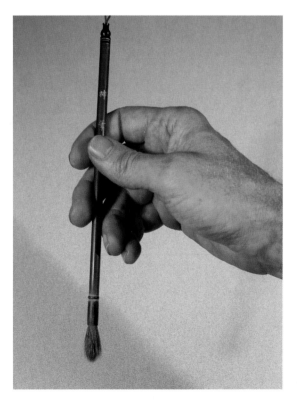

The proper way to hold a sumi brush.

The four basic sumi brush strokes.

brush the same as before, but use the back of the brush as the pivot point, keeping the tip at the outside of the circle. This results in a dark circle with a light center, and it's the most difficult sumi stroke. Precision and control are what's called for in this stroke.

Bamboo is probably the easiest and most natural thing to paint with a sumi brush. Traditionally, it's the first of the Chinese "Four Gentlemen" to be taught. The others are plum blossom, Chinese orchid, and chrysanthemum. These four represent winter, spring, summer, and fall, respectively.

Pens and Pencils

Lettering and calligraphy can be done on fired glaze, using a traditional lettering or drawing pen loaded with thin china paint. Both pointed and flat nibs are useful, and the marks they produce are quite different from those made by script brushes. These marks are more precise and mechanical in feeling, and the tools are much harder to control.

Mapping or quill pens have very fine pointed nibs with a split tip, and make thin lines of even width. Drawing pens often have a larger bowl-tipped nib, making it easier to vary the width of lines. Calligraphy or lettering pens are squared-ended, and come in many widths and degrees of flexibility.

If you're used to using a pen on paper, drawing on a hard glazed surface can be a little disconcerting. The nib makes a harsh scratching noise, and there is no absorbency to help modulate changes in speed or pressure. If the two sides of a split fine point are even slightly misaligned, color dumps off to one side of the stroke. With a little practice, you can produce any effect with china paint on glaze that you can with ink on paper. Besides lettering, pens are used in china painting for outlining, for cross-hatching and line textures, and for dot patterns.

The hardest part about pen work with china paint is getting a medium of the proper consis-

Paul Lewing, "Heron & Bamboo," 10" x 14", porcelain tile with extruded porcelain border.

tency and drying speed. The color must be very well ground with the medium as well.

Occasionally you will see a color-filled mechanical pen in china painting supply catalogues. These are not usually successful because the powdered color, no matter how finely ground, eventually separates from the medium, and the mechanism clogs. Pens filled with gold luster are readily available, and work well because the gold is actually dissolved in the medium, rather than being just suspended in it, as china paint is.

In her seminal 1877 book, *China Painting: A Practical Manual,* M. Louise McLaughlin mentions overglaze crayons or pencils made by the Lacroix Company in France. I have never seen anything like these, but it would be very possible to make your own by mixing china paint into melted wax or gum tragacanth.

In addition to pens and pencils for applying china paint, you will need some kind of tool to sketch your design onto the ceramic object. There are a huge variety of pens, pencils, and markers

A. L. H. Robkin, "Archiloches 103." Penwork on porcelain tile, wood frame, 8" x 10." *Photo: Paul Lewing.*

Pens and pencils for china painting. Top to bottom: two lettering pens with changeable nibs, wax-based china marker, two markers marketed to china painters, pencil marketed to china painters, laundry marker.

on the market. Almost anything that will leave a mark on glaze is usable in some china painting situation.

Ordinary graphite pencils usually will not leave a strong enough mark, but china paint suppliers sell very soft ones that will. It takes a softer pencil to mark on a glossy glaze than a matte one. China markers and grease pencils will work on any glazed surface, but they may resist water-based paints.

Most felt-tipped markers will also work on glaze, but you need to choose the right marker to go with your painting medium. Oil-based colors will usually cover a water-based marker line, but solvent-based markers, like laundry markers, will often resist a water-based paint. This can be very useful if you want fine white lines in a field of color, but annoying if you don't.

Ute Henne (Germany), "Cup and Saucer," porcelain. Saucer, 7⅞". The motif was drawn with a pen and fired, color added with a square shader and stippled then fired, liquid bright gold applied with a pen, burnishing gold applied on rims.

Many marker lines will disperse into color applied over them. This is a little distracting, but usually makes no difference to the fired result. Occasionally you can find markers in china paint supply catalogues that will not disperse in either water or oil, and will fire out. It's best to stock up on these whenever you find them.

It is sometimes astounding to see how prominent a pencil or marker line is after firing. It's almost impossible to predict which colors or composition of tool will leave a trace on which glaze, fired to which temperature. Usually these traces are faint and easily rubbed off, but occasionally a marker or pencil will leave a prominent line that cannot be erased after firing.

Wipeout and Blotting Tools

The one thing that makes china painting very different from all other painting and ceramic mediums is the ability to easily wipe off the unfired color. You can make an unpainted mark that is soft or hard on the edges. You can remove large areas or very fine lines. You can remove the color entirely, or you can move the wet color off to one side of your wiped mark.

China paint and ceramic suppliers sell a wipeout tool that has a flexible rubber tip on each end, pointed on one end and broad and flat on the other. Some catalogues carry wipeout tools in a variety of shapes, sizes, and flexibilities. These are very versatile and indispensable tools. If your

Wipeout tools. Top to bottom: homemade foam rubber tool, foam makeup applicator, rubber tool from paint store, three commercial wipeout tools, homemade tool made from credit card.

paint is completely dry, they will remove the color cleanly. If it's still wet, they will move the color aside. The flat end makes marks just like a flat or bright brush, but in the negative. Ceramic supply houses also sell many rubber tools made for shaping clay that are just large versions of these wipe-out tools. You can also make your own wipe-out tools from erasers, wood, bamboo, old credit cards, and many other things.

Foam rubber is an excellent choice for making wipeout tools to leave a soft edged mark. Makeup applicators are perfect for small areas. I use a lot of pieces of egg-crate pattern foam mattress for both blotting and wipeout. They need to be periodically washed out, but a wet one makes a different mark than a dry one, so it's best to have plenty on hand. Ceramic suppliers sell a wide variety of foam and sponge shapes and sizes, attached to all kinds of handles.

Foam rubber also makes a good blotting tool, for water-based (and some oil-based) paints. Often you want to spread an area of color quickly, but you don't want the resulting brush strokes.

Patting the area with foam will leave a smoother texture than a stencil brush, and can even result in an effect similar to spraying. Continued daubing will begin to remove color, especially water-based paints. You can achieve remarkable control of color intensity in large areas this way. Certain oil mediums may deteriorate foam quickly, however.

When painting with water, the foam needs to remain dry, so it's best to have a selection of foam pieces for blotting, too. Wet foam will splatter tiny droplets of paint several inches around itself.

The traditional material for blotting out brush strokes and fading colors with oil-based paints is silk, wrapped around a ball of cotton. If you're painting with water as a medium, this doesn't work as well, since it gathers the color to the center of the pad and leaves a dark spot where the pad is picked up. Chamois skin is another traditional blotting material.

Stencil and Stamp Materials

A hard smooth glaze makes an ideal surface for adhering all kinds of stencils and masking compounds.

Any kind of thin soft paper, such as newsprint or butcher paper, can be used as a stencil if it is dampened. It will stay in place for only a few minutes, but that may be long enough. Tearing the paper stencils can make interesting shapes.

Self-adhesive labels, and many kinds of tape, make ideal stencils for china painting. For overlapping stenciled patterns, you need to fire between each layer, but this process of slowly building layers of pattern works well. For larger stencils, the low-tack adhesive film sold in art supply stores is perfect, although the contact paper sold in grocery and hardware stores to cover shelves works almost as well.

Watercolorists use a liquid masking fluid that dries hard and peels off. It's similar to the liquid rubber emulsion that some potters use as a glaze resist. This is great for masking out areas and

patterns. Potter's liquid wax resist is too fluid to adhere to a slick surface.

Stamps might be thought of as negative stencils. Almost any material can be coated with color and touched to the surface. Foam, sponge, rubber, and linoleum all work well. You could even make traditional fish prints, by painting a real fish with china paint and laying it on the surface.

Stamping, in my experience, works better with an oil medium than with water. Water-based paint gathers to the center of the stamp as it's lifted, and tends to splatter. It also often leaves bubbles that do not smooth out in the firing.

In the 18th and 19th centuries, many dinnerware factories developed very intricate and beautiful stamped patterns, made up of dozens of component shapes and colors. They are a wonderful blend of the handpainted and mechanical looks.

A selection of foam rubber application and blotting tools, some commercially made, some homemade.

Paul Lewing, "Rescued" bowl, 8" diam. Blue: foam rubber stamp. Green: round adhesive label resist. Beige: tape resist.

CHINA PAINT & OVERGLAZE

The author's palettes—a good example of how NOT to organize your palette.

Many china painters mix colors on a grinding glass and transfer them to a well-organized palette. Courtesy of Betty Fox. *Photo: Paul Lewing.*

Palettes and Palette Knives

Any palette designed for oil paint or watercolor will work for china painting. It must be smooth and non-porous, and it's best if it's white, so any porcelain, glass, or plastic surface will work. Palettes specifically designed for mixing paints, of the kind sold in art and china paint supply places, are probably best but not necessary, especially if you're not using many colors.

Many china painters use an ordinary ceramic tile on which to mix their colors, and clean it off after each session. Others prefer a square of glass, usually etched or sandblasted to give a little roughness to mix against. If you use glass, paste white paper to the back of it for a better background color.

If you prefer to mix large quantities of some colors and keep them moist using a mixing medium, a covered palette is essential. In a very tightly closed container, china paint mixed with this kind of medium will stay moist for as long as a year. For this approach to mixing colors, a separate jar for each color works just as well.

Palette knives, used for mixing the color with the medium, come in both straight and offset shapes. I prefer offset blades myself, but it's purely a matter of personal preference. They also come in several sizes, and I use both large and small ones.

Steel knives are the most common, but many of the old manuals caution against using a steel knife to mix certain colors, particularly yellows, as they would affect the fired color. They recommended a knife made of horn, bone, or ivory. These days, plastic would be more easily available, and stainless steel would work as well.

Miscellaneous Tools & Supplies

If you've ever done much work in other painting or ceramic mediums, you probably have all the other convenient tools for china painting.

Many artists like to draw a very detailed mockup on paper, and transfer it to the work using graphite paper. The graphite paper sold by china

paint suppliers works better than carbon paper or regular graphite paper for this purpose, as it is less waxy. Good quality tracing paper is also very handy for this step. Some artists prefer to transfer their designs to the work by running a toothed rowel wheel along the drawing lines, making perforated patterns. After the drawing is taped in place, loose charcoal is pounced on, and the drawing carefully removed, leaving black dotted lines.

Another paper product that can be very handy to decorators of plates and bowls is a plate divider. You can make your own by folding a paper circle, but china paint suppliers sell, for about $1.50, a pattern that will divide plates up to 12 inches in diameter into as many as 14 equal segments.

Eyedroppers, hypodermic syringes, or small squirt bottles are very handy for dispensing small amounts of medium. I like ear or enema syringes for doling out a few drops of water at a time.

Very fine sandpaper or abrasive pads are handy for removing tiny unmelted granules of china paint, which appear as a rough surface after firing. A quick sanding and a refire will give a glossy surface.

There are a number of tools and supplies designed to work with metallic luster. A glass brush is the traditional tool for polishing gold or silver. Roman gold is often burnished with an agate etcher, although some artists prefer to use burnishing sand. A special gold eraser is also a good investment.

If you plan to draw bands on round pots, a banding wheel is essential. One that wobbles or comes to a stop quickly is worse than useless. Get a good heavy one that spins true for a long time. Buy the biggest size you think you'll ever use. You can make a round bat that will fit on top of your banding wheel, but it will never be as solid, or spin as true, as a good banding wheel. Most banding wheels have concentric lines inscribed in their surface, which is a big help in centering your work on the wheel. If yours doesn't, you may spin the

A variety of palette knives of different sizes, shapes and materials.

Complete Chapman-Bailey china painting kit, ca.1965. Includes colors, medium, grinding glass, silk, carbon and tracing papers, palette knife, and brushes. *Courtesy of Kurt Johnson.*

Drawing a circle on a tile using a banding wheel.

Using a plate divider to section a plate into 9 equal portions.

Drawing a line on a plate using a banding tool.

wheel and draw them on fresh each time with a pencil.

Some mechanism for supporting your hand while making bands is also a good idea, especially on those days when you've had too much coffee.

Some china paint catalogues carry a device for making bands that is a small piece of metal with flanges that hook over the rim of the piece. A series of holes drilled at different distances from the edge accommodates a brush or pencil point. Moving the pencil or brush around the rim consistently, without wobbling, is awkward, however. These tools are useful for objects that are not round, but are nowhere near as good for making circles as a wheel.

Mediums and Solvents

China paint is most often bought as a very fine dry powder. In order to apply it to a glossy glazed surface, you need to mix it with some form of liquid, preferably a sticky one. This is what's known as a medium. A solvent is a substance that will dissolve the medium and color mixture, and clean it out of brushes and other tools.

We don't know what the first china painters used as a medium, but you can bet that any oily or sticky liquid, be it animal, vegetable, or mineral, has been tried as an overglaze medium somewhere by someone. Chances are it worked to some degree in some situations.

There is no "right" or "best" medium for china painting. Several factors influence the decision on a preferred medium, notably drying time, hardness of the dried coat, and stickiness. Your style and manner of working will determine which medium is best for you. If it feels right to you, and the fired results are what you want, it's a good medium for you. I personally have never had any lessons in china painting, so I never learned that water alone would not work as a medium. It's what I use almost all the time on my tile work; however, it does not work well on a vertical surface.

Traditionally, china paint has been mixed with mineral or vegetable oils or resins, but there are water-soluble mediums that work just as well. The biggest advantages to water-based mediums are that there is less odor and less tendency to provoke allergic reactions, which are usually triggered by the solvents rather than the mediums themselves.

Mixing and Painting Mediums

Some china painters prefer to mix and store a fairly large quantity of paint and take out only as much as they need for any one session. The large quantity must be mixed to a thick consistency like toothpaste, with a medium that will stay wet (or "open" as china painters call it) for a long time. This is known as a *mixing medium*. Colors mixed with such a medium and kept tightly covered will stay open for many months.

When it comes time to paint, the thick paint is diluted with a thinner, more fluid medium, to the proper consistency to apply with a brush, pen, or other tool. This substance is known as a *painting*

Paul Lewing, "Rescued Pot," 9 inches in diameter. China paint, mixed with a traditional painting medium of balsam of copaiba and lavender oil, applied with a rubber stamp.

Joyce Sandberg, "Geometric Blue Gingham Plate," 9" diam. Blue pen lines, three cone 016 firings, cream and blue enamel dots fired to cone 017. *Photo: Keith Olson.*

medium. Many china painters dispense with mixing mediums altogether, and mix only as much color as they need with a painting medium each time.

Those artists who like to fire their work between coats can use a mixing medium, but those who like to fire only once need their paints to dry hard enough to apply another coat without disturbing the first layer. These artists will prefer a closed, relatively fast-drying medium. Back in the days when a lady did not have her own kiln, a medium that dried hard and fast meant fewer smudges and nicks, and fewer trips to the kiln. Today, when most people either have their own kiln (or work where the kiln lives), this is not as great an issue. Now the choice is more likely to be made based on whether or not the artist likes to dust additional color or flux onto the unfired painting, in which case an open medium would be preferred.

No one medium will suffice in all situations. You may choose one substance for color washes, another for large thick brushstrokes, and others for fine detail, pen work, or wipeout work. Another factor that will influence your choice is personal painting style. The perfect medium for a slow and careful artist will only frustrate a loose and spontaneous one. Those who favor stiff brushes will require a different feel than those who like soft brushes. Thick applications of paint will require a different medium from thin washes.

Oil-Based Mediums

As mentioned earlier, we have no way of knowing what the first overglazers in China used as a medium, but it's pretty certain that very early on, the artists of northern Europe settled on a number of products from the surrounding evergreen forests. Many of these products are still in wide use today.

Turpentine is distilled from the sap of pine trees. It's cheap; it dries quickly and hard; and is still the most commonly used solvent for all oil-based mediums. It's used to clean tools, and is added a drop or two at a time to get painting mediums to the ideal consistency. You can get it at any paint, hardware, or art supply store. Many people are allergic to turpentine, while others object to the smell. The newer odorless turpentine works just as well as the old-fashioned kind, and may be less allergenic.

Fat oil of turpentine, also known as *Dresden fat oil*, is thickened turpentine. You can make your own by letting an open container of turpentine (covered with a cloth to keep out dust) evaporate to the consistency you like, or you can get it from china paint or printing supply houses. Fat oil is the basis for a number of specialty mediums, and is always recognizable by its strong odor. It is toxic if taken internally, and anyone who is allergic to turpentine will be even more affected by fat oil.

You may use fat oil as a painting medium by

Paul Lewing, "Rescued Pot," 11 inches in diameter. China paint applied with foam stamps. Some were inked using water, others with propylene glycol.

itself if you like a thick consistency, or thinned with turpentine for a more fluid, quicker-drying coat. To slow its drying time, add a little mineral oil, or a vegetable oil like olive or linseed oil.

Balsam of copaiba has largely replaced fat oil as the basis for most painting mediums since the 1970's. It's a golden brown, oily resin derived from the sap of a large leguminous tree native to South America. It dries fast and hard, and is thinned with turpentine. Some people use it alone as a painting medium, but most modify it with a small amount of essential plant oils to control its flow and drying time. It may also be used alone as a *grounding oil*, particularly in the heavy variation. The copaiba tree (*Copaifera Officianalis*) is named after the Copaiba volcano in northern Chile, and balsam of copaiba, in addition to its lovely name, has some very special properties. It is sold in natural medicine and health food stores as a diuretic, stimulant, and antibacterial agent. It has been used for centuries in South America to heal cuts with very little scarring, and is said to be particularly

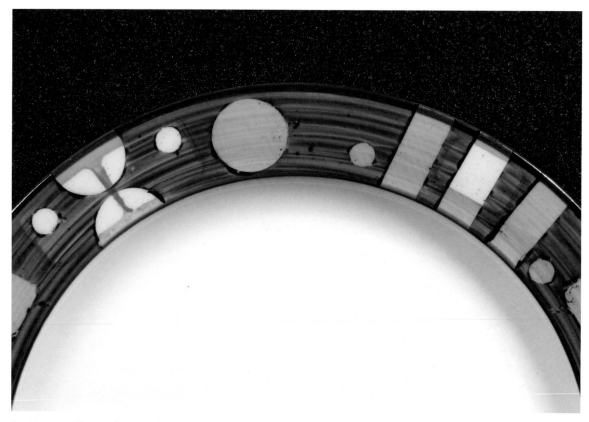

Paul Lewing, "Rescued Pot," 8" diam. China paint mixed with water or polyethylene glycol, using adhesive label resists.

effective in treating the lesions caused by eczema, psoriasis, herpes, syphilis, and gonorrhea.

Lavender oil is one of the two oils most commonly added to balsam of copaiba to make a painting medium. Alone it dries fairly quickly, and is used in place of turpentine in medium mixtures, to speed drying. It is also commonly used to thin lusters, and is available at pharmacies as well as china paint suppliers. Oil of lavender is sometimes used to clean brushes, and a drop or two is often added to a painting medium for making thin washes of color. There are three grades of lavender oil. *Pure lavender oil* is the most expensive, and dries in about 12 hours. *Artificial lavender oil* is cheaper and dries more slowly. *Spike oil,* which

has camphor added, is the fastest drying agent of the three.

Clove oil, the other common ingredient in painting medium mixtures, has the opposite effect of lavender oil. It dries very slowly, so the oils of clove and lavender are balanced to control drying time. A natural preservative, it has a strong distinctive smell, and is available in pharmacies and overglaze supply catalogs. Alcohol is its solvent. It will burn your skin and may dissolve some plastics.

Anise (or aniseed) oil, also stocked in pharmacies, is often added to make the paint flow more freely, and therefore is a common ingredient in *pen oils*. It is also useful as a solvent for cleaning natural-hair brushes.

Olive oil may also be added to balsam of co-paiba to retard drying. It is non-toxic and soluble in turpentine. The medicinal grade of olive oil carried in pharmacies is preferable to the food grade, because it is much thicker. Food grade olive oil is too thin to make a practical painting medium, but does work well as a mixing medium.

Sewing machine oil is a light, non-drying oil, soluble in turpentine, which may be mixed with other, heavier mineral oils.

Mineral oil and its more refined version, *baby oil,* are non-toxic, heavy, clear oils, which make excellent mixing mediums. Both are widely available in drug stores and supermarkets. Once dried, paint mixed with mineral oil is very hard to reconstitute.

Kerosene, or lamp oil, is a term used to denote a number of refined mineral oils. They can vary widely in viscosity, but some are useful as a painting medium, if you don't mind the smell. Kerosene is a good brush cleaner and is useful for restoring the proper consistency to paint that has dried out too much. You may add a few drops of kerosene, mix thoroughly, let the kerosene evaporate, and remix with your regular painting medium.

Linseed oil is sold in at least five grades or varieties, usually at paint stores and art supply houses. It is moderately useful as a painting medium, but is tricky to use. If it is not thoroughly dry when it goes into the kiln, it may run or boil and splatter.

Stand oil is a polymerized form of linseed oil that is often used for grounding. It dries slowly to a hard finish, and tends to flatten out as it dries, which helps eliminate any unevenness or marks made by padding. It is also an excellent medium for stamped designs and dry grounding.

Damar varnish has many of the characteristics of stand oil, but is usually a bit thinner. It makes a good oil for wet grounding if a little lavender oil is added to hasten the drying, and is soluble in alcohol. The varnish sold in art supply stores for covering oil paintings is Damar varnish. Before

Paul Lewing, "Rescued Pot," 11" in diam. Black and red china paint mixed with glycerin, then combed with a whirley brush.

Paul Lewing, "Rescued Pot," 8" in diam. Blue and brown china paint in propylene glycol, spattered with isopropyl alcohol.

Paul Lewing, "Basket Weave," ceramic tile, 4¼" x 4¼," screen-printed, using diethylene glycol as a medium.

the advent of modern polymer varnishes, it was used as a cover varnish for making decals.

Many other oils have been used in conjunction with china paint, with varying degrees of success. The oils of **carnation, walnut, peanut, pine, castor bean,** and **lemon** are those most often mentioned. Lemon oil is sometimes used to thin lusters, and is a good brush cleaner. **Varnish** and **motor oil** have also been used, but produce objectionable odors when fired.

Water-Based Mediums

Water is what I've always used as a painting medium. It has some advantages over stickier mediums, as well as some limitations. It dries very quickly, both on the palette and on the work, so painting must be fast and spontaneous. Cleanup is very easy, usually no more than a quick rinse in a bucket of water and a pat on a rag to dry. I usually do not grind my colors with the water. I find that the powder and water mix very evenly with just a few brush strokes on the palette.

However, I would not be able to use water alone as easily if I worked on vertical surfaces. I paint primarily on tile, which is laying flat when I work on it. When I do have to work on a vertical surface, I use a different medium. Unless the paint is mixed quite thick, it will run before it dries, which makes thin washes almost impossible. The unfired surface is also incredibly delicate; the slightest touch with even a dry brush or the edge of a piece of paper will remove it completely. I usually mix very small amounts of paint at a time because, while the paint is perfectly usable once it has dried into a soft crumbly mass, it never mixes with water quite as smoothly ever again.

Water is the most variable medium of any I have mentioned. I have always used tap water, but where I live (Seattle) our municipal water comes from melted snow in the nearby mountains. There is chlorine added, but it contains virtually no minerals. In many parts of the world, particularly in desert and coastal areas, there may be a high concentration of mineral salts, which can affect

Paul Lewing, "Rescued Pot," 8" in diam. Rose china paint mixed with polyethylene glycol, dried, then wiped out with a stiff tool.

the fired color of china paint. If you find that certain of your colors are not firing out to their true shade, try distilled water.

Glycerin, a remarkable substance that may be mixed with either oil- or water-based substances, has many uses for china painting. It may be used as a mixing medium, and thinned with water for painting. It may also be mixed with oil, and used as a painting medium. Thinned with water, it may be used as a pen oil, but it tends to attract water from the air, which blurs the lines. A small addition of clove oil seems to help counteract this. Glycerin, a common food additive easily found in drugstores, does not dry out. Adding alcohol to glycerin (four parts alcohol to one part glycerin

works well) will produce a nice closed medium. Alcohol spattered onto wet glycerin-based paint will react spectacularly.

Glycols are a large class of chemicals known as double alcohols, the most common of which are propylene glycol and ethylene glycol. They are similar to glycerin in that they are clear, colorless, viscous liquids that do not dry. There are important differences among them, however. The most difficult aspect of using the different glycols may be that their names are confusingly similar.

Propylene glycol is widely used as an additive in food, cosmetics, and toothpaste, and is non-toxic. It dries very slowly, and colors remain suspended in it readily. I do a lot of outlining in black, so I

Paul Lewing, "Airbrushed Leaves," ceramic tile, 4¼" x 4¼," sprayed using alcohol as a medium.

keep a mortar and pestle charged with this mixture handy. Over the course of weeks it may dry to a jelly-like consistency, but a squirt of water and a quick stir restore it to usable consistency. It is often the main ingredient in environmentally friendly antifreeze. Some ceramic suppliers also carry it to be used as a glaze additive to prevent runs and drips.

Ethylene glycol is the smallest of the glycol molecules, and thus the most toxic. Its sweet taste makes it an especially dangerous substance to leave open in a studio with small children and pets, particularly cats. The main use for ethylene glycol is as antifreeze, which makes an excellent painting and screening medium, although the added coloration may be a bit distracting.

Diethylene glycol is similar to ethylene glycol, but its toxicity is lower. It is used in some photographic processes, and may sometimes be obtained from photographers' supply houses. It is my favorite medium for screening, if I do not need to apply a second color without firing first. There are other forms, of glycol such as ***triethylene*** and ***tetraethylene glycol,*** but they are rarely seen, and must be obtained from chemical supply houses.

Polyethylene glycol is different from the others, in that it does dry in a moderate amount of time, because it contains some water. This makes it perhaps the most useful of the glycols as a painting medium for vertical surfaces. I like it for making very clean sharp wipeout marks. It can often be found in medical supply houses, under several brand names, where it is sold in large jugs as a pre-surgery laxative.

Glycerin and all of the glycols, except polyethylene glycol, make excellent screening mediums, although their openness means that you cannot print a second color without firing first.

Paul Lewing, "Dinnerware Match," screen-printed and hand painted ceramic tile, 6 " x 6" each, 1988. Gum arabic and water comprised the printing medium.

Polyethylene glycol does not stay well mixed with powdered color at the thick consistency necessary for screening, and becomes lumpy.

Alcohol is more useful as a solvent and cleaner than as a medium. Many china painters give their brushes a final rinse in alcohol at the end of a session, after a thorough cleaning in turpentine. However, alcohol's very short drying time can make it useful as a medium for spraying and airbrushing, as it helps prevent runs. Different combinations of alcohols with other water-soluble mediums can produce dramatic results when alcohol is spattered or brushed onto a wet painted surface.

There are several easily obtainable forms of alcohol, which have slightly different characteristics and responses to other mediums. *Isopropyl,* or *rubbing alcohol,* is the most readily available, and is derived from propylene, a petroleum product.

Ethyl alcohol is derived from grain, and is the form present in alcoholic beverages. *Denatured alcohol,* or mentholated spirits, is a mixture of ethyl alcohol and a denaturant, which makes it unpleasant to drink. *Methyl alcohol,* also known as methanol or wood alcohol, is distilled from wood, and is a common gasoline additive. All the alcohols are colorless liquids. All except the highly toxic wood alcohol are only mildly toxic. Ethyl and methyl alcohol are flammable.

White glue may be used as a painting medium if it is thinned a bit with glycerin, gum, or one of the glycols. Thinned with water, it makes an excellent pen oil, with the advantage that it dries quickly to a hard enough surface to be painted over.

Acrylic medium, or almost any of the acrylic polymer substances sold in art supply stores for use in acrylic painting, may be used as a painting medium if thinned with water or glycerin.

CHINA PAINT & OVERGLAZE

Jeremy Jernegan, "Full Weight" and "Second Division," ceramic, steel, homemade overglaze, 96" x 26" x 32," 1999. Jernegan uses CMC gum (with water) for a medium, relying on its shrinking during drying to produce the "peeling paint" look. Thick application and fast drying promote the effect.

Acrylic medium dries quickly to a very hard finish, although retardants are also available to slow this down. This hard finish makes it a good choice for those painters who like to apply multiple coats without firing in between. However, care must be taken not to let acrylic medium dry in your brushes. Acrylic medium may be clear, matte, or gel, all of which will work, although some have diatomaceous earth added, which will make the fired result matte.

Sugar is one of my favorite mediums for painting and pen work. It dries fairly quickly to a hard surface. I usually just mix dry sugar (powdered sugar dissolves better than granulated) and paint into water to the desired consistency. Normally I

Jeremy Jernegan, "Full Weight" detail.

Celina Clavijo Kashu (Japan), "Cebollar," thrown porcelain, 5" diam.

use about twice as much paint powder as sugar. Many painters like sugar as a pen medium because it dries hard enough that they can paint over it with oil-based paint without firing. Those brands of powdered sugar substitute that are based on dextrose will work identically to sugar.

Some painters prefer the sugar dissolved in the water in the form of syrup. You can make your own by boiling sugar and water, in the ratio of two parts water to one part sugar. Or you can let soda pop (preferably a clear flavor to avoid the distraction of colorants) evaporate to the right consistency, although it must be sweetened with either sugar or one of the artificial sweeteners that contain dextrose. Corn syrup from the grocery is too thick to be used alone as a painting medium, and will become gummy if not thinned with considerable amounts of water. If it's too thick, it will bead up and refuse to cover some fired colors, and may result in a matte surface.

Detergent may be used as a mixing medium, although it may make the paint more matte after firing. Choose a clear detergent rather than an opaque one because the cloudy ones have wax added. The wax may melt before it burns off, causing the paint to run before it has a chance to sinter. You may thin detergent with water for use as a pen medium. Rinse your pen or brush occasionally to prevent build-up of color. I once tried detergent as a silk-screening medium, and it was a disaster, since it printed as froth. Washing the screen out was a foamy adventure, too. All in all, detergent ranks low on my list of medium preferences for any situation.

Gum arabic, which is derived from the sap of a species of acacia tree, is non-toxic and water-soluble. It is carried in art supply stores as either a powder or a liquid, and dries in a moderate amount of time to a hard surface. It may be used as a medium for pen work or painting, and I have

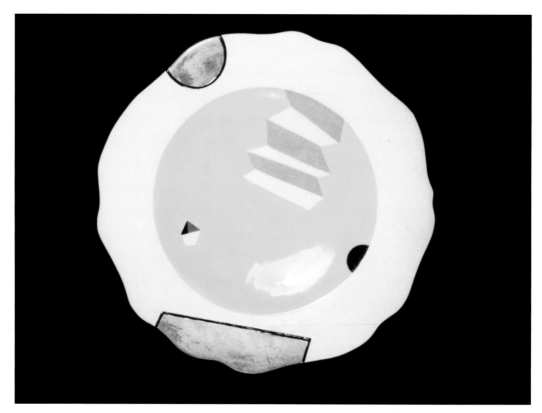

Joseph Detwiler/Lorene Nickel, "Plate", porcelain, underglazes, overglaze enamels, luster, 9" diam., 2003.

used a mixture of gum arabic and water for years as a silk-screening medium, when I want to print multiple colors without firing between colors. Its use as a painting medium is limited, however, by its tendency to peel off if applied too thickly. Gum arabic comes mostly from Sudan, and is indispensable in many food and beverage products, particularly soft drinks.

Gum tragacanth is similar to gum arabic, and may be used as a binder for making china paint crayons or pencils. Just mix china paint and gum, in almost any proportion, and let it dry. The mixture may be mixed quite stiff and rolled into a cylinder, or mixed thinly and poured into a tube such as a paper drinking straw. The more gum in proportion to the paint the harder the crayon will be.

Carboxyl methyl cellulose (CMC) is another form of gum commonly available from ceramic suppliers, and works as a painting medium with characteristics similar to the above gums.

Milk, excellent as a painting and pen medium, is often used as a medium for raised paste and enamel, and is said by many to be the very best medium for spraying. It dries hard, especially in its more high-fat varieties. It does, however, spoil quickly and produces a noticeable odor in firing. To avoid spoilage, many china painters prefer to use powdered milk.

Green tea and *seaweed* have long been used in the Orient as overglaze painting mediums. They are boiled in water to make a strong infusion, and strained to remove any stray leaves. Green tea was the preferred medium of the great Japanese potter Shoji Hamada for his overglaze work.

The products sold by china paint suppliers are specific combinations of the above ingredients, mixed in such proportions as to make an ideal mixing or painting medium, or an ideal grounding oil, pen oil, or medium for enameling or raised paste work. For the beginner, or the artist who only needs very small quantities of a specialized medium, it's probably best to just order these. Many china-painting teachers have developed proprietary mixtures, available only through them, that work better for a particular technique than anything else on the market. However, with a few basic ingredients, you can make any of these concoctions in your own studio. Below is a list of some of the most common oil-based mixtures for various procedures.

Painting mediums

Some suppliers sell as many as six different grades of painting medium, all of which are mostly balsam of copaiba modified with the oils of lavender and clove to control drying time and hardness. The most common formulation for a medium to mix with fresh powdered color is:

8 parts balsam of copaiba
1 part lavender oil
1 part clove oil

To make the mixture dry faster, add one more parts of lavender oil; for slower drying, add one more parts of clove oil. The parts are usually measured by volume. Some artists prefer a medium that is almost entirely balsam of copaiba, and may mix these three ingredients in proportions up to 32:1:0.5. Those painters who want their paint to dry hard usually add an amount of fat oil equal to the balsam of copaiba.

Mixing mediums

Fat oil of turpentine is the most common primary ingredient in mixing mediums, often adjusted by the addition of small amounts of clove or lavender oil. For those who object to fat oil's smell, medicinal grade olive oil may be used to replace fat oil in the same proportions with these oils. Another good choice for a mixing medium is mineral oil, or its more refined cousin, baby oil. It may or may not be modified with clove and/or lavender oils. Glycerin and the glycols are also good mixing mediums, with the additional advantage of water solubility.

John W. Hopkins, "T-Rowing the Great Wave of Hokusai," earthenware, sandblasted, china painted, 32" diam., 1994.

Pen oils

Pen oils need to flow more freely than other mediums. They need to dry quickly, so that the line will not spread, but not so fast that they build up on the pen point. Anise oil is usually added to oil-based mediums to promote flowing, and it's common practice to add anise oil to your favorite mixing medium until the mixture drips slowly from the palette knife.

A workable water-based pen oil may be made by mixing:

2	parts gum arabic solution
1	part glycerin
1	part white vinegar

For a pen oil that dries harder than this combination, add 2 parts white glue.

Paul Lewing, "Rescued Pot," 11" diam. Black lines made with a lettering pen, color mixed with oil-based pen medium.

Ruby Tobey, "Hummingbird Box," 8" diam., 2000. Pen work lines and brushed china paint. *Photo: Picture Perfect Photos.*

Royal Vienna plate with gold applied over solid rose ground. Collection of Ann Cline.
Photo: Ann Cline.

Grounding oil

Grounding oil for dry grounding needs to dry in a reasonable amount of time, but not completely. In order to hold the dry powder in place, it needs to remain slightly tacky. Fat oil of turpentine is the standard for this application, and nothing else works as well. What is sold as grounding oil is often nothing more than fat oil alone. Other workable grounding mediums are stand oil (the polymerized version of linseed oil), and heavy balsam of copaiba. Another recipe for grounding oil consists of:

8	parts balsam of copaiba
16	parts mineral oil
⅓	part oil of cloves

In 1909, *The Class Room #1*, a china painting text, gave this as a recipe for grounding oil: "3 parts boiled linseed oil, 6 parts essence of turpentine, 4 parts asphaltum. Boil one half hour, stirring constantly with a stick upon the end of which is fastened a bag of litharge (lead oxide)." This would definitely not be a recommended procedure today.

Recipes

Celina Clavijo Kashu (Japan), "Begonias," thrown porcelain, 4¾" diam. Kashu has developed an "overglaze sgraffito" technique, using CMC, gum arabic, and traditional Japanese gums based on fish (*nikiwa* and *akifu*) and seaweed (*funori*) glues.

Johanna De Maine (Australia), "Golden Dawn over Coonowrin," square platter, 7" diam. Wheel thrown porcellanous clay, with luster and raised enamel, 2004.

Nancy Froseth, "Stove 11," white earthenware, underglaze, overglaze and raised paste, 2½" x 4" x 10," 2002. *Photo: Hans Froseth.*

Mediums for raised paste

Mediums for raised paste are used to make the relief shapes that are usually covered with gold or silver luster. They typically dry very slowly and retain their shape, and they must be completely dry before firing. Light balsam of copaiba or pine oil may be used alone as a raised paste medium. For a water-based medium, try equal parts glycerin and Isopropyl alcohol; for an oil-based medium, equal parts fat oil and Damar varnish will work. Another mixture that works is equal parts of fat oil, pine oil, and heavy balsam of copaiba.

There is nothing more difficult for a truly creative painter than to paint a rose, because before he can do so he has to first forget all the roses that were ever painted.

—Henri Matisse (1869–1954)

Painting with Overglazes

Many artists come to china painting with extensive experience in other art forms, particularly oil and watercolor painting. A few come from a ceramic background, seeking a more painterly approach.

Overglazing is a special art form in several ways, and occupies a distinctive niche in the continuum from painting to glazing. Painters will enjoy the depth, luminosity, and permanence of china painting. Potters will delight in a medium that is more like painting than any other ceramic technique, and offers a full range of colors. Both groups will appreciate the fact that the raw colors are almost identical to the fired colors.

What makes china painting truly unique is its application onto a glossy surface. This creates special challenges, but also special possibilities. The material is a powder suspended in a medium, and as such, is adaptable to any of the techniques used with any form of paint or ink. It may even be used dry, like metal enamels.

As in all art forms, there is no right or wrong way to use china paint. There are only those methods that work for you.

What to Paint On

Any fired ceramic object may be decorated with china paint. Whether it's high- or low-fired, glazed or unglazed, you can china paint it somehow. Whether it's handbuilt, thrown, slip-cast, or pressed, you can china paint it. Porcelain, stoneware, earthenware, terra cotta—you can china paint them all. Pots, sculpture, tiles, sinks, toilets—you can china paint them all. If you could

Kevin Myers, "Totem," raku, thrown and altered with china paint and lusters, 38" high, 1997.

fit a porcelain bathtub into your kiln, you could china paint it. Many artists use china paints, lusters, and other overglaze techniques to embellish their high-fired work. Refiring will not destroy body or glaze reduction effects, but it will destroy post-firing smoked effects, such as the blackened body in raku.

You may, however, need to make some adjustments in fluxes and firing temperatures to get china paint to successfully bond to your work. If you want a smooth, glossy, consistent finish, you will need to work on a glossy glaze. The higher the underlying glaze was fired, the hotter the china paint firing must be to fuse with it. Keep in mind that any flaws in the glaze, such as crazing, will show in the overglaze.

Gregory Aliberti, Westlake Transit Center, Cleveland, Ohio, north view. Silk-screened and relief tile, 1999.

Kevin Myers, "Totem," detail. Myers resmokes his pieces after each china paint and luster firing to preserve the glaze's crackle pattern.

Gregory Aliberti, Westlake Transit Center, detail.

Celina Clavijo Kashu (Japan), "Dragonfly," Kakehashi River Promenade Tiles, porcelain, 2004.

Paul Lewing, "Hummingbird Sink," china paint on porcelain sink, 16" x 12", 2004.

Paul Lewing, "Shipwreck," china paint on ceramic tile, 39' x 10', 2003. *Photo: John Gussman.*

You may even fire china paint onto used ware from secondhand stores, although if it's been in heavy use, it may develop black spots under the glaze after firing, which china painters refer to as "mildew." Some or all of this problem can be eliminated by boiling the china for half an hour in water to which baking soda has been added. Used china may also break in firing, the glazes might bubble, and your results from used china may not translate well to other ware.

Traditionally, china painters have not made the objects they decorate. It began as a manufacturing medium, and the division of labor inherent in factory work persists. Ever since china painting became a popular recreation in the late 19th century, china painters have relied on their favorite china manufacturers.

Old books on the subject give advice like "the French china is always preferable to that from

John Baymore, "*Yunomi*," stoneware wood-fired to cone 11 with Shino glaze, gold chloride red and copper green lead-free overglaze enamel, electric fired to cone 017 with 4 hour soak, 3" high, 2005.

Charles Krafft, "Andrea Doria," overglaze on scorched china, 1993. *Photo: Dan Walter.*

Garth Johnson, "Sale Ordeal (Light)," collector's plates altered and china painted, 42½" x 34," 1999.

England." Unfortunately, it is impossible to know which factories, clay bodies, glazes, or manufacturing processes they meant by statements such as that. Gladys Burbank Nelson, writing in her *Anthology of a Porcelain Artist*, ranks all the types of china familiar to her, from the hardest to the softest, as:

> Japanese and Chinese China
> German China
> French and Danish China
> English China
> Some Stoneware
> American Porcelain
> Other Stoneware
> Beleek
> Pottery
> Satsuma

This is hardly specific information, and ignores the fact that there were many manufacturers in most of those countries. Even today, there is no general agreement on what constitutes "porcelain," or even "ceramic."

Transferring Designs

Very few china painters begin a painting without some preliminary sketch on the glazed piece. Some draw directly onto the work and proceed from there, while others like to make a very detailed study on paper, and transfer the design exactly to the glazed surface.

Those who draw directly on the piece will usually make their choice of instrument based on what their painting medium will be. Your sketch should not dissolve into your painting, although this is usually more distracting than harmful. The sketch marks also should not resist the painting medium, and should disappear in firing.

The traditional treatment for oil-based mediums is a light sketch with a china marker, followed by a more detailed drawing done with India ink and a brush. After the ink has dried, the marker may be washed off with turpentine, leaving the ink to be covered with paint and later disappear in firing. Some wax china markers may resist both oil- and water-based mediums, and may not disappear in firing, although they will usually wipe off even after firing.

Felt-tip markers are based on a wide variety of solvents, such as alcohol, ketone, xylene, and glycol ethers. They may dissolve into a like medium, and may not always fire out, so you should test fire before using them on an important piece. Their tendency to resist a medium unlike themselves may be annoying when they're used to sketch, but can be used to advantage as a painting tool.

Ordinary graphite pencils are usually too hard to make a distinct mark on a smooth glaze, but softer varieties work well. If you wipe the surface of the glaze with a cloth dipped in turpentine and allow it to dry, a residue will be left that is hard enough to mark easily with an ordinary pencil. China paint suppliers sell a variety of pencils and markers specifically for this purpose. They are almost all designed to work best with oil-based mediums.

To transfer a design exactly to your piece, draw it on paper first. You may cut around it to help position it on the work. Sometimes just tracing around this shape is a sufficient guide. If you prefer a more detailed transfer, you may tape your drawing in place, then slip a sheet of graphite paper under it. Carbon paper or graphite paper with a waxy surface will not transfer designs as well as paper coated with pure powdered graphite. Tracing over your drawn lines with a pencil or other pointed object (a dried-out ballpoint pen

Graphite paper is taped in place between the original drawing and the tile.

The drawing transferred onto the tile.

The finished tile, a reproduction of a high school artist's work, on left.

point works very well) will reproduce them on the glaze in a light gray. You may also choose to cover the back of your drawing with graphite using a soft pencil, essentially turning your drawing paper into graphite paper. If you're using a traditional oil painting medium, washing the piece with turpentine or lavender oil prior to doing the drawing will allow you to make more distinct graphite lines. Whichever method you use to sketch your design, keep it to an absolute minimum.

Your Palette

China paint is typically mixed for use in very small quantities. Potters accustomed to decorating with glazes or underglazes will be astounded at how little material it takes to produce a strong color. The amounts are more like those used in watercolor painting. Individual colors may be mixed with an open medium and stored in small jars, but in order to blend and mix colors, you need a palette.

Special palettes are sold by china paint supply houses, and the covered ones are particularly nice for keeping your paints open between painting sessions. A flat palette is more useful than one with small depressions in it, as you can more easily blend colors. A sheet of glass or white plastic works well, as do white tiles.

Most times you will be using only a few colors for a particular subject. It is best to lay the colors out with the most similar next to each other, as in a color wheel. This will minimize muddying the colors. Do not crowd the colors, but leave plenty of room for them to spread, and for test strokes.

When you start to learn china painting, it's best to limit yourself to a small number of colors. Most colors may be mixed together, but there are exceptions, which you should keep in mind as you lay out your palette. For example, the gold-based colors sometimes will not mix with some of the iron-based colors. However, some particular combinations will mix well, and gorgeous rosy reds

may be obtained by layering gold-based pink or ruby with iron reds, firing between layers.

One of the unique characteristics of china paints is that there are three groups of colors: those which rely on gold as a colorant, those based on cadmium, and all the others. Pinks, purples, lilac, ruby, and the like come from gold. Cadmium colors include bright reds and oranges, and a few maroons and yellows.

Cadmium colors will almost never mix with non-cadmium colors. Sometimes the mixture will fire out as a bubbly mess, but more often the result will be the total disappearance of all colors. A few companies sell blues, greens, black, and whites labeled as cadmium colors, made specifically to mix with the cadmium reds and yellows.

Many china painters believe that the gold colors also will not intermix with the other groups, but this is not entirely the case. The basis for this belief is probably the fact that mixing any other color with the deep, clear rubies, pinks and purples will muddy the color.

Paints mixed originally with an open (non-drying) mixing medium may be scooped back into the jar at the end of the session, even if a painting medium has been added. Some closed (drying) painting mediums will dry hard enough that the paint cannot be reconstituted. Paint mixed with plain water is usable after it dries, but it may become grainy. When you've finished painting, clean your palette with the appropriate solvent, or at least cover it. Dust in the colors may fire out as dark or blank spots.

Brushing

China paint is almost always applied with a brush, even if the brush strokes are not apparent in the finished product. The difference between good and bad brushwork often lies as much with the brush as with the artist, so buy the best brushes you can, and take good care of them. You will need a flat or bright brush, a round, and a liner. There are

Andreas Knobl (Germany), "Rockhopper Penguins," porcelain tile, 7⅞" x 5⅛".

many other shapes available (see the section on brushes in Chapter 3, "Tools and Equipment"), all of which are useful and sometimes indispensable, but these three are the minimum. The most common mistake in acquiring brushes is buying ones that are too small.

Traditionally, most china painters have used an oil medium, and favored one of two systems for mixing their colors. Some prefer to mix a substantial quantity with a mixing medium that stays wet, or "open." A small quantity is then dabbed on the palette in a shape like a small mountain with a reservoir at the bottom. Dip the brush into a painting medium, deep enough so the medium

fills the heel of the brush. Lay the brush on a clean tile and wiggle it back and forth to distribute the medium into the bristles, then lightly press it to a clean cloth to remove excess medium, and then load the brush from the reservoir. Others simply mix the powdered china paint directly with a painting medium, prepping and loading their brush in the same way.

Whichever system is used, the paint is ground into the medium with a palette knife until it is completely free of lumps, and about the consistency of toothpaste. Certain colors seem to need more grinding than others, particularly dark browns and the gold-based colors. Some artists

grind their paint on a grinding glass and transfer it to the palette; others mix directly on the palette. If you use an oil medium, mix the color and medium to a thick paste, and thin with turpentine. Some painters like to grind the powder with turpentine, alcohol, or lavender oil, and then let it dry before mixing with a painting medium.

You have a wide range of oil mediums from which to choose (see chapter 4), but most china painters now use some combination of balsam of copaiba and the oils of lavender, clove and anise. The decision is based mostly on how quickly they like their paint to dry and how thickly they like to apply it. Turpentine and fat oil are seldom used today except for techniques like traditional Dresden style painting. There are also water-soluble mediums. I almost always mix my colors with plain water, or one of the glycols. Regardless of the medium, you'll soon develop a feel for how thick you like it to be and how fast you want it to dry.

The proportions are critical. If there is too much oil, the paint will appear transparent and shiny before firing, and will run on a vertical surface. If it's too thick, it may chip off after firing. Intense colors are best achieved by firing multiple layers of paint.

In this operation, you may be adding minute amounts of medium and solvent. Small squeeze bottles, eyedroppers, and ear syringes are handy tools for this. If your vials have cork stoppers, insert a toothpick into the bottom of the cork to pick up just a few drops at a time.

For water-based mediums the procedure is almost the same as for oil, with the solvent being water, and the medium being one of the sticky substances such as glycerin, one of the glycols, sugar syrup, etc. You may continue adding water to these indefinitely as they dry.

When I use plain water as both medium and solvent, I lay out a small pile of dry powder, drip a little water next to it, and blend the two together with a brush to the proper consistency. It dries

San Do, "Macaw" tile, 10" x 14." *Photo: William Newberry.*

very quickly, but I just keep adding a few drops of water. Mixing paint with your brushes is very destructive to them, but I maintain this bad habit because it is so much faster than grinding colors with a palette knife.

Before you load your brush with paint, dip it in the appropriate solvent and dry the tip on a rag, otherwise the brush will not load completely. Rinse your brush thoroughly when changing

Paul Lewing, "Reef," china paint on ceramic tile, 6½' x 14', 1992. *Photo: James Cohn.*

A section of "Reef," first coat, unfired. The tiles at the top have been sprayed with cornstarch in preparation for a sprayed coat of blue.

The first coat, after firing. The black marker lines have burned away.

The second coat, after firing, with colors shaded and intensified.

"Reef," detail, after third firing for outlines. *Photo: James Cohn.*

colors. The chemical interactions between different mineral colors may change them more than their unfired appearance would suggest. The yellows are particularly susceptible to being muddied by a tiny amount of almost any other color.

The raw colors of unfired china paint are almost exactly the same as the fired colors, except that they appear matte and powdery. This will be the biggest treat for potters used to other forms of glazing, and it removes one of the biggest hurdles for painters wanting to fire their paintings. Usually several firings are necessary to achieve shading and intense colors.

After that, china painting is just like any other form of painting. Anything a brush will do in any other form of paint or ink, from oil and watercolor, to sumi painting, ceramic oxides and underglazes, or house paint faux finishes, it will do with china paint.

At the end of your painting session, rinse your brush out completely in clean solvent (either water or turpentine) and let it dry flat without resting it on its tip. Many china painters who use oil mediums like to give their brushes a good washing with soap and water after cleaning with turpentine, with a final rinse in alcohol.

Painting Roses
Celeste McCall

Among china painters, no subject matter approaches the rose in appeal. Asked to show off her masterpiece, almost every china painter will choose a rose painting. This mystique dates back to F. B. Aulich and Franz Bischoff, "the King of Roses." Celeste McCall, one of today's most renowned rose painters, believes that the challenge of depicting a multi-layered subject is what most attracts painters to roses.

Celeste has always loved art in all its forms, and still does work in oil, watercolor, acrylic, gourds, and several other media. She took up china painting when a friend began taking lessons in a shop in Borger, Texas. After three years of lessons, she began teaching, and today has taught in most states, usually at china painting schools. She did have one college art class, but almost never went because of the schedule. She says, "If art was on Saturday mornings, I figured it was for someone else other than myself."

While Celeste knows that the attraction of multi-layered subjects like roses lies in their complexity ("Like a man in a hat," she says) she believes that people will tackle them if they can see all the parts.

Celeste McCall, tray, 12" wide.

Ribbon Rose. Most roses will fit within a pentagon shape.

Baby rose. Wipe out highlights on the petals and make some cuts on the ribbon rose, to "mess up" the top.

Birdhouse rose. Begin by blocking in the shape and darkening the center and under the bowl. Each petal is cut toward the center of the petal below it. Then pull out some interesting edges on the rims of the petals.

Cuts made with a dry brush on the bowl of the rose.

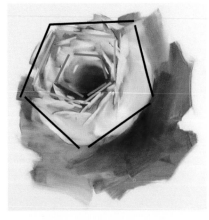

The shapes of the tiers of cuts maintain the pentagonal shape.

The finished birdhouse rose blossom.

She considers even portraits to be easier than roses, and so has developed three styles of roses, to suit her students' levels of expertise.

The simplest she refers to as "ribbon roses". These are based on a ball shape with a spiral, and are usually painted quite small. Bigger spirals are added to make the bloom larger. Slightly more complex is the "baby rose", which is based on the ribbon rose. "Wipe-out roses" or "birdhouse roses" (named after their shape), are the most complex, and are

softer and more free form. These wipeouts (called "cuts") are done by taking an unloaded brush and "cutting" it across the wet paint, removing the paint and creating a petal. She points out that all roses are shaped like a Chrysler logo, and recommends starting with the easiest and progressing to the more difficult styles.

When choosing forms on which to paint, Celeste selects simple shapes, as she seldom embellishes her pieces with raised paste or gold, preferring the

Celeste McCall, plate, 8" diam.

painting to stand on its own. She prefers ovals or rectangles to squares or circles, because they are less formal, and have a built-in contrast between long and short sides.

Several aspects of Celeste's painting technique are unusual. For one thing, she does not sketch her designs first and transfer them to the piece. In fact, she often has nothing at hand to look at when she begins. She draws the initial design directly on the shape, using china paint and a scroller or liner brush. She likes to watch the individual components of her design develop as they wish, "like actors on a stage."

Celeste's painting medium is also very unusual. She uses nothing but Turpenoid Natural®, a common solvent and brush cleaner. She likes its smooth feel and quick drying time. It also leaves no brush strokes or runs, and is non-toxic and non-flammable. However, she points out that you must have brand new, or very clean, brushes or they will become "pregnant" at the ferrule. One disadvantage to this medium is that the paint dries to an unworkable hardness within a day.

Occasionally, Celeste will finish a piece in two or three firings, and may even do a single fire as a demonstration, but she prefers to let her paintings develop slowly. Typically, her work is fired five to ten times. She fires no hotter than cone 016 or 015, as she does not like a high shine, and her pieces are not intended for daily use.

Celeste McCall's medium and technique may be unusual, but she has used them masterfully to solve china painting's classic problem, the painting of roses.

A Bouquet of Roses

No subject fascinates china painters quite like the rose. Since the earliest days of European overglazing, roses have been prominent in the work of most factories and individual artists. Here are a few outstanding examples.

Anne Albright, framed tile, 12" diam. 2001. Collection of World Organization of China Painters. *Photo: Mary Early.*

Jean Sadler, plate, 8" diam.

Ann Cline, tray, 14" x 10".

Cherryl Meggs, framed tile, 18″ x 12.″

Hilda Palmer, small plate. Collection of Cherryl Meggs. *Photo: Cherryl Meggs.*

Jean Helm, tray.

Gisela Bylund, vase, 18" tall, *Photo: Steve Wilson.*

Loretta Joslin, "Yellow Roses," white stoneware, glaze, china paint, 11" x 11" x 2½," 1999.
Photo: Walker Montgomery.

Grounding and Tinting

It's very difficult to obtain a perfectly smooth wash of color with china paint, as even the finest brushes leave tracks on the smooth glaze surface. It is particularly hard to get a deep color of smooth texture, without firing on multiple layers of over-glaze. Several techniques have been developed to achieve an even area of solid or graduated tone.

Dry grounding or powder grounding

Dry grounding or powder grounding is used much less frequently than in the past. The method was perfected quite early in the development of European overglazing, and the Sèvres factory, in particular, was renowned for the brilliance and depth of its grounds. The technique is messy, hazardous, and difficult to control, but it remains the best way to get a solid, deep color in a single firing.

The method involves spreading a sticky oil where you want the color to be, letting it dry until it's tacky, then spreading a dry powdered color evenly on the surface.

Traditional grounding oil is composed primarily of fat oil of turpentine, perhaps modified to control drying time and hardness. In this case, it's probably best to rely on a commercially prepared mixture as nothing else works quite as well.

Grounding oil, unless it has been tinted by the manufacturer, dries almost clear, so grind a bit of the desired color into the oil before you start to make it easier to see exactly where the oil is and how evenly it is applied.

Thoroughly clean the piece with alcohol before applying the grounding oil. Brush the oil over the whole area to be colored, and pad it smooth with a piece of silk wrapped around a ball of cotton or lamb's wool, or with a piece of fine-textured foam rubber. Change silk frequently, and if you hear a clicking sound and the silk appears to pull a bit, stop and rest the piece for a few seconds. As you blot the oil, it will get thinner and more even.

Ann Cline, "Monochrome Plate," 7½" diam. with enamel and gold. The dark border was dry-grounded.

There must be no brush marks or bubbles remaining, or they will show in the fired color.

Allow the oil to dry, in a dust-free place, until it is evenly tacky. This may take from a few minutes to several hours, or even overnight, depending on the composition of the medium and atmospheric conditions. It's a good idea to spread a test swatch on another piece of china, as the best way to judge the tackiness of the surface is by touching it, which will leave a mark. If you add the color while the oil is too wet, it will be uneven; too dry and it will not adhere properly. If the oil is too thin, it will not hold enough color; too thick and it may blister during the firing.

When the oil is ready, dry powdered china paint is spread on the surface. Most people use a dry brush for this purpose, usually a large mop brush or a cosmetic blusher. Others use a wad of cotton or lamb's wool, while others initially put the color onto the surface by sifting it through a strainer or shaker, in much the same way as metal enamels are applied. A china paint vial with a piece of nylon stocking secured over the end with a rubber band makes a good sifter for this purpose.

This is the messy and hazardous part of the operation. Cover the work area with paper or plastic to catch the excess powder, as it is still usable. If you plan to recover the excess paint, avoid using cotton balls, as lint will contaminate the paint. Wear an appropriate dust mask and provide adequate ventilation, as this is a dusty procedure.

When the surface is entirely covered with powder, use a soft brush to gently move the color around evenly, taking care not to leave any brush marks. The brush must not touch the bare oil directly; there must always be a layer of powder in between. Just dab lightly; don't rub or bear down. Shake or tap the work to remove loose grains, or blow it off if you have good ventilation, making sure there are no large grains remaining. When the coating is perfect, it will have a texture like velvet, with no dark or shiny spots indicating insufficient powder. Do only as much area as you can conveniently cover in one application, as any overlaps will also show. Very carefully clean any unwanted grains of color off the ungrounded areas with a cotton swab, taking great pains not to mar or scratch the ground.

A graduated color may be achieved by dusting a color onto one area, and another onto an adjacent area. By carefully moving the two piles of color together, you can get a blend, although it is very difficult to get an even transition with this technique.

Check the whole surface very carefully before firing, as it cannot be repaired or patched if there are flaws. The best remedy prior to firing is to remove all the color and start again. After firing, you may have to apply another layer to the entire area to cover a small flaw.

Some colors, such as greens, lend themselves to this technique more readily than others. The gold-based colors, such as pinks, purples, and rubies, are the hardest colors to dry ground evenly. Dark cobalt blues are also particularly difficult, and the iron reds are unpredictable and inconsistent. Certain colors seem to always be usable just as they are, while others require a bit of dry grinding to rid them of lumps. Others may even require straining through a fine copper or brass screen. Fire dry grounded work slowly, especially if the grounding layer is heavy, and cool the kiln completely before opening it.

Wet grounding or tinting

Wet grounding, or tinting, is the more common method of obtaining an even coat of color today. It's a much easier and less hazardous procedure than dry grounding. Mix color with your favorite painting medium, to a consistency slightly thinner than for painting, and brush it on the area to be tinted. Then remove the brush marks by padding or blotting the area.

In the classic method for wet grounding, you place a small amount of Dresden thick oil or fat oil of turpentine in one corner of your palette, and a pile of dry paint near it. Grind oil into the paint until all granules are well mixed and the paint has a consistency like piecrust (stiff and difficult to grind). Add a few drops of clove oil and grind well, then add more clove oil gradually until the mixture is soupy and a little runny. Apply the paint with a large brush, and pad smooth.

The traditional tool for this padding is a piece of fine silk with no surface texture, wrapped around a ball of cotton or lamb's wool. If your choice is cotton, it's best to wrap the cotton ball in plastic wrap, then in silk, to prevent cotton fibers coming through the silk. When the silk gets soiled with an oil-based paint, soak it in turpentine to remove the china paint, and then wash it. If your

Bridget Chérie Harper, "Come Play With Me," china paint on porcelain, 18½" x 8" x 5," 2004. Front view.
Photo: Doug Crouch.

Bridget Chérie Harper, "Come Play With Me." Back view.
Photo: Doug Crouch.

medium is water-based, just wash it. Wrinkles will leave marks in your paint, so iron the silk before using it.

Foam rubber also works well as a blotting tool, or even as a tool to apply the tint. It comes in several textures, all of which are usable for certain techniques. It's easily cut to shape and usually free. Some foam cannot be used with paint that has been mixed with turpentine, however, as it will destroy the foam. Fine pore cosmetic sponges work well with turpentine.

Stencil or stippling brushes used for padding leave a slightly coarser texture than silk or foam, and produce a different texture when wet than when dry. Small stencil brushes tend to be too stiff for my taste, so I make my own by cutting the tips of old round brushes to a flat or "deerfoot" shape.

The more you pad an area, the lighter it will become. Eventually all the color will be removed. This happens quite quickly if you use water alone as a medium. Unfired china paints appear almost

San Do, "King of Thailand"
tile, 12" x 16."
Photo: William Newberry.

exactly as they will fire, however, so it takes very little practice to know when to stop padding. The most sensitive use of tinting probably is in portrait painting, where delicate shading is crucial. Holding the piece in your hand rather than laying it on a hard surface makes for a softer effect, as it lessens the impact of the pad.

Tinting colors must be mixed thoroughly with the medium, or there will be specks or streaks. Specks may be removed with a needle before firing; streaks just require more padding. Dark cobalt blues are particularly hard to keep free of specks, and some metallic paints are almost impossible

Mercedes Guibernau de Campos (Uruguay), "Mother Teresa," plate with raised pasted and gold border. Collection of World Organization of China Painters Museum. *Photo: Mary Early.*

John Page, "Bunny Bowl," 12" diam., 1985. Yellow and green overglazes were airbrushed, the bunny shape was airbrushed through a stencil, other colors were brushed.

to apply evenly with a brush. Black will appear much richer if a layer of another dark color, such as cobalt blue or iron red, is fired onto the area first. This will also lessen the tendency of black and some other very dark colors to chip off after firing.

Blending colors is much easier in a wet ground than in a dry ground. Use a medium that stays wet long enough for you to apply all of the colors, and then blot them into each other. It's best to apply the lighter colors first, and blend the darker ones into it. You may also brush two wet colors into one another with a dry brush. You may combine the techniques of wet and dry grounding by dusting a different color onto a wet colored ground.

Manipulating a dry or wet ground before firing may make interesting textures. For a marbled surface, mix your paint with balsam of copaiba as you would for a wet ground, apply it normally, and let it dry. Mix one part water and two parts denatured alcohol, and apply this mixture on the dry paint with a pad.

Turpentine dribbled or spattered on any oil-based paint will produce runs or spots, with dark edges and light centers. Water will produce the same effect on a water-based paint. Interesting textures can be made by padding the wet ground with wadded plastic or paper, by dry-brushing it, or by drawing in it with any type of soft or flexible wipeout tool. Test colors before using them for wet grounding, as some will fire to a different color than they will when brushed. Many artists prefer to fire the first layer of a grounded color a cone or two hotter than the final coat.

Paul Lewing, "Birds at Mowich Lake," china paint on ceramic tile, 11' x 6½', 2002.

"Birds at Mowich Lake," detail. Dark green was wiped with a pointed rubber tool to create the effect of grass.

"Birds at Mowich Lake," detail. Black was feathered with a dry brush to create the effect of hemlock branches.

Stencils, Resists, and Wipeouts

One of the advantages of working on a slick surface is that blocking, manipulating, and removing paint is much easier than on a more porous surface. Tape of all kinds adheres well, and various kinds of tools will completely, or partially, wipe the paint off.

Any kind of adhesive label or tape can be used to make negative patterns on the work, and intricate patterns can be built up in successive firings. Any kind of brush or pad may be used to apply the color, using almost any medium. Stencils must be peeled off before firing, as any color remaining on top of the mask will fire onto the work when the mask burns away. Some cleanup may be required after the stencil is removed, as paint may build up under the edge.

Color may also be applied through open areas of a stencil, using a stencil brush or a pad. Paper can be used to make stencils, but longer-lasting ones may be cut from acetate, thin metal, leather, plastic, or gasket material. Patterns may be applied through screens or expanded metal sheets.

The clear plastic self-adhesive film frisket used by graphic artists is a very useful material for intricate one-off stencils. Contact paper, used to cover pantry shelves and books, is a less expensive alternative that works just as well. Draw your pattern on the work, adhere the clear sheet over it, and cut out the areas to be painted with a sharp, pointed knife.

Areas may be blocked off by painting on a liquid resist. Liquid wax resist and melted paraffin, so beloved by potters, are not good choices for this, as they rely on the absorbency of the bisque to dry. Liquid latex is a better choice, but a masking fluid is probably the best. The masking fluid used by watercolorists is usually too thin to stay on a vertical surface, but there are masking fluids made specifically for china painting. Put on a thick coat, let it dry completely before painting over it, and remember to peel it off before firing.

Ruby Tobey, "Mountain Scene," pen work on porcelain plate, 10" diam., 2003. Photo: Picture Perfect Photos.

Almost anything my be used to move or wipe off china paint, whether dried or still wet, including your hands. Franz Bischoff was renowned for creating highlights on his roses using his fingernail. China paint and ceramic suppliers sell a variety of wipeout tools in a wide range of sizes, materials, and degrees of flexibility. The most common are rubber or soft plastic. The rubber dental picks on the ends of toothbrushes work as well as any tool designed specifically for this purpose. You can make your own from erasers, foam rubber, wood, bamboo, or other materials. Old credit cards are easily cut to almost any shape. A medium that dries hard can be cleanly removed with a lettering pen.

Most china painters working in the "American style" use either a piece of silk wrapped around their finger, or a clean brush slightly wet with medium or solvent. The strokes made by a wipeout tool in dry china paint tend to remove the color completely, while those made when the paint is wet usually move the color to one side, leaving a blank area with a dark edge. My choice of medium is sometimes determined more by what kind of wipeout mark I want to make than by what kind of brush mark I want. If you're using a water-soluble medium, a softer wipeout stroke can be made using dampened foam rubber. Makeup applicators are particularly useful for small spaces.

Pen Work

China paint may be applied with a pen in exactly the same way as ink would be. Most artists use an old-fashioned quill, or a steel nib of flat, bowl, or pointed shape. A large feather, with the tip cut at a steep angle and the point split, will hold more paint, and release it more slowly, than a steel pen point, but the marks may not be as precise.

Calligraphy is an obvious use for the pen. Certain alphabets are better executed with a script brush, but those that feature thin accents and long, even, wide lines are best done with a flat lettering pen. A pointed nib makes long lines of even width far better than even the best liner brush, and is much easier to use with a ruler or guide for precise lines. Split nibs will make a thicker line when more

pressure is applied. For small, detailed work, pens are decidedly easier to control than brushes.

Pens may be used for drawing, outlining, crosshatched shading, or textures composed of repeated line shapes. They may also be used to apply dots of color, or even complete designs in a pointillist style.

Mediums for pen work need to flow easily but not run, dry quickly so the line will not spread, and not separate from the color. Traditionally, anise oil is added to an oil painting medium to make it dry harder and faster. Pen work done with a medium made from sugar and water may be painted over with oil paints, without firing first. However, the pen work may or may not resist the covering coat evenly.

Paint should be mixed thinner than for brush painting, and be remixed often. There are several commercial lines of colors that perform well in a pen, sold premixed in jars or tubes, in both oil and water bases.

The precise nature of pen work demands that the surface be perfectly clean and that guidelines be kept to an absolute minimum, so they don't resist or interfere with the pen line. Clean the nib often, as paint will dry quickly in it.

Do not simply dip the pen point into the paint, but rather load it onto one face of the pen. Some artists prefer to turn the pen upside down and scoop the paint up onto the underside of the nib. Others like to load the top side of the pen. Whichever loading technique you use, touch the pen point to the lip of the container or the palette to release any drop from the point before you begin your stroke. Make sure the hole in the nib stays free of paint. Keep the pen full and work slowly, but deliberately. Any hesitation or indecision will be obvious, especially when lettering. Keep the point moving whenever it's in contact with the glaze surface or you will get blobs. Hold the pen at a sharp angle to the work, rather than straight up, and let the paint flow easily from the pen.

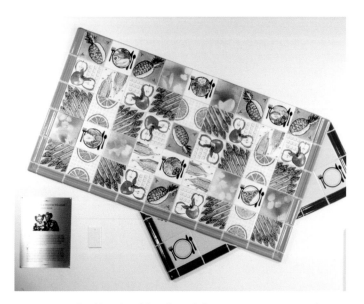

Paul Lewing, "Comforter," china paint on ceramic tile, 75" x 57," extruded porcelain border. Williams Food Bank, Fremont Public Assn. Headquarters, Seattle, WA., 1998.

Stamping

Stamps are a convenient way to make repeated designs, providing the shapes are not too intricate. In the late 19th century, stamping was used by relatively unskilled workers to quickly reproduce designs, some of which were quite detailed.

Almost any slightly flexible material may be used to make stamps. Rubber, linoleum, leather, felt, cork, even wood, all make usable stamps. Foam of all kinds, hard or soft, is probably the easiest material to work with, if you use a water-soluble medium. It may be cut with scissors or knives. Wetting and freezing the foam first makes it less resilient and easier to cut. A hot wire or knife will dissolve certain types of foam, but since this produces noxious fumes, do it outside or in a well-ventilated room. You will want to adhere a handle to the back of your favorite stamps to keep your hands clean.

Paul Lewing, "Comforter" detail. The hats, AIDS ribbons, cat faces, and keyboard were screen-printed; the leaves were airbrushed.

Gregory Aliberti, "Ed's Diner," screen-printed tile, each 8" x 8," depicting vintage diner cars, 1997.

Gregory Aliberti, "Parker's," screen-printed tile, each panel 68" x 28," 1998.

Mark Burleson, "Deer, Star, Gun," screen-printed tile and mixed media, 2000.

Water alone does not work well as a stamping medium, as it leaves bubbles in the paint. A more open medium, such as oil or glycol, is a better choice. Stand oil is particularly effective.

The paint may be applied directly to the surface of the stamp with a brush or roller, or you may spread the paint evenly on a grinding glass with a palette knife or brayer, and dip the stamp into it. Mixing two colors side by side and rolling them together with the brayer will achieve a graduated color.

To get a clear print, touch the stamp lightly but firmly to the work, taking care that all parts of the stamp contact the glaze evenly. Push straight down and lift straight up, without sliding the stamp on the surface.

Screen Printing
Silkscreen printing may be used to reproduce an intricate design in china paint, but the technique only works on a perfectly flat surface, such as tile. To get a printed design on a rounded surface, you

Exposing the screen. Acetate stencils are laid on the screen, held down with glass, and exposed to strong light.

must first print it as a decal, and then transfer it. Some round shapes are screen printed by industry, but this requires specialized equipment. The best way to learn silk-screening is to take a class at an art center. The technique for printing with china paint on tile is exactly like printing with ink on paper; only the composition of the ink is different.

To make your screen, build a frame out of 2×2 wood, slightly larger than your image. Staple the mesh to the underside of the frame, stretching it tight. Tape the edges about ½ inch out onto the fabric, on both the front and back of the screen, with brown paper tape, and varnish the tape and the wood to make them durable. Take care not to get any varnish on the mesh, as it will block the screen. The fabric is polyester, and I use a medium

density 12XX mesh. Drill a hole near one end of a short piece of wood slat, and affix it loosely with a screw to the middle of one side of the frame. This is called a kickleg, and it swings freely to hold the screen up off the work, freeing both of your hands.

Silkscreen stencils work by blocking the areas where you don't want color, leaving the mesh open in the places you do. Simple stencils may be made by taping cut paper to the back of the screen.

One traditional way of making stencils, and still a good way to reproduce brush marks, is with tusche and glue. Tusche is a thick oil-based liquid, and the appropriate glue is water-based. Your design is brushed onto the screen with tusche and allowed to harden. The whole screen is then covered

CHINA PAINT & OVERGLAZE

In the middle of the second print run (black) on one of the Totem series. The red has been printed but not fired yet. Notice the open areas on the screen. There are two stencils for each of two images on this screen.

The finished Totem series, each 6" x 6." Framed in wood.

with the glue. Once the glue has dried, the tusche is washed out with solvent, leaving the brush design open to print.

In the 1960's, a method was invented to make silkscreen stencils photographically. It was an exacting, tedious process, requiring a darkroom and very careful control of water temperature.

Today there is a much easier system produced by Speedball®. It uses a photosensitive emulsion, which does not require a darkroom, and comes as a kit with complete instructions.

To make a stencil, you must first render your design in opaque material on a clear sheet. If your design has only one color, you may draw it in ink on paper, and have it photocopied onto sheet acetate. Designs of more than one color require a separate stencil for each color. Computer graphics software can easily separate the colors, but lacking such a program, you must trace each color onto a separate sheet. Use opaque pigmented ink, rather

John Britt, "Fly Cup," porcelain with china paint and decal, 4" high, 2000.

Rimas VisGirda, tumblers, white stoneware, overglaze, homemade decals, and vintage Czech and Homer Laughlin decals, 4" high.

125

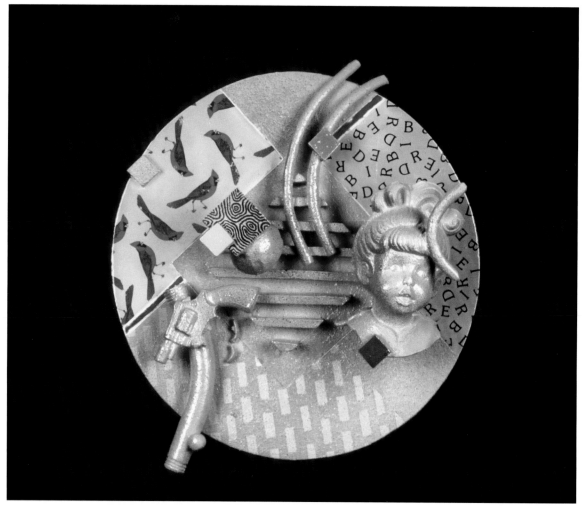

Michael Hough, "Red Bird," plate with sculpted and press-molded additions and commercial decals, 18" diam., 1998. *Photo: Ellen M. Martin.*

than transparent dye-based ink, in a drafting pen or brush. Rub-on transfers work well as stencils, and provide an easy way to make patterns and letters.

Mix the two-part emulsion and apply a smooth coat onto the back of the screen with a silk-screening squeegee. After letting it dry in a dark place, you're ready to transfer the stencil to the screen.

Lay the stencils face up on the inside of the screen, holding them down with a piece of glass, and expose them to a strong light. The relation-ship of light intensity, duration, size of screen, and distance of the light from the screen, is critical. Consult the chart that comes with the kit. My screens are 19 inches square, and I use a 250-watt bulb, 18 inches from the screen, for 15 minutes. The light hardens any area it hits, leaving the areas under the opaque parts undeveloped and soft, to be washed out in a forceful stream of warm water.

When the emulsion dries completely, it's ready to print, with either water- or oil-based mediums.

Garth Johnson, "Creation," 8½" diam., digital laser decals, 2000.

To completely clean your screen for reuse with another image, wash it out with household bleach.

To print, the screen must be fastened with hinges to a table or board, using either removable-pin hinges, or specially made hinges with built-in clamps. This allows the screen to come down in exactly the same place every time. It must lay flat on the surface to be printed. To print on tile, I tape a piece of ¼-inch plywood to the bottom of each hinge, and one at the front edge of the base board.

To register each succeeding tile in exactly the same place, move the first tile around under the screen until the image is in just the right place, and affix stops at the corners of the tile. I use L-shaped pieces of ¼-inch hardboard, held down with Velcro™.

Dribble a line of ink across the far side of the image, and drag it firmly across the tile with a squeegee. This will force the paint through the open areas of the screen onto the tile. Lift the

You can print any substance that's ground fine enough to go through the holes in your screen, assuming it is the proper consistency. The ink should be about as thick as mayonnaise, although finer detail may require thinner ink. Only experience will tell you what's right.

I've used dozens of different mediums for screening. For very fine detail, nothing beats fat oil of turpentine, perhaps modified to adjust the drying time. However, cleanup is messy and smelly, and the printed image never dries hard enough to lay the screen back down on it for a second color run without firing first.

For coarser detail, I prefer diethylene glycol, ethylene glycol, or glycerin. If I want to print more than one color without firing, I use gum arabic, thinned with water. If your medium dries hard, you may print one color next to another without firing, but never one over another. The second color will lift the first off the tile onto the screen, blocking the open areas.

To mix the ink, I simply put some of my chosen medium in a small jar, and mix in dry china paint with a palette knife until the consistency seems right.

Decals

Some of the most interesting and exciting overglaze work being done today employs the use of decals, both hand-made and off-the-shelf. Several ceramic suppliers sell supplies for making your own decals (see Resources). The steps for printing the decals are the same as those for printing directly onto tile.

The image is printed onto special paper and then covered with lacquer or spray acrylic.

To apply the decal, cut around the image, and soak it in water until the paper loosens from the lacquer. Lay the printed sheet of lacquer on the work, and smooth it out with a sponge. There must be no wrinkles in the decal, and no pockets of water, dust, or air under it. Anywhere the decal does not contact the glaze, it will burn off.

Harin Lee, "Untitled," porcelain, china paint, lusters, commercial decals, 11" x 15" x 7," 2005. *Photo: John Carlano.*

screen, let the kickleg hold it up, remove the tile, put another tile in the guides, and repeat any number of times. Wash out the screen with the appropriate solvent for your medium, and repeat the process for each color.

Rain Harris, "Rapunzel," porcelain, luster, hair, Plexiglas, beads, commercial decals, 12" x 12" x 12," 2004. *Photo: John Carlano.*

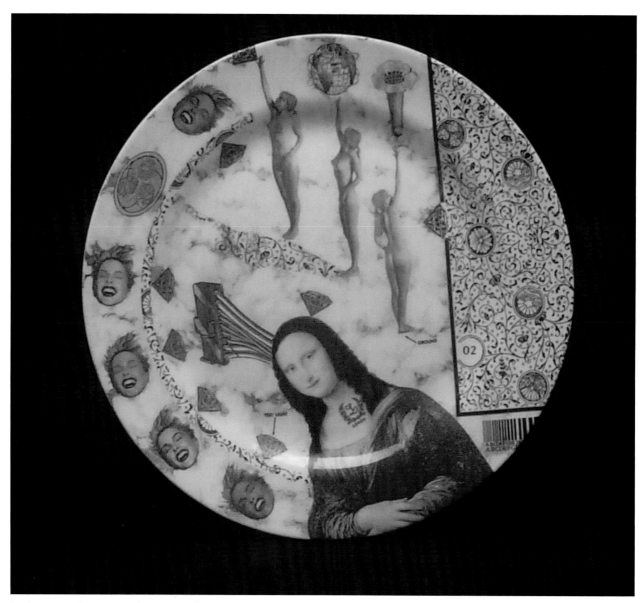

Les Lawrence, "Faux Lenox" series, 11" diam., laser print decals.

Making Decals
André van de Putte

André van de Putte in his studio.

One half of a two-part *Ceramics Monthly* article got André van de Putte started on the process of making his own photo-ceramic decals. He was a junior at the State University of New York at Stony Brook when his professor, Michael Edelson, suggested he combine his newfound interest in photography with ceramics, a discipline he had discovered several years earlier under Toby Buonagurio. During his subsequent studies toward an MFA with Doug Huston at the School of the Art Institute of Chicago (SAIC), he developed more sophisticated four-color decals.

After graduate school, André worked as an administrator, gallery curator, and teacher at Lasell College and the Massachusetts College of Art in Boston until his return to Chicago in 1998. He is currently the Director of Graduate Admissions at SAIC, and continues his ceramics practice.

Imagery has always been more important to André than process. He is inspired by popular culture and has an obsession with collecting, multiples, and labor-intensive processes. He loves to challenge notions of what is "high" and "low" art, and values clay's ability to mimic other materials.

André's work is constructed of low-fire white clay, primarily in the form of tiles, but sometimes with

Tracing the flag image on the film transparency, in reverse.

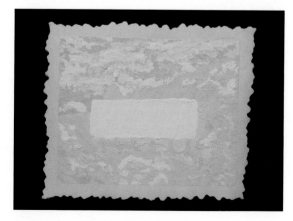

Earthenware tile with underglazes, fired and ready to accept a black background decal.

Tile with black decal fired on, ready for the colored decal of the flag to be applied over.

Screening supplies. The screen will be clamped into the hinges on the edge of the table for registration.

Washing out the screen after exposure.

Spraying cover coat of varnish on the finished two-color decal.

Finished decal, with three scenes taken from postcards of Holland, Michigan.

additions of extruded or slip-cast parts. His finished images resemble hand-colored photographs, but he reverses the process by blocking in the "hand-colored" areas in underglaze, firing the pieces with a clear glaze to cone 04, and applying the decals last. To make sure the decal will register with the finished image, André traces the image in reverse and transfers it to the tile, using graphite paper.

The decal-making process is much like any other silk-screen printing. First, a high-contrast transparency is prepared, using Kodalith sheet film or a laser printer. This becomes the "mask" for the screen. The screen is then exposed and developed, opening up areas for the china paint to pass through.

Next, he mixes china paint and medium to the proper mayonnaise-like consistency. He has used both oil- and water-based mediums, but prefers the water-based ones for their lack of toxicity and

Soaking the decal in water.

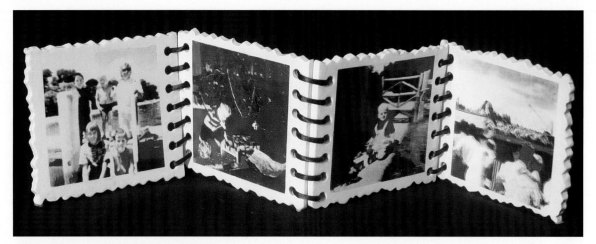

"Family Album," open. Each tile 3¾" x 4¼" x ¼."

"Holland, Michigan Album" tiles, fired and laced together, each tile 4" x 5¾" x ¼."

ease of cleanup. He currently uses a medium and paper sold by Brittains (see "Resources").

The image is then screened onto decal paper, which has been specially prepared with a gum coating. Once it dries, a layer of varnish is applied. Historically, a copal varnish was screened on, but plastic varnish in aerosol cans has largely replaced

that practice. André sprays several light coats, letting the decal dry in between, and then a heavy coat. If the cover coat is too thin, the decal will be brittle.

For transfer to the ceramic surface, the decal is trimmed to leave about ⅛-inch of clear varnish around the image, and immersed in lukewarm

Chapter 5

"Mineola Diner" tile, 5½" x 7½" x ¼."

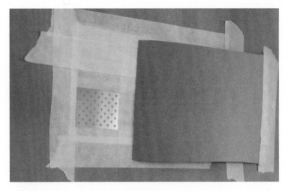

Masking off the area of the flag
image to be printed in blue.

Blue paint on the screen, ready to be printed.

water. It initially curls up, but relaxes flat again as it soaks. André tests it by gently trying to get the varnish/image layer to slide easily off the paper. When the whole image will slide, he adheres one edge of the decal to the piece and gently slides the paper from under it, pressing it onto the surface evenly with a sponge or a piece of wet decal paper.

The decal must contact the glazed surface completely, as any air or water pockets left under it will burn away, leaving gaps in the image. Any bubbles are worked gently to the edge of the decal, or to a clear area in the image, where they may be pricked with a sharp tool and flattened down.

After the decal is dry, it is fired to cone 018 in an electric kiln. The lid is left propped open a bit through the first fifteen minutes of the "high" setting, in order to vent fumes from the burning varnish.

Though decalcomania is a technique for producing multiple images, André's pieces are "one-offs." He enjoys the ironic idea that a tedious and exacting process has been used to make an object that closely resembles the most mass-produced

of commercial products. He gravitates to "found object" images, such as postcards, family snapshots, and yearbooks. His current work is a series of "books" based on postcards from tourist-trap towns like Holland, Michigan. Deckled edges and black photo corners refer to the source imagery and add an element of whimsy.

Having grown up in Amsterdam adds to André's fascination with such quintessentially American images. Critics have said that his Dutch citizenship has a lot to do with his love/hate relationship with kitsch.

While the surface of the clay form may be quite convex or concave, there should be no ridges or depressions under the decal, as it will wrinkle. Fire slowly to burn off the lacquer.

Several companies manufacture a wide range of decal images, usually printed by the offset lithography process. A number of artists have used these commercial decals to great artistic advantage.

There are also companies that will make your designs into custom decals.

Spraying

China paint is very rarely applied with an airbrush or sprayer because it's difficult to get it to stick to a glossy surface, especially a vertical one. The material is also toxic when inhaled, and the usual oil mediums have an unpleasant odor.

Andreas Knobl (Germany), "American Dream Cars." The blue background is airbrushed.

John Page, "Mad Dog Platter," 18" diam. 1985. Black overglaze airbrushed over stencils, accents added with a brush.

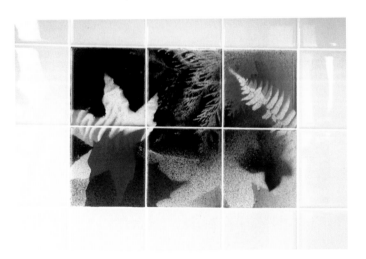

Paul Lewing, "Sprayed Leaves," china paint on ceramic tile, 13" x 8½," 2003.

To eliminate the smell, and to get the color to dry very quickly, use denatured alcohol as a medium. Keep the mixture tightly capped, as the alcohol will evaporate, causing the paint to thicken quickly.

To spray water-based china paint onto tile, I have used a method which mimics the drying qualities of glaze on bisqueware. After very carefully cleaning the tile with window cleaner, I spray on an even coat of a thick solution of water and cornstarch. I speed the drying of this coat by using alcohol, or by drying it with a hair dryer. When it's dry, it leaves a layer of fine powder, which holds the spray of china paint in place.

Spraying china paint onto a glossy surface is extremely tricky, because it takes very little excess to make it run, regardless of the medium. Every drip, spatter, or dust spot is glaringly obvious, and very difficult to patch. Multiple thin layers are much easier to control than one thick coat. Sprayed china paint may emerge from the firing a bit rough, as the tiny beads of color may not completely melt. A light sanding with fine sandpaper or an abrasive pad will usually smooth it out sufficiently, although it may need refiring.

It is possible to find a limited color selection of china paints in aerosol cans. Ceramic suppliers and paint stores also sell aerosol cartridges that fit on refillable glass containers. Airbrushes, mouth atomizers, and all types of paint sprayers will work with china paints, with no difference in procedure from ordinary paint or other kinds of glaze, other than those previously mentioned.

Matte Paints

Matte paints are a variation on china paints that do not develop a glossy finish in firing. They may be applied to a glossy glaze for contrast, or they may be used on an unglazed fired surface, where they will produce a finish much like the bare clay itself. Sometimes referred to as gouache colors, these overglazes were originally developed by the Royal Worcestershire Porcelain Works.

Paul Lewing, "The Hunt," matte paint on porcelain tile, 7½' high, 2005.

Dorothea Warren O'Hara, Beleek pitcher. From *Keramic Studio*, Vol. XIV #10, February 1913, p. 206.

Marcia Stivelman, "Egg," Russian design in raised paste, gold, and enamel, 9" x 6," 1999.
Photo: Andrew R. Goldstein.

Matte paints are chemically very similar to regular china paints, with the addition of zinc oxide. You may make your own from any shade of china paint, but each color requires a different amount of zinc oxide, so much experimenting is needed. Some china painters introduce the zinc oxide into the paint in the form of zinc-based sunscreen ointment. China paint suppliers provide a fairly complete spectrum of colors, although not nearly as varied as the regular paints.

Matte paints are applied almost exactly as regular paints are, using all the traditional techniques. The one exception to this rule is in lightening a color. Instead of applying a thinner layer to get a paler color, matte paints are lightened by adding an opacifier (usually the white matte paint) and applying the paint thickly. They are fired exactly as regular paints are.

Flux is never added to matte paints since this would destroy the matte quality. They are inappropriate for dinnerware, as silverware will stain them and make unpleasant sounds during use.

Raised Enamels

This is the material that china painters refer to simply as "enamel." The term seems to have come into wide usage in 1913, when Dorothea Warren O'Hara published *The Art of Enameling on Porcelain*. Prior to this, all overglazes were commonly referred to as "enamels." At the time, so-called "conventional" designs were gaining in popularity, and the slow and meticulous methods demanded by raised enamel lent themselves nicely to this symmetrical, abstracted style of depicting natural subjects, particularly flowers. A form (or brand) of enamel known as *Aufsetzweiss* was common back then, but is seldom seen today. It was a higher-fired variety of the material, much like what is now known as "hard enamel," and was often mixed with softer enamels to raise their firing temperature.

Although it is fluxed enough to bond to the underlying glaze, raised enamel has much more

Johanna De Maine (Australia), "Birds of a Feather," porcellanous clay, luster, raised enamel, sandblasted etching, 7" high, 2004.

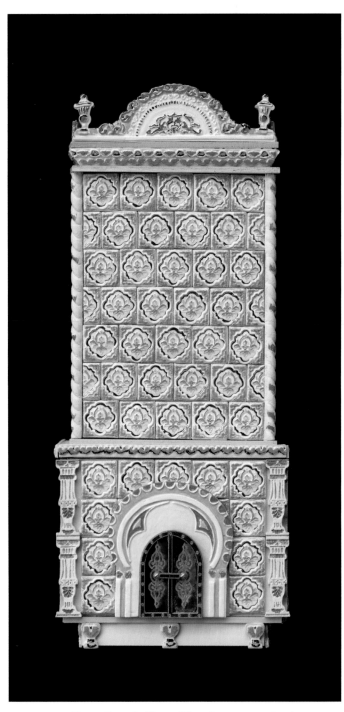

Nancy Froseth, "Stove 8," earthenware, underglaze, raised paste, luster, 10½" x 4" x 2," 2002.
Photo: Hans Froseth.

"body" than china paint. When it's done right, it looks like a tiny coil laid on the surface, almost round in cross-section, like trailed slip.

This is a very difficult material to master, since consistency is critical and it dries quickly. It may be applied over painted, fired areas, or on bare glaze. It is usually the last thing to be fired. Enamel is fired to a lower temperature than china paint (cone 017 or 018, depending on the hardness of the underlying glaze) and, until recently, tended to chip off if fired more than one or two times. There are now some enamels on the market that resist chipping and will handle more firings.

Fat oil of turpentine is the traditional medium to mix with the powdered enamel, and special enamel mediums are often only this. Grind a small amount of the powder with the oil and thin with a few drops of turpentine, or lavender oil if you need the material to stay open a bit longer. The easiest way to get the material to the proper consistency is to mix it with medium to a crumbly texture like piecrust, then roll it into a ball and knead it until it's like putty. Store this in an air-tight container, and pull off small pieces to thin to working consistency.

When the consistency is just right, it forms a high, round dot. If it's too wet, it sinks and spreads. Too dry, it forms pointed "tails" that remain sharp after firing. When the consistency is perfect, it is said to "string" nicely, enabling you to make long, graceful scrolls. If it's just a bit too runny, try breathing on it to add the tiniest bit of moisture. When it starts to dry, add a bit more turpentine or lavender oil, but you may only do this a few times before it makes the enamel too oily and prone to bubbling in the firing.

It's almost impossible to apply enamel properly with a loose, free brush stroke. It's better to dip a brush or pointed tool, such as a toothpick, into the wet enamel, and let it just flow off onto the work, without the tool even touching the glaze surface. Clean your brush or tool often to remove any dried enamel.

Rosa Maria Plancarte (Mexico), "Peacock," porcelain with raised paste and gold, 6½" x 9," 1986. Collection of World Organization of China Painters Museum. *Photo: Mary Early.*

Keep the work flat as you apply the enamel, and don't move it until the material is dry, or it will run. Enameling all the way around a vessel is incredibly time-consuming, as each side must dry before it can be rotated, and it cannot be laid down on the unfired enamel. An easel that supports the pot from inside is essential here. Enamel will also run or blister in the firing if it's not completely dry. It has a dull surface when it's dry enough. Do not artificially dry enamel in your oven or with a hair dryer or it may bubble.

Enamels come in a selection of colors or you may tint the white enamel yourself. If you want a pale color, use a tiny amount of a dark color rather than more of a pale one. Keep the china paint content to a minimum, as the flux in it will cause the enamel to relax in the firing. Be aware when mixing in china paint that enamels will fire much darker than they appear when raw.

Enamel is also available in squeezable pen-like dispensers. The lines they produce are not quite as thick as traditional enamel, and they are frustratingly hard to control and quick to clog. Immersing them in a cup of hot water will usually restore them to a usable free-flowing condition, however.

Raised enamels may be classified as "hard" or "soft," depending on their firing temperature. Hard enamels are usually fired to cone 015 or 014, and are applied onto high-fired glazes, while soft enamels, fired to cone 017 or 016, are fired

Marci Blattenberger, "Sea-Ra," plate, 10" diam. "The background was done with overglaze paints mixed very thin and then dripped with liquid paraffin. Dust and cat hair were thrown into the still wet paint to pull in color for added texture. After several firings, small curved areas were masked out and base for gold was applied with a rough sponge, then structure paste mixed with water was applied with a palette knife and pulled into river-like texture paths. Paste was applied thicker in some areas and pieces of dichroic glass were embedded in the thicker paste. The piece was fired to mature the paste and fuse the glass. The structure was then covered with liquid bright gold and fired again. Small freshwater pearls were glued (unfired) to the piece."

onto lower-fired glazes. On very high-fired porcelain, you may need to add a bit of tin oxide to get a hard enamel to adhere better.

Raised Paste and Other Structure Pastes

Raised paste is more opaque and less glossy than enamel, as it is a clay slip-like material. Its normal use is in the form of scrollwork on rims and the frames for areas of painting, as a base for unfluxed

Roman gold (see next section). For this reason, some manufacturers tint the raised paste a deep yellow, so that thin or missed spots in the gold will not show. Some china painters will mix raised paste and enamel, for a glossier finish using a lower quality gold, but the results are not as rich. Liquid gold is not appropriate for use on raised paste, since it turns the paste black.

Atelier Flugel (Germany), "Butterflies," porcelain vase with fiberglass drape and gold luster, 7½" x 5," 1990. Collection of World Organization of China Painters Museum. *Photo: Mary Early.*

Hancock's Powder, a proprietary mixture of kaolin, flux, and a little color, has been manufactured since the early 1800's. Most raised paste is either straight Hancock's Powder, or a variation on it. Some artists like to make their own additions to it, such as tin oxide for extra hardness.

Some companies supply raised paste premixed. Mixing your own is harder, but gives a better result. The traditional method is to grind the powder with fresh turpentine, let it dry, and then add enamel medium or fat oil. As with enamel, the consistency is critical. It must be just thin enough to flow (unlike enamel) but thick enough to keep its shape. If you add too much oil, it will flatten out, will not dry, and will bubble in firing. If it's too thick, you may add a few drops of turpentine. The material needs to be remixed every few minutes. Mix it a bit thicker if you're making lines than if you're applying dots.

A few artists use syrup or glycerin as a medium for raised paste, and M. Louise McLaughlin (1914) recommends using alcohol instead of turpentine. This counteracts the tendency of the lines to spread, but also evaporates quickly. While it's easier to get the perfect consistency, it doesn't stay that way long.

To apply the paste, insert the point of a good liner brush under the surface of the paste, scoop some up, and lay it on the surface. Raised paste should flow off the brush, rather than being

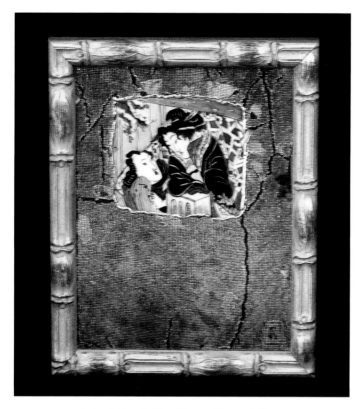

Antonia Acock, "Edo Figures," framed tile,
8" x 10," minerals and fiberglass on porcelain, lusters.

are a number of products in between that may be referred to as texture pastes or structure pastes. They are all various proportions of kaolin and flux, with other possible additions. Most are proprietary formulations sold only by their inventors, with trade names such as I-Relief®.

The structure pastes are typically white, but may be tinted with china paint (up to one part color to two parts paste). If tinted, they will generally fire about twice as dark as they appear when raw, unlike china paint. They will often separate into interesting pebbly textures, and may be covered with china paints or lusters. They are generally fired to cone 015, and may be either glossy or matte, depending on the brand.

Structure pastes may be mixed with the same oil-based mediums as raised paste for gold or raised enamels, but are often mixed with water or milk. They are intended for a freer application style than either paste for gold or enamel, and can be applied very effectively with a palette knife.

An intriguing use for structure pastes is as an adhesive for applying other materials to fired glaze, such as sticking pieces of glass or porcelain ("jewels") to the work. They may be treated just like a thick glue such as epoxy, and will maintain their shape after firing.

All of the paste-like materials contain clay (usually kaolin, but sometimes ball clay), and lead-based frit. Most also contain zinc oxide, and particular formulations may include the oxides of tin, calcium (whiting), or boron, as well as silica or cullet (ground glass). A very simple version may be made by combining equal parts of kaolin, frit, and zinc oxide.

The addition of sheets of fiberglass onto fired surfaces is another interesting possibility. Unlike "jewels," the adhesive is usually not structure paste, but regular china paint flux, spread under the fiberglass and fired to cone 010.

brushed on. It may also be applied with a palette knife, much like oil paint. For long thin lines, a pen may be the best tool, in which case the paste should be a bit thinner than for brushing.

Dry the raised paste slowly, without added heat or draft, which may take several days. Fire it (usually to cone 018) only after it is completely dry. As it is designed to have gold applied over it, it will take refiring better than enamel, but no more than three times. For this reason, complete all the firings for painting before you begin to apply raised paste.

If you think of raised paste as one end of a continuum, with raised enamel at the other, there

Raised Paste for Gold
Barbara Jensen

When asked why she likes such a difficult and temperamental technique as raised paste for gold, Barbara Jensen replied, "I'm part gypsy, part magpie-if it sparkles, I like it." A former art teacher, Barbara has also done weaving and metal enameling, and has been china painting since 1973.

Raised paste is a labor-intensive medium, with a tendency to crack or pop off. It takes a steady hand and a light, sure stroke. It is a clay slip-like product, unlike the more glass-like raised enamel. Raised paste retains a sharp profile after firing, whereas enamel relaxes a bit. The two materials are sometimes mixed in order to achieve a glossier finish with a lower quality gold, but the results are not as rich.

Barbara selects plain lightweight china, with no embossing or piercing, and a smooth hard glaze. She says the piece will tell her what it wants as decoration. "I've had one piece for twenty years, and it hasn't told me yet," she says with a laugh.

Mixing paste to the proper consistency for storage.

Thinning paste to proper consistency for application.

Brush loaded with paste.

Applying paste over drawn lines.

Applying gold over fired paste.

Burnishing fired gold with sand.

If there is to be any painting on the piece, Barbara finishes and fires that work completely before beginning the paste, as there is a limit to how many times the paste may be fired without chipping off. She fires her painting quite hot, to cone 014, which requires her to test every color. She has found that cadmium colors will not work at that temperature, and therefore avoids them.

Jensen sometimes sketches out her paste designs, especially if they are combined with painting, but often works directly on the china.

Graphite, wax, or grease pencils will sometimes resist the paste, so she uses a fine marker to draw her patterns. She has found a copy machine to be a useful tool for sizing and flipping designs.

To prepare a batch of raised paste, Barbara blends four parts Hancock's Powder with one part tin oxide, measuring by eye. The tin makes the paste harder and more resistant to chipping. She then grinds this as a slurry with denatured alcohol (isopropyl alcohol will leave a residue) until it is completely smooth. It is then dried to a putty-like

"Raspberry" tile, 9" diam.

consistency. She says that you should be able to roll it into a ball and press it flat without it cracking, but it should not be sticky. She then stores it in an airtight container.

To work with the material, Barbara takes out a pea-sized ball and thins it with clean, fresh turpentine. She prefers to buy her turpentine at a hardware store rather than china paint suppliers, because their turnover is faster. The original medium for raised paste was fat oil of turpentine, and some is still needed to make the material stretch as it needs to. Barbara markets her own proprietary Medium for Raised Paste, whose composition she has perfected through years of experimentation.

The paste is mixed with this medium to a consistency appropriate to the type of brush stroke. Barbara lists four types of strokes, which require increasingly thicker consistencies: dot, pulled dot, curved dot, and string. Only experience can tell you the right consistency for each kind of stroke.

She likes to apply the paste with a sharp-pointed natural bristle brush, such as a #1 scroller, with bristles at least one-half inch long, and a needle point. She skims the surface with the loaded brush, in a light delicate touch. As a clay material, raised paste has a plastic memory, and will not allow going back or touching up.

Barbara's kiln is small, with only on/off switches. She likes to fire slowly (1½–2 hours) to cone 016, and to cool slowly, with the lid closed and the peephole plugs out. She says raised paste will tolerate no more than three firings.

She usually uses fluxed gold paste, with about 35% gold content. She once used some 90% gold, which she reports was wonderful, but expensive. To thin the gold paste, she uses Dresden Gold Essence

"Snowberry" plate, 9" diam.

(usually sold as a thinner for liquid bright gold) and mixes it to the consistency of heavy cream. She prefers this essence to turpentine, lavender oil, or gold facilitator, as she finds they leave a residue.

The gold is brushed on the paste areas in a thin coat, fired to cone 017, and cooled slowly. Two thin coats, with firing between, are better than one thick one, as the gold may chip off. To burnish the gold, Barbara prefers dry sand to a glass brush or an etcher.

On some of Barbara Jensen's work, the raised paste and gold stands alone; on other pieces, it complements the painting. Either way, it suits a self-described "girly girl, who likes jewelry."

Pat Brick, "Casserole," porcelain with china paint, luster and Roman gold, 12" x 10" x 10," 2005. *Photo: Paul Lewing*

Roman Gold

A hundred years ago, it was common for china painters to prepare their own gold in powder form, by dissolving gold coins in aqua regia (equal parts hydrochloric and nitric acids), then precipitating the gold powder on either mercury or protosulphate of iron (FeSO$_4$·7H$_2$O or *copperas*). Using mercury was cheaper, as it precipitated more gold from the solution, but copperas produced a more durable product. Even today, some gold is touted as being mercury-free. The precipitate was then mixed with nitrate of bismuth and pulverized borax to flux it.

An alternative method was to dissolve gold in ammonium chloride (NH$_4$Cl or *sal ammoniac*) and nitric acid. Then a solution, made by heating mercury in nitric acid, was added to precipitate the gold. Needless to say, these procedures are rare today!

Today there are several methods of applying gold accents to fired glaze. Liquid gold luster (either bright or matte burnished) is far easier to use, but Roman gold is more durable and richer in appearance, since it is applied much thicker (0.3–1.0 microns) and has a much higher metal content. Using fired gold on porcelain dates back to the

Marcia Stivelman, "Satsuma Cup & Saucer," china paint and Roman gold, cup 3" high, saucer 6" diam. *Photo: Andrew R. Goldstein.*

very earliest days of china painting in Europe. The liquid form has been on the market since the late 19th century.

Roman gold is sold in three forms—powder, paste and pat. Paste and pat are premixed forms of Roman gold, and are sold fluxed or unfluxed. The choice depends on how hard the underlying glaze was fired, as some flux is needed to bond it to a harder glaze. The fluxed form is more versatile, as it may be applied on unpainted china and raised paste in the same firing, but is never applied over china paint, whether fired or unfired. Unfluxed gold will give a higher shine when burnished, but cannot be applied over glaze alone. It must have a layer of china paint or liquid bright gold fired on first. Assume it is fluxed if it doesn't specify.

To use the powdered form (which is very seldom seen today), put some on a glass slab, and add fat oil until it's a brushable consistency, thinning it with turpentine if necessary. It must be mixed very well, using a non-metallic knife, as any oxidized metal will darken the gold. Old books recommend a knife made from horn, ivory, or bone, but today plastic would be the most convenient choice. The material will be a dark chocolate color prior to firing. It may also be dusted over liquid bright gold or regular Roman gold, for a richer look.

Any excess of this very expensive material left on the palette should be saved. Scoop it into a jar, cover with turpentine, and shake well. Let it settle and decant the turpentine, taking the fat oil with it. Dry it and regrind it later as if it were fresh material.

To use either the pat or paste form, scoop some onto a grinding glass and thin with what is sold as "gold facilitator." This is generally accepted as the best substance for the purpose, but some artists use lavender oil, turpentine, lemon essence, or other solvent to soften the paste. Mix it very well, as any thin spots will come from the firing as an ugly purple. Make certain that the surface is very clean before application. Many artists warm the work in an oven or with a heating pad before painting on Roman gold, as it makes for easier application and a better bond. Two or three coats may be necessary, firing in between. If the gold is laid on in one thick layer, it is likely to chip off.

The gold emerges from the firing a reddish brown or yellow color, and must be burnished to bring out the shine. It may be polished to a glossy or matte finish. Do not touch the areas to be burnished or the gold will discolor. Burnishing is easier if the piece is warm. To achieve a bright finish, rub it with an agate burnisher or glass fiber brush, taking care to use very light pressure, lest it rub off. Be very careful with the glass brush, as any stray fibers will work their way into your skin and clothing, and will spoil any future painting they settle on. For a matte finish, rub it with moistened burnishing sand or pumice powder, using the tip of your finger or a cotton ball. A piece of rubber or polished hardwood will get into tight areas where your finger will not reach. Some artists use baking soda or toothpaste as a burnishing medium.

For a finish which resembles Roman gold, you may also use liquid burnish gold. It is applied just like liquid bright gold, but must be burnished like the other forms of Roman gold.

Liquid Bright Gold and Other Lusters

Bright gold is by far the most commonly used luster color, although lusters come in several other metallic finishes, a wide range of colors, and several special effects. The application techniques and firing are identical for all of these.

All lusters are applied in layers so thin (0.05–0.1 microns) that they take on the characteristics of the surface under them. To get a glossy result, you must put them over a glossy glaze. This is not surprising since, for example, the gold in bright gold makes up only 8–12% of the mixture. You can achieve a matte finish by firing bright gold onto a matte glaze.

There is a relatively new product on the market, Micropure gold M-472G, which, unlike other

Ken Turner, thrown porcelain vase, 7" x 7" x 14." Black, cone 10 reduction glaze, liquid bright gold applied with a brush, allowed to dry, then covered with water-based marbleizer exposing black glaze. *Photo: Tom Holt.*

forms of gold, will not arc in microwave ovens.

Lusters are metal salts suspended in an oil medium (usually oil of lavender) fluxed with bismuth nitrate. Before firing, most are brown and sticky.

It may be best to keep a special set of brushes for luster work, because they are difficult to wash out completely. It may even be a good idea to reserve a different set of brushes for each color, as some colors will not mix. Lusters may be removed from your brushes by washing them in successively cleaner bottles of acetone.

Shake the vial of luster well before using, to mix the color and medium. If it's too thick, it is best to thin it with a special luster essence, although other solvents may work. Never thin gold with turpentine, or it will turn purple. The essence is used only to thin the luster, never to paint with. Never

Joan Takayama-Ogawa, "Deco Beaded Teapot," earthenware with underglazes, glazes, china paints and luster, 9" x 9" x 4," 2001. *Photo: Steven Ogawa.*

Joan Takayama-Ogawa, "Deco Beaded Teapot," detail. *Photo: Steven Ogawa.*

Joan Takayama-Ogawa, "Tea Towers," earthenware with engobe, china paints and luster, 12" x 8" x 8", 1998.
Photo: Steven Ogawa.

Shane M. Keena, "Untitled,"
earthenware, glaze, multiple
firings with maroon luster,
12" x 12½" x 18", 2005.
Photo: ETC Photography.

Shane M. Keena,
"Untitled," detail.
Photo: ETC Photography.

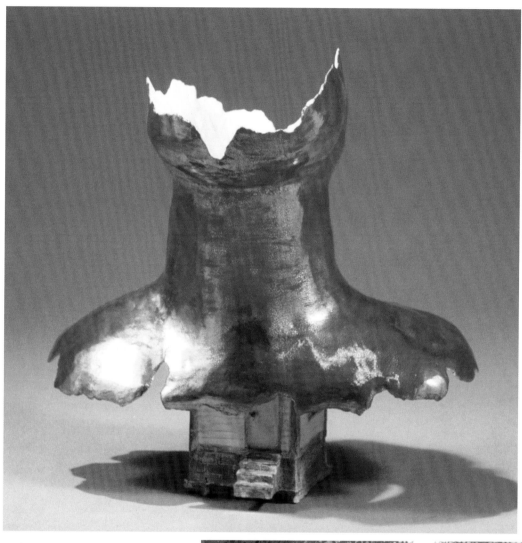

Linda Litteral, "My House: Storyteller Series," stoneware, red glaze, gold luster fired to cone 010 to cause crackle.

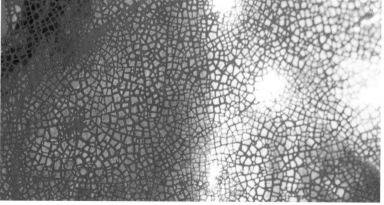

Linda Litteral,
"My House: Storyteller Series," detail.

Patz Fowle, "Rush Hour…Rodeo," porcelain, stoneware, underglaze, oxides, stains, platinum luster, nichrome wire, 6½" x 9" x 4½," 1987. *Photo: Joseph D. Sullivan.*

apply luster over, or touching, unfired china paint. Colored lusters and gold may each be applied over the other with firing in between, but gold over some china paint colors, particularly greens, may result in dark spots.

Since gold is so expensive, it's usually purchased in very tiny vials. Secure a bottle of luster in a holder of some kind to prevent its tipping over (a lump of clay works very well for this).

Some people airbrush their lusters, and many artists use a pen to lay down fine lines. You may also buy special gravity-feed pens specifically made

for luster, or special pens preloaded with gold or a few other colors.

When brushing luster on, cover the whole area evenly at one sitting, as overlaps show. If the gold is too thin it fires out as purple. If it's too thick, it will be black and dull. Lusters of all colors are best applied in several thin layers, firing in between. Avoid dust at all cost, as the tiniest grain will be apparent in the fired luster.

Lusters are usually the last things fired onto a piece, and it is recommended that they be fired to cone 018 or below. However, many people main-

Ken Turner, "Running Man Shield," thrown porcelain, 21" diam. Rim: trailed glaze on stained bare clay, copper luster fired, then gold luster. Center: glaze, copper luster, halo luster. *Photo: Tom Holt.*

Ann Cline, "Lemonade Pitcher," 7" high. Design drawn with china paint and pen oil, china paint, Roman gold, "pebbles" added with pen and china paint.

tain that lusters are not nearly so as delicate as that, and fire them repeatedly as high as cone 015.

Make sure the luster is completely dry before firing. Leave the kiln lid propped open for the first part of the firing, until the noxious odor disappears, and provide good ventilation in the kiln room. Some artists leave the kiln lid propped open throughout the firing.

If a piece comes from the kiln with smudges or fingerprints, they may be removed with a special gold eraser, or with iodine.

In addition to gold, metallic lusters are made of copper, bronze, platinum, and palladium. Other lusters are also available in about twenty transparent colors, as well as opal and mother of pearl. Several colors of halo lusters produce large spots of color in a colored matrix. A few colors are also available in a runny, crackled, or hammered effect.

Mother of pearl and opal lusters must be applied in a swirling motion to achieve a nice oil-slick-like distribution of color on the fired piece. If they are applied in straight lines, ugly yellow streaks result. They also must be applied very thinly or they will burn off.

Metallic Paints

These are a form of overglaze colors that resemble metal-flake car paint without the gloss.

John W. Hopkins, "Composition #49," earthenware, sand-blasting through layered china paints and lusters.

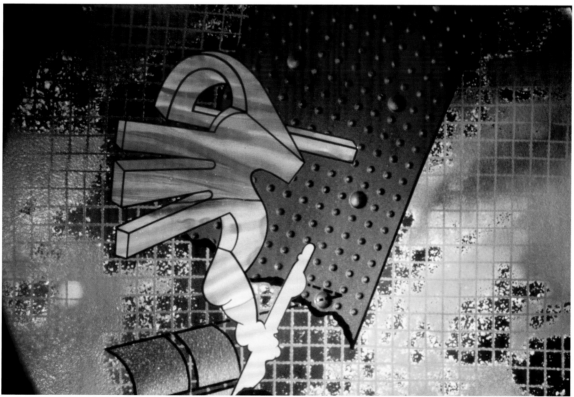

John W. Hopkins, "Composition #49," detail.

Johanna De Maine (Australia), "Rose Garden," thrown porcellanous clay, luster, raised enamel, sandblasted etching, 7" high, 2003.

Mica is added to produce the iridescent effect. Consequently, they are very gritty and difficult to brush freely, and are usually applied like a powder ground. In fact, they take to this technique much more readily than china paints.

Alone they are quite matte, but they may have a layer of clear "glaze" fired over them. They may also have colored china paint fired on top of them, but this will mask the iridescent look. Liquid gold on metallics often fires to a black color.

Prepared colors are quite pastel, but you may add colored china paint to them; however, this will also mask the distinctive effect. The colored metallics are semi-opaque, so they may be applied over another color. The metal colors, such as copper and gold, are more opaque, and have a look like glittery luster.

Metallic paints need to be fired hotter than other forms of overglaze, usually to cone 015. If after firing, they feel gritty, or a small amount rubs off on your finger, they need to be fired hotter.

Glaze

Glaze for china painters means something different than what potters refer to as glaze. In chemical composition, glaze is similar to "flux," e.g., a lead frit. Unlike flux, which is added to china paint to lower the firing temperature and increase the gloss, glaze is fired under or over the china paint to do the same thing. It can be, essentially, an overglaze for overglazes.

It may also be applied like a ground on unpainted ware, to make any painting done on top of it glossier. The shine will intensify with each subsequent firing.

Used over fired paints, glaze may be brushed on and padded smooth, or it may be used like a dry ground, either in a separate firing or on wet china paint in an open medium. It is usually put on quite thinly, as it will cause certain colors to fire out. Iron reds, flesh tones, and some browns are particularly susceptible to this, and may disappear entirely if covered with too thick a glaze.

Ute Henne (Germany), porcelain vase, 7" high. The gold band was roughened with incising paste before the gold luster was applied.

Richard Milette (Canada), "Vase Sirénes with Banana Handles", decals, luster, 17⅓" high, 1993.
Photo: Raymonde Bergeron.

Glaze comes in three variations: clear, ivory, and lavender. The ivory and lavender are slightly opaque and are used to soften the painting under them. Ivory glaze is usually applied over paintings done in predominantly warm tones, while lavender is used over cool colors.

Removing China Paint

Occasionally you may want to remove all or part of your fired china paint, either because you're not satisfied with the result, or for effect. As china paint is not nearly as integral a part of the piece as glaze, it is much easier to remove.

The most common method for removing fired gold, luster, china paint, or any other kind of overglaze, is by using dilute hydrofluoric acid. This is sold as a rust remover, under the trade names of Whink® or Rust Ban™. The liquid is brushed on and allowed to sit, then wiped off, taking the overglaze with it. This process usually also etches the underlying glaze. If you want to remove the paint in small areas only, you must mask those areas off. Nail polish works well for this, and the polish can be easily taken off later with nail polish remover.

Hydrofluoric acid is an extremely toxic and corrosive material, and great precautions should be taken when using it. Always wear heavy rubber gloves and protective clothing. Avoid applying it with tools that have absorbent handles, such as cotton swabs with wood or paper stems. The acid will seep up the stem and burn your hands. The burns from this acid are particularly nasty, as you often will not feel them until after extensive damage has been done. The burns are extremely slow to heal, and the fluorine molecules can be absorbed into the body, possibly resulting in heart failure.

Proper disposal of the acid is also very important. If you pour it into a sink or toilet, it will etch the glaze. Neutralize the acid before disposal by adding baking soda to it until no more bubbles form, and then flush it down the drain with lots of water. However, only the application of calcium gluconate gel will completely neutralize the acid.

As a rule, trying to save a painted piece by removing fired china paint is a false economy. The piece never looks quite as good again, and if you can paint it once, you can paint it again.

A slower and less extreme product for removing part or all of the china paint is ammonium fluoride paste, used to etch the surface of glass and metal. It is slightly less toxic and much easier to control than the liquid acid. A similar, if not identical product is called incising paste, which is normally used to roughen the surface of glaze or china paint, rather than completely remove it.

Sandblasting results in much the same surface as etching, and is far less toxic. China paint is a much more delicate surface than glaze, so proceed slowly and carefully, if you do not want to completely remove it.

"C-Monster"
Mural

This was an interesting project for several reasons. It involved a number of special techniques, and the subject matter and setting were quite unusual. What made it unique was that the design was someone else's.

Cindy, my client, wanted a whimsical mural set in a field of stone, as a backdrop to a backyard barbecue. Her concept was a play on the words "sea monster," depicting a creature among objects beginning with the letter "C," surrounded by a border based on words.

The Design Process

Cindy located me through my web site, and came to my studio with books by a favorite artist who uses word games as a creative starting point. She also brought some rough sketches by Shannon Noel, an illustrator and set designer, whom she knew through their children.

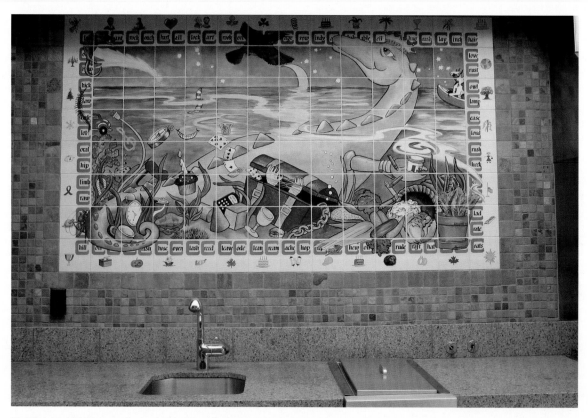

The finished "C-Monster" mural 7' x 4' installed over a barbecue grill.

Shannon Noel's proposal drawing, my sketches for the calendar, and the acetate "C" stencil.

Copying the drawing onto the tiles using a china pencil.

She asked me to design an image with a border. Her idea was that the border would incorporate a calendar (one of the items beginning with "C") or some form of word play. Her suggestion was for a series of words beginning with the "C" sound, but not necessarily the letter, such as "series," or "cease." We ultimately decided that Shannon would elaborate on her sketch, producing a full-color finished drawing, which I would then reproduce on tile. It would be my responsibility to design the border.

We decided that the central image should overlap the border to make it more interesting and dynamic, and that the border would incorporate both a calendar and a word game, in two tiers.

Each of the forty 6" x 6" tiles on the outer row would have a symbol depicting a national holiday, a family occasion, or an important date in the Jewish or Catholic year, as these were their religions.

My idea for a more graphically interesting word game was a pattern of two repeated "C's" on each tile, with a word lettered inside each. They were to be words that stood on their own, but made another word with the "C" attached, such as "clean,"

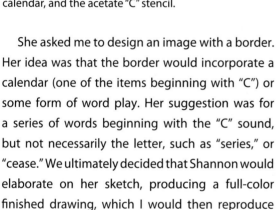

Blotting the paint with a foam rubber tool.

"chair," and "cease." I would have preferred the more visually dense "C" border to be outside the sparser calendar, but it was much easier to keep every tile clear for all the dates on the outside tier.

Since the piece was to be outside, we chose a frost-proof tile, with an off-white matte glaze.

Beginning the Mural

The easiest way to make the border appear to be behind the central image was to fire one coat of china paint onto the central image, then complete the border pattern, wiping it off wherever it overlapped. I then went back and completed the painting of the central image.

Texturing a background color with a stencil brush.

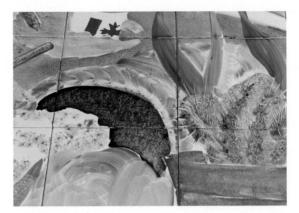

Detail of part of the central image after the first firing.

The central image after the first firing.

The first step in painting any mural is numbering the backs of the tiles. I use an underglaze pencil to write two numbers and an arrow on each tile. The first number is the horizontal row, starting at the bottom. The second number is the vertical row, starting on the left. The arrow points up.

After numbering the tiles, I wash them to remove any dirt or grease. I used a commercial window cleaning spray, since I chose water as the painting medium for the first coat. Had I chosen oil, I would have used alcohol or turpentine to clean the tiles.

After the tiles dried, I copied the scale drawing onto them freehand, using a special pencil made for this purpose. The marks made by a regular graphite pencil sometimes remain after firing, and many markers will resist water-based paints.

The mural was then transferred in manageable sections to my painting table. I always work from the top down, or from the background forward, so the sky was the first thing to be painted.

In order to leave the constellations (Cassiopeia, Cygnus, and Ceres) white, I coated them with a latex masking fluid made for watercolor, and let them dry. The blue was brushed in, padded with sponge rubber, and allowed to dry. The masking fluid was then pulled off.

Painting continued until the entire central image was done. In some areas I left brush strokes showing; in others, they were blotted with sponge rubber or a stencil brush; still others got a texture wiped into them. A few images were painted with more than one color, but most were single background colors. The piece was then fired to cone 016, the first of eight firings on the mural, all to that same cone. I fire my tiles in mullite tile setters for easy and efficient kiln stacking.

Printing the "C's." Everything but the green "C" has been fired once.

Peeling the clear film off the painted forms.

After the fourth firing, the calendar symbols are finished, and the "C's" are fired on.

Lettering the words inside the "C's" with a pen.

Wiping out the clef image. The images above my hand have already been wiped clean of the blue background color; areas below my hand have not. The black lines are marker, and will burn out in the firing.

The Borders

In the second firing, I laid on the yellow background for the "C's." I could have sprayed this color, but chose to brush and blot it, wiping off any part of the central image which overlapped the border. The yellow background needed to be fired before the "C's" could be screened over it. For this firing I also painted the first coat on the calendar symbols.

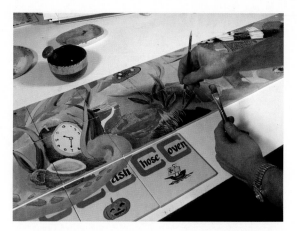

Using a double-ended rubber wipeout tool to create a grass texture.

I originally drew the "C" on graph paper with a pen. This design was then copied onto sheet acetate to make a stencil for silk-screening the image. For instructions on screen printing, see earlier in this chapter.

In the third and fourth firings, I fired the printed "C's." Had I used a closed medium I could have printed both of the "C's" on each tile without firing in between, but I opted to try glycerin. It worked well as a screening medium, but did not dry, so I needed to fire between print runs. If both of the "C's" had been in the same quadrants of every tile, I would have made a stencil that incorporated the two letters. The fact that both "C's" needed to be next to the central image meant that they were in different orientations on each of the four sides of the mural.

To facilitate removing any printing that would overlap the already-fired imagery, I covered the painted shapes with a clear adhesive frisket film, and cut it to the outline of the underlying image. I then printed the full "C" and peeled the film off.

In these two firings, I also completed the calendar symbols, deepening color and adding texture in

The seventh kiln load, fresh from the firing and still in the tile setters.

Adding black outlines with a liner brush.

Detail of a section of the central image after its second firing.

Detail of a section of the finished mural.

one firing, and painting the outlines in the other.

The next step was hand-lettering the words inside the "C's" for the fifth firing. I experimented with a number of mediums and tools for this job, and ultimately chose a commercial pen oil in a #0 flat lettering pen. The pen oil flowed more easily than any water-based or homemade oil-based medium. The pen made a more even and cleaner mark of appropriate size than any brush I tried.

I made a cardboard template to ensure that the letters were even and straight, drawing the top and bottom lines with a pencil. The china paint and oil were ground together on a tile, picked up with a palette knife and put into a small container deep enough to load the pen.

Finishing the Mural

The sixth and seventh firings were used to apply additional shading, deepening colors and emphasizing textures. I might have fit the whole mural in a single firing, but timing, and a hunch that I might need to do more work on certain areas, led me to use two.

I always feel that the "real work" of painting on any area happens in the second firing. In the first firing, the base has been established, and shapes have been roughly defined with as much detail and texture as possible. These forms are delineated as exactly as possible in the second firing. Colors are intensified and modified on a colored base, rather than on a white background.

In many areas, such as the sky, I simply intensified the color by adding a second layer of the same shade, blotting it as I did in the first firing. Other shapes had a second color added as shading to define shape. Texture was sometimes emphasized by adding color only to the dark areas and repeating the same technique as in the first firing. In other cases, a solid first color serves only as a background, with a second color brushed over, which is then either drawn into or wiped out to create textures and imagery.

I often use a dampened foam makeup applicator to wipe out small areas. Paint mixed with water is easy to wipe off using this technique. However, if I need to draw lines through a wet color, I prefer to use something stickier. In the case of the cat's cradle, I used propylene glycol.

In the eighth and final firing, I added black outlines to make certain shapes stand out, and to hide any ragged edges. This operation really shows the importance of a good brush for making long, expressive, even playful, lines.

For this step I used black china paint ground in propylene glycol with a mortar and pestle. I have found this to be much more efficient than grinding it on a palette with a knife. The paint remains evenly mixed for a long time, unlike using water alone. It also dries slightly on the sides and rim of the container, giving me a range of color intensity.

After Cindy's enthusiastic approval of the finished mural, the "C-Monster" and its surrounding stonework were adhered to the concrete structure of the barbecue with thin-set cement by a professional tile setter. The installation was finished with a gray sanded acrylic grout.

Kilns are as capricious as women, and you know well what that means.

—Charles Fergus Binns (1857-1934)
Addressing the National League of Mineral Painters, 1899.

Chapter 6

Kilns and Firing

While Binns may or may not have been joking with his opinion of women, he was serious in his assessment of the kilns of his day. During the early days of overglazing, in both Asia and in Europe, ware was fired using the same fuel as in the glaze firing, usually wood or charcoal. Wood was more problematic, as it produced ash and smoke, and made it hard to maintain an oxidizing atmosphere in the kiln chamber. Reduction spoils some over-glaze colors and causes fritted lead to volatilize, resulting in a dull surface. Charcoal was the preferred fuel until the advent of liquid fuels such as kerosene, propane, and natural gas in the early 20th century. In fact, the great Japanese potter Hamada Shoji fired his overglaze work in a charcoal-fired kiln well into the 1970's. However, since the middle of the 20th century, the overwhelming majority of china painted work has been fired in electric kilns.

The first major improvement in the firing of small kilns to low temperatures was made by Johann Gregorius Höroldt, who became the second director of the Meissen factory in 1723. He protected the pieces in his kilns with muffles, which are refractory shields that partially or completely enclose the ware. This blocked the flames and ash deposits, but did nothing to guard against reduction.

China painting's enormous popularity in the late 19th century was aided by the appearance of small, relatively portable and affordable charcoal kilns, whose designs were soon adapted to liquid fuels. Until then, most china painters did not have

their own kilns, and either worked in community centers or schools which had kilns, or shipped their work (sometimes hundreds of miles) to be fired. These painters developed mediums which dried very hard, and painted multiple layers, to be fired only once.

M. Louise McLaughlin describes one of these kilns and its firing regimen in her 1914 book, *China Painting: A Practical Manual*. "The one in

Ad for Wilke Kilns, from *Keramic Studio*, Vol. VII #11, March 1906, p. 260.

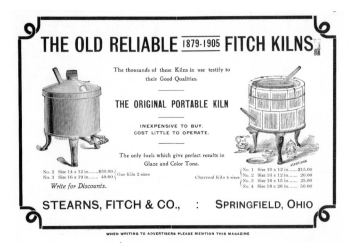

Ad for Old Reliable Fitch Kilns, from *Keramic Studio*, Vol. VII #11, March, 1906, p. 259.

A kerosene-fired Revelation kiln from the very early 20th century. Collection of World Organization of China Painters Museum. *Photo: Paul Lewing*

most general use consists of an iron pot with a cover in which the china is placed, and around which, between it and an outside wall of fire clay tiles, is a space of three or four inches to contain the fuel. The pot, as well as the cover, is provided with a vent from which a short iron pipe proceeds. The whole apparatus is elevated upon three feet." The kiln also featured an iron pan below the firing chamber, and a separate perforated iron basket. The ware was stacked in the iron chamber and the lid put on, a fire was started in the iron basket to get the charcoal lit, and the hot coals were then shoveled around and on top of the iron pot. When the desired heat was achieved, a grate in the bottom of the chamber was pulled out, and the coals fell into the iron pan. Heat was usually gauged by observing the color inside the chamber.

Many a lady was badly burned when her long dress caught fire in the process of moving burning charcoal, and many a stilted pot fell over while the kiln was being stoked. The advent of liquid fuels meant firing was safer, easier to control, more predictable, and less affected by wind, rain, or cold. The liquid-fueled kilns could even be installed indoors, with proper ventilation.

As early as 1900, people were experimenting with electricity to fire kilns, and by the 1920's a few kilns were being fired using silicon carbide rods, called Globars®, rather than wire elements. These kilns required large transformers, and the Globars were expensive and delicate, but they worked well in industrial applications.

By the 1930's, insulating soft brick and nichrome element wires had appeared, making small electric kilns feasible for use in schools. These kilns could only handle low-fire temperatures, but they were ideal for the lead glazes that were then in fashion.

The resurgence in popularity of china painting in the 1950's and 1960's was boosted enormously by the invention of the top-loading round or octagonal kiln. It was relatively small and portable;

it could be wired into a residential electrical system; and it heated and cooled quickly. Kilns of this design are ubiquitous today, and their design has changed little in fifty years. Most of their improvements have been in temperature regulating and monitoring systems.

The first of these systems was the KilnSitter®, a device that utilizes two automated shutoff mechanisms, one controlled by a pyrometric cone and the other—a backup system—by a timer. Kilns now usually come equipped with a digitally-controlled temperature regulation system that automates the entire firing with preset or operator-designed firing programs.

Buying and Firing a New Kiln

The first consideration when buying a kiln is size. Choose one that is large enough to hold a reasonable quantity of the type of work you like to do, but not so large that there will usually be a lot of empty space in the kiln. Firing a single small piece in a large kiln will waste electricity, but this will not affect the fired results. If you like working on very small objects, such as jewelry, you may be able to use a kiln that plugs into a normal residential wall outlet.

Top-loading models of electric kilns are by far the most popular design, but many manufacturers also make a front-loading model. These may be a better choice for those with back problems, or short individuals who have trouble reaching the bottom of a top-loader. A counterbalance on the lid of a top-loader is a good idea even if its weight is not an issue for you.

Place and install your kiln according to manufacturer specifications. If you buy a used kiln, and you did not get the original owners manual, contact the original manufacturer or go online and download the appropriate instructions.

Loading a China Paint Firing

Since china paint is fired to such a low temperature, pieces may be stacked in the kiln. Unless

Revelation kiln, showing the asbestos-lined door, and one of the two removable muffles that fit just inside the door. Other muffles are barely visible inside the chamber. *Photo: Paul Lewing*

the underlying glaze is very soft, it will not melt enough to stick pieces together. The china paint itself does melt, however, so any contact between pieces must be limited to undecorated areas.

Flat shapes, such as plates and bowls, may be stacked with stilts or wads between them, up to a point. Position the points of these spacers directly above one another to minimize stress. Too much weight concentrated on a few points will cause the ware to break. You may lean several plates against each other, separated by hooking a three-sided double-point stilt over the top edges. Many china paint manuals recommend firing both plates and tiles vertically. If you fire a lot of plates, you may want to invest in specially designed mullite plate setters.

23″ and a 28″ diameter top-loading electric kilns. The larger size will be too large for all but the most prolific china painter. *Photo courtesy of Seattle Pottery Supply/ Crucible Kilns.*

It is often recommended that shapes with recessed feet be fired on stilts to avoid trapping air underneath, as this will cause cracking. The true cause is more likely the difference in cooling rate between kiln shelf and air, which causes some parts of the piece to cool faster than others.

Tiles are stacked most easily and efficiently in mullite racks designed for the purpose. There are a number of tile setter designs, some of which hold the tiles vertically, and some horizontally. Keep in mind that the setters must be heated as well as the ware, so try to keep the mass of the furniture to a minimum. Vertical stacks of tiles in racks will fire much more quickly than the same number of tiles laid flat on kiln shelves.

Make sure your painting is completely dry before firing. Some mediums will run during the warm-up cycle if they are still wet. Take care also to avoid touching the decoration while loading. More work is ruined by smudges during loading than any other way.

It's a good idea to position a number of cones inside the chamber, at least in the first few firings of a new kiln. Use large cones, either self-supporting or embedded in a wad of clay at about an 8° or 10° angle. Place one where you can see it inside each peephole, as well as several in the middle of the load, on each level. A small freestanding cone, placed in a cone pack or wad of clay, will not bend at the same temperature as the same numbered cone or bar inserted in the kiln sitter, but a full-sized one should.

At least in the first firing, it's also a good idea to place two more cones with the large cone behind the top peephole. One should be one cone number lower than the target temperature, the other one cone number higher. This will give you a better idea of how much colder or hotter your kiln fires, should it not correspond exactly to the number of the cone in the kiln sitter. If you find that your kiln fires cooler on the very bottom than in the rest of the chamber, place a kiln shelf on the floor of the kiln with a ½- or 1-inch post under it.

Firing China Paints

When it comes to firing, china paint is as easy as ceramics gets. Firings are short and inexpensive, the results are consistent and predictable, and the firing cycle is very forgiving. Every clay artist has a relationship with the kiln that falls somewhere on a continuum from partner to tool. If wood firing is the ultimate in the view of the kiln as a partner, china paint is the ultimate on the opposite end of the spectrum. The kiln is a tool.

However, china paint is still a ceramic medium, so there are pitfalls and anomalies. It may be as

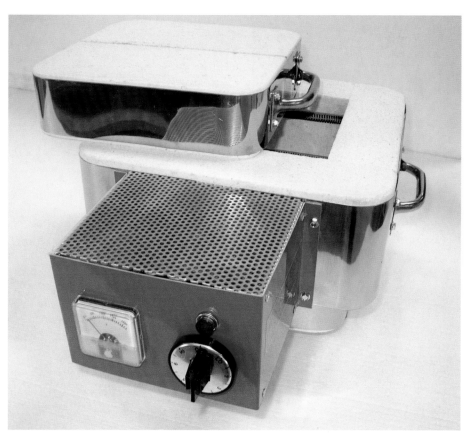

This tiny (6″ x 6″ x 4½″) kiln comes apart completely. It would be suitable for a bead maker.
Photo: Jen-Ken Kilns.

close to paint as you can get while still having to fire it, but it's not paint. The variables are mostly limited to temperature, color chemistry, and the underlying glazes. China paint is always fired in oxidation, eliminating the variability of reduction firing. Different heating and cooling cycles have very little effect, as they do in firing matte, micro-crystalline, or macrocrystalline glazes. Glaze flaws such as pinholing, crawling, crazing, and shivering are eliminated in a previous firing.

Color Chemistry

The most prominent peculiarity of china paints is that, unlike either paint or other forms of glazes, they are comprised of three distinct color groups:

colors based on gold, those based on cadmium/se-lenium, and all the other colors. Problems often occur when the groups are intermixed, and each fires best at a different temperature.

The gold-based colors (ruby, violet, purple, li-lac, and many shades of pink) like the most heat, as do dark cobalt blues. For best results, they need to be fired to cone 016 or 015. The gold-based colors will be yellowish if underfired, and bluish if overfired.

The cadmium/selenium colors (bright reds and oranges, maroon, and some yellows) need the least heat, and are best fired to cone 018 or 017. They may be washed out or disappear entirely if fired

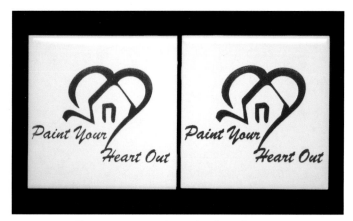

These two custom logo tiles, from the same print run, were fired in the same kiln load. The tile on the left was on top of a stack of tile setters with plenty of air above it. The tile on the right was fired in the top slot of a tile setter, very close to the underside of the setter.

too hot. Cadmium reds need special consideration in kiln loading, just as they do in application and firing. If a cadmium red is placed too close to kiln furniture or other ware, the red color may come out dull and purplish. It is best to leave several inches of space around any large area of this color. When I fire a kiln load with a lot of cadmium red on tiles, I try to leave every other tile setter slot empty. Cadmium oranges and maroon do not seem to be affected in the same way.

The group that includes all the other colors is the most forgiving, and is generally fired to cone 016 or 017. Iron reds are particularly sensitive to heat. If they are fired too hot, they may turn brown, and the more yellow shades may disappear completely.

Metallic colors are generally fired a cone or two hotter than china paints, while lusters are fired a cone or two lower, perhaps even as low as cone 022. Lusters generally are not nearly as temperature-sensitive as their labels would indicate.

Many china painters fire each color group separately, beginning with the hottest cones and working their way down to the lower ones. To build up enough intensity of color and shading, they may do several firings at each temperature, painting only those areas of their design that include a particular color group.

I have never been able to think or work this way. I need to work on a whole piece at once, and I need to finish it as quickly as possible. I usually do three firings to build up shading, texture and intensity, and fire all three times to cone 016. Other artists prefer to do their initial firings to a relatively low temperature, and fuse it all together in a final hotter firing.

The maturing temperature of most (but not all) colors may be lowered a cone or so by the addition of a little flux, and colors that come out matte due to underfiring can usually be made glossy by the application of a coat of clear "glaze." There is some variation among manufacturers as well, so it is possible to have the entire spectrum mature at the same temperature by picking some colors from one company and others from another.

Underlying Glaze

To bond completely with the ware, china paint requires just enough heat to soften the glaze it's applied over. Probably the entire surface of most glazes does not soften in the firing; rather the very powerful fluxes in the china paint slightly melt any glaze they come in contact with.

The difference between the melting temperature of soft glazes (fired originally to a temperature below cone 1) and that of hard glazes (fired above cone 6) may mean that the china paint firings need to be one, or perhaps even two, cones higher or lower than usual.

Unless you have made and glazed the object yourself, it is often impossible to know how hot it was fired. Some experimentation may be necessary to find the optimum temperature for a particular ware. If you are in doubt, it's best to fire a little cooler than you think you may need,

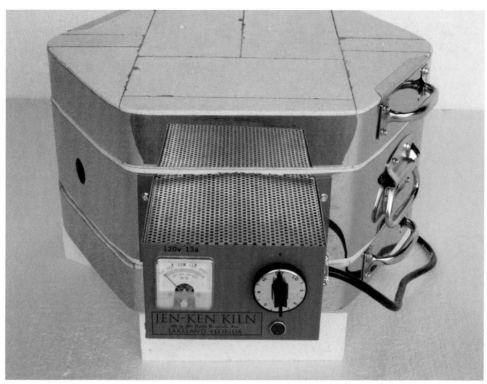

A portable 120V, 13 amp kiln that will fire up to 2000°F. *Photo: Jen-Ken Kilns.*

as you can always refire to a higher temperature, but if you have overfired, there isn't much you can do to remedy things. Sometimes another coat of the same color applied onto an overfired color will come out as you intended, but not always.

Firing Cycles

The timing of china paint firings is hardly critical in most cases. The only danger is in things breaking if they are fired too fast, since china paint requires firing just barely past the point of quartz inversion at 1063°F (573°C). As long as the ware is eased past this point on heating, and again on cooling, it hardly matters how fast the firing goes, and there is no need for any downfiring or soaking cycle. Some colors, particularly the bright cadmium reds and oranges, achieve their maximum brilliance in a very fast firing.

Materials other than china paint itself may require more careful firing, however. Most artists who use liquid lusters warm them very slowly to allow the smelly medium to burn off completely. Additions of thick materials like raised paste, structure paste and enamel need very slow cooling to avoid chipping off.

Digital controllers are great for regulating heating and cooling cycles, and are especially helpful when you want to maintain the same firing cycle regardless of how full the kiln is. Each particular brand of controller has its input regimens, but they're all pretty straightforward.

If you use an oil-based medium and you do not have a downdraft venting system (recommended), prop the kiln lid up a bit during the warm-up phase of the firing to properly carry away the fumes. You may notice that your painting turns a dark brown as it gets warm. This is only the oil

CHINA PAINT & OVERGLAZE

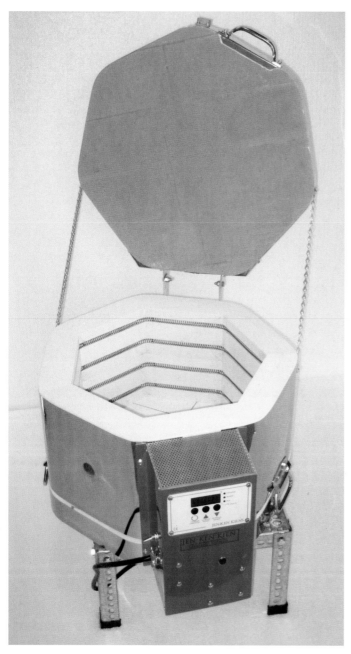

A small modern kiln with digital controller, suitable for the hobby china painter. *Photo: Jen-Ken Kilns*

medium beginning to burn, and nothing to worry about. Water-based mediums do not do this.

The main variable affecting the length of firings is the density of the load. A kiln that is almost empty will fire several hours faster than one that is densely packed. It's a good idea to always warm your kiln up on the same schedule, so that you soon get an idea of how long a firing should take.

Let the kiln cool undisturbed until the temperature falls at least below what may be reached in a kitchen oven. Many china painters will not even open the lid, much less unload the kiln, until it has reached room temperature. I'm more impatient than that, and often need gloves to unload my kiln, with no ill effects to the work.

My firing schedule is fairly typical of china painters, although perhaps a little fast for some people. My kiln is a typical 23" top-loading octagon, with three element rings and one blank ring. I prop the lid open with a brick, and turn all three rings to "low" for 20 minutes. I then turn all three to "medium," leave it for 20 minutes, and then close the lid. Twenty minutes after that (one hour after the first switches were turned on) I turn all three switches to "high," and let my KilnSitter™ shut it off when it reaches temperature. I have fired my kiln so many times that I can predict, within 10 minutes, when it will shut off. If there is hardly anything in it, it will take about two hours; if it's really packed tight, about 4½ hours. When firings begin to take longer than that, I know it's time to change the elements.

If you fire using a pyrometer or a computerized controller, you may notice that your work is coming out over- or underfired, although you are getting a reading of the correct temperature. This is particularly likely to happen if you fire either very quickly or very slowly. This discrepancy occurs because, while pyrometers (and controllers regulated by pyrometers) measure temperature, cones actually measure "heat-work," a function of both heat and time. Therefore, there may be a real

difference in the appearance of china paint fired to a pyrometer reading of, for instance, 1458°F (792°C, or cone 016) in two hours, and that fired to the same reading in five hours. The longer firing is likely to produce much glossier surfaces.

Another source of confusion may be that the "end-point" (the temperature at which the tip of a standing cone bends over far enough to touch the shelf) of a large cone is different from the end point of a small standing cone of the same number. Our previous example of 1458°F (792°C) would theoretically be cone 016, if a large cone were used, but 016 measured by a small standing cone requires 1517°F (825°C) to slump over, as it has less mass to pull it down. Neither of these numbering systems takes into account the weight of the kiln sitter rod pushing a small cone or bar down.

The end-point temperatures assigned to cone numbers are predicated on a certain rate of temperature increase, specifically 270°F (150°C) per hour for large cones, and 540°F (300°C) for small cones. If you fire much faster or slower than that, your results may not correspond to what color manufacturers intend.

Kiln Maintenance

Today's electric kilns are incredibly reliable and long lasting, but they do occasionally need some routine maintenance. Your kiln's most common housekeeping requirements are cleaning, and repositioning elements.

Periodic vacuuming inside the chamber is particularly important in china paint firing, because even the smallest particle of dust can cause glaring flaws in the painting. Dust doesn't get stirred up and blown around the chamber as it does in a fuel-burning kiln, but it will rise on heated air currents and deposit itself on the work. The bricks of the kiln itself are the main source of dust and larger particles, which may fall on the painting and fuse.

Vacuum along all the grooves that hold the elements, as well as the floor and underside of the

Front-loading electric kiln, a good choice for those with back problems. *Photo courtesy of Seattle Pottery Supply/Crucible Kilns.*

lid. Be sure to vacuum inside the KilnSitter tube, since corrosion from the metal rod can build up there and hamper the operation of the kiln sitter. To avoid sucking the two small metal pieces that support the cone out of their slots, remove them for this operation.

No matter how securely element wires are pinned in, they eventually begin to sag out of their grooves, and need to be put back in. Contact between the wires and any other surface during firing will drastically shorten their lives, if not break them immediately.

Element wires should only be moved when they are hot enough to glow or they may break. Either unplug the kiln or switch off its circuit breaker when handling elements. To move a sagging element, heat it up with a propane torch until it glows and use a non-metal tool to gently push it

Mullite tile setters of various sizes and configurations.

back into place. Pin it immediately with a small piece of high-temperature wire before you lose your place.

If you fire to china paint temperatures only, you should occasionally (every 100 firings or so) fire the kiln empty to around cone 04. This will help preserve the oxidized coating on the elements.

Periodically, your kiln will need new elements and/or switches. If you decide to do this repair yourself, follow the manufacturer's instructions carefully. It's a tedious job that requires attention to detail and some hand strength, but not a difficult job.

Your first sign that an element may be failing is that firings begin taking longer, or will not reach temperature at all. China paint firings are so fast, and require so little power, that most kilns will eventually reach the required temperature even without all the elements working properly.

Replace all the elements at one time, as the failure of one is usually a sign that the others are close to failing. However, if you decide to replace only one, you need to determine which element has failed. Turn one element at a time up through the cycle of low, medium and high. Never turn a switch directly from off to high, as the surge of power may damage the switch. Hold your hand near the wire, without touching it, to see if it heats up, or hang a small piece of paper on the element to see if it chars.

If the element has failed because the wire has broken, it may be fixed temporarily by hooking the broken ends together, but this is a stopgap measure at best.

The outcome of any serious research can only be to make two questions grow where only one grew before.

—Thorstein Veblen (1857–1929)

The Chemistry of China Paint

China paints are the lowest-firing form of glaze possible. They are essentially a very highly colored frit. Glaze chemists working at higher temperatures will notice the absence of some familiar elements and the appearance of some new ones. As firing temperatures in oxidation decrease, base glazes become much simpler, while color chemistry becomes increasingly complex. The chemistry of the uncolored base glazes has changed very little in the medium's 1000-year history, at least up until the 1970's, but there have been major developments in color production.

However, china paint chemistry is only simple in relation to that of higher fired glazes. It is still a fantastically complex system, and one about which very little has been written. Information is especially hard to find because much of it is, and has been from the art's earliest days, proprietary.

It is impossible to know what proportions of which elements are in a particular brand or shade of china paint. The number of possible permutations of fluxes and colorants is almost infinite; suppliers often do not know that information themselves, and they wouldn't tell if they did. Dozens of companies make ceramic stains, each with their own secret recipes and processes. Distributors may even be using stockpiles of chemicals that have been out of production for decades. To understand and control the medium, we can only educate ourselves about what each of the ingredients might do.

It is possible to make an approximation of china paints by mixing frits and commercially produced

stains, but the whole point of china painting is consistent color across the entire spectrum. The quantities you need are small, and the variety of commercial colors is enormous. While mixing your own may be an interesting experiment, it is ultimately pointless for the vast majority of artists.

The Basics of Glaze Chemistry (Much Simplified)

Glazes are essentially glass, which is mostly silica (SiO_2, or silicon dioxide). However, silica melts at a very high temperature, much higher than we can attain in our kilns. To lower the melting temperature, a more fusible material must be added to the glass-forming silica. This is called a flux. These two are all that's needed to make glass, but we need to apply our glass to a ceramic surface, so it must be made stiffer so that it doesn't run off the surface. The primary element that does this is alumina (Al_2O_3, or aluminum oxide),* the primary ingredient in clay. In glaze chemistry terminology, this is called a stabilizer.

> ***Note**: Very few of the ceramic elements can exist alone, uncombined with other elements, gold and the other "royal metals" being notable exceptions to this rule. Before firing, most are combined with some other element, usually oxygen and/or carbon, occasionally sulfur or nitrogen. These often burn away in firing and, in most cases, we are left with an oxide in the fired glaze. For the sake of brevity, I will refer to these elements by their name only, without the modifier "oxide," unless I'm discussing properties unique to an oxide configuration. For instance, in the statement "cobalt usually produces blue," you may assume that what is actually present in the fired glaze is cobalt oxide.

John Britt, "Recipe Cup," thrown porcelain, celadon glaze, decal, 4" high, 2002. This side of Britt's cup shows a recipe of raw materials for the glaze on the cup.

John Britt, "Recipe Cup," thrown porcelain, celadon glaze, decal, 4" high, 2002. This side shows the glaze's flux unity formula and percentage by weight analysis, with other information.

In the late 19th century, the Director of Research at the Berlin Royal Porcelain Factory, Hermann Seger, developed a method for analyzing the composition of a molecule of fired glass that is still used today. The method starts with the atomic weight of each element, which determines the molecular weight of a molecule of each raw material. It then subtracts the weight of any element that burns away in the firing (mostly organic material and chemically combined water), counts how many molecules of each oxide are present in the quantity of each raw material specified by the recipe, and separates these oxides into three categories: RO oxides (alkaline fluxes), R_2O_3 oxides (neutral stabilizers), and RO_2 oxides (acidic glassformers). A "glassformer" is an oxide that can retain the amorphous property of its molten state

on cooling, rather than reverting to a crystalline state. The R stands for "Radical" and represents any element. The units that are represented by these numbers are called "molecular equivalents." The O stands for oxygen, and the numbers indicate how many oxygen atoms and how many of the radical atoms are present.

If at this point in the mathematical operation, we were to adjust the totals of all these oxides, in all three categories, to add up to 100, we would achieve an analysis called "molar percentage," which is used occasionally by some glaze chemists.

Seger added one more step, which makes his method especially valuable to the study of glazes. Since the fluxes are the most variable and interesting part of glazes, he adjusted the numbers so that all the oxides in the RO column add up to 1, with the numbers in the R_2O_3 and RO_2 columns representing their relation to the total fluxes. This system of analysis is called "flux unity," and is the most common way potters analyze their glazes. The main function of modern glaze calculation software programs is to convert back and forth between recipes of raw materials and flux unity analyses of fired glaze molecules.

While it's still helpful, Seger's method of flux unity analysis does not predict the behavior of china paints nearly as well as it does that of glazes fired to higher temperatures. One reason for this is the much higher percentage of colorants in china paints, which usually are not included in the analyses. Some colors need to contain significant portions of base glaze oxides (such as alumina or zinc) as part of their crystal structure, and these inevitably affect the behavior of the glaze as a whole. In addition, china paints are made to fire onto glaze, not clay, and so contain virtually no alumina or other stabilizer.

Seger's method also does not deal well with the fact that some elements do not fit neatly into the categories of flux, stabilizer, and glassformer. Several of them (boron and bismuth, for example) may be more than one in different situations, or even at the same time. Others, though the proportion of R oxide to oxygen puts them in one column (as in the case of phosphorus) their action is never that of the typical elements in that column.

A different system of analysis, more common among chemists, geologists, and other scientists, is called "percentage by weight." In this system, once the number of molecules is established, they are weighed rather than counted (as in the flux unity and molar percentage systems) and all the oxides present are made to add up to 100.

When you look at a glaze formula, if all the numbers add up to 100, chances are it's a percentage by weight analysis, unless it says otherwise. If the fluxes add up to 1, it's a flux unity analysis.

Jeremy Jernegan, "Storm Warning #1", ceramic and steel with homemade overglaze enamel, 45" x 30" x 13", 2001. Red area was fired, then white enamel applied and sanded, then fired.

RO Flux	R_2O_3 Stabilizer	RO_2 Glassformer
K_2O Potassium	Al_2O_3 Alumina	SiO_2 Silica
Na_2O Sodium	B_2O_3 Boron	
Li_2O Lithium	Bi_2O_3 Bismuth	
PbO Lead	P_2O_5 Phosphorus	
ZnO Zinc		
BaO Barium		
SrO Strontium		
CaO Calcium		
MgO Magnesium		

Figure 1. Common Flux, Stabilizer, and Glassformer Oxides.

THE COMMON CERAMIC ELEMENTS AND THEIR SYMBOLS

Ag	Silver	Na	Sodium
Al	Alumina	Ni	Nickel
Au	Gold	P	Phosphorous
B	Boron	Pb	Lead
Ba	Barium	Pr	Praseodymium
Bi	Bismuth	S	Sulphur
Ca	Calcium	Sb	Antimony
Cd	Cadmium	Se	Selenium
Co	Cobalt	Si	Silicon
Cr	Chromium	Sn	Tin
Cu	Copper	Sr	Strontium
Fe	Iron	Ti	Titanium
K	Potassium	U	Uranium
Li	Lithium	V	Vanadium
Mg	Magnesium	Zn	Zinc
Mn	Manganese	Zr	Zirconium

Base Glazes for China Paint

Figure 1 shows all the most common oxides used to make base glazes at any temperature. They are separated into the three categories according to their chemical composition and function in a glaze.

Glassformers

Although several other oxides used in glazes would fit into the glassformer column in this system of analysis, they do not function as glassformers. These include the opacifiers tin (SnO_2), titanium (TiO_2), and zirconium (ZrO_2), as well as the colorant manganese (MnO_2).

Silica is the only oxide that is always a glassformer. The lower the firing temperature of a glaze, the less of the very refractory silica there may be.

In highfire glazes, up to 70% of the weight of a glaze may be silica, representing as much as 5 times as many molecular equivalents as the total fluxes. In china paints, the silica may constitute only 20% of the weight of the glaze, or two times the number of flux molecules.

Quartz, flint and sand are the usual sources for silica, although ground glass (cullet) is sometimes used, if its flux is an appropriate one.

Stabilizers

As in the RO_2 column, there are usually oxides listed in the R_2O_3 column which do not act as stabilizers. These include iron (Fe_2O_3), antimony (Sb_2O_3), and chromium (Cr_2O_3), which are colorants. Bismuth (Bi_2O_3) is a very active flux and glassformer. Phosphorus (P_2O_5, a glassformer and minor flux at this low temperature) and vanadium (V_2O_5, a colorant) are also usually listed in this column, even though their structure does not exactly fit the R_2O_3 model. Boron (B_2O_3) is also listed in this column, and will be dealt with at length later. In discussions of colored stain production, many other oxides are referred to as stabilizers, but the word's usage is not quite the same there. In that case, the term refers to making the color consistent and impervious to variations in atmosphere or temperature.

Alumina is really the only stabilizer in glazes, and is present in amounts ranging from 20% by weight, or 0.55 molecular equivalents, in highfire glazes, down to levels approaching zero in china paints. Alumina is one of the most refractory materials in the glaze chemist's arsenal, so very little can be added to such a low-firing melt. This is especially true in bright colors, as the presence of alumina will lighten them. Alumina is also useful in the production of matte paints, especially in those colors that are affected by zinc. Alumina's other important function is in controlling the coefficient of expansion, as its COE is one of the lowest of any of the ceramic oxides.

Sharon Snook, "Elephants", 12" diam. 2005. Collection of World Organization of China Painters Museum.
Photo: Mary Early.

Aluminum hydroxide (or "hydrated alumina," as it is often called) may be the source of alumina, but clay is a more common source, although clay introduces silica as well. Kaolin is the usual clay of choice, because of its lack of impurities.

The ratio of silica to alumina determines a lot about the fired surface of a glaze; the more silica in relation to alumina, the glossier the surface will be. Also, the amounts of silica or alumina present may have dramatic effects on the shades produced by certain colorants.

Fluxes

The flux oxides are divided into two categories: the alkali metals and the alkaline earths. In Figure 1, the alkali metals are listed first (Na_2O, K_2O and Li_2O), with the alkaline earths below. Strictly speaking, only the bottom four are alkaline earths, but lead and zinc are often lumped with them for convenience. Notice that the three alkali metals have two R ions for each oxygen atom, while the others each have one. All the flux oxides in the RO column have a pH number above neutral, but the alkali metals are more alkaline. Bismuth, the flux listed in the R_2O_3 column, is amphoteric (capable of being either acidic or alkaline).

Each of the flux oxides has unique characteristics besides its alkalinity. Each melts at a different temperature, giving it a certain fluxing ability. In Figure 1, they are listed in approximate descending order of fluxing power (ascending order of melting temperature). In addition, each has its own rate of expansion and contraction (coefficient of expansion or COE) when heated and cooled, which determines how well they will fit on a particular clay or glaze. Each also has its own particular, sometimes pronounced, color response to different colorants.

An important concept relevant to fluxes and glazes is that of eutectic mixtures. Generally, adding one material to another results in a mixture with a reduced melting point. When more than two substances are present, it is possible for more than one composition with an especially low melting point to occur. Any addition will lower the melting temperature, but that particular ratio of any two ingredients that melts at a lower temperature than any other combination is called a eutectic mixture. As an example, lead oxide melts at 1616°F (880°C) and silica at 3110°F (1710°C), both above the firing temperature of china paint. However, a mix of 90% lead and 10% silica melts at 950°F (510°C), well below even cone 020. Many frits used in china paints, particularly those without lead, have more than one flux oxide, to lower the melting point even further.

Lead is the most common flux in china paints. It is used for many good reasons, despite its hazards. Overglazes were originally adapted from Chinese lead glazes of slightly higher firing temperatures. Almost all colorants produce brighter colors, and some colors are only possible, in a lead base. Lead glazes are unparalleled in their gloss, their wide firing ranges, and their ability to fit a wide range of clays and glazes. Lead oxide is also plentiful, cheap, and easy to mine and process.

Several forms of raw lead oxide, as well as lead carbonate, have been used as the source material for lead in glazes, but today lead is always added to the batch as part of a frit. Frits are synthetic glaze materials usually made by melting the raw materials, pouring the molten glass into water to break it up, and then grinding it to a fine powder, although a few frit compositions are made by an entirely dry process. The process of fritting was in widespread use in China as early as the Tang Dynasty (618–909 AD).

Frits are more expensive than mined materials, but they have many advantages. Their composition and particle size are consistent, and carefully controlled. Some ions, such as sodium, potassium, and boron, exist alone in nature only as a soluble form, which is undesirable in a glaze batch. Fritting a soluble material such as salt (NaCl) yields only sodium ions. In the case of lead, another advantage is gained by fritting. Raw lead will volatilize at china paint temperatures, while fritted lead will not.

There are hundreds of different frits, made by several manufacturers, each designated by a unique number. Virtually all of the flux oxides may be obtained in fritted form, in many combinations with various other oxides.

In many china paint formulations (although obviously not those listed as low-lead or lead-free) lead may be the sole flux oxide. In fact, in the old days there may have been nothing more in a china paint base besides lead and silica, as in the frits lead monosilicate ($PbO \cdot SiO_2$), lead bisilicate ($PbO \cdot 2SiO_2$), or lead sesquisilicate ($2PbO \cdot 3SiO_2$). Today, all base fluxes for china paints contain other flux oxides besides lead. However, in almost all china paint bases that are not specifically billed as low-lead or lead-free, at least 80% of the weight is some combination of lead and silica. The exceptions are the gold-based colors, which may contain as little as 45% lead and silica combined.

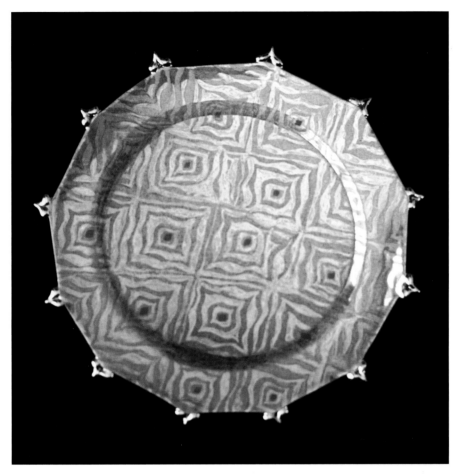

Keith Campbell (Canada), "Twelve Good Hearts," porcelain, glaze, red glass enamel, gold and mother of pearl lusters, 13¾" diam.

Keith Campbell, "Twelve Good Hearts," detail. The iridescence in mother of pearl luster is attributable to bismuth.

Potassium and sodium are present in small quantities in many lead-based frits, but they assume a larger importance in the production of lead-free and low-lead flux mixtures. Their melting points are similar to that of lead, but each has problems associated with it that lead does not.

Sodium is the most active flux across the entire firing temperature range, and begins to melt at 1472°F (800°C), right at the top of china paint temperatures. It has a marked effect on some colors, producing blue with copper or iron, and purple with manganese. In a melt containing boron, borax ($Na_2O \cdot 2B_2O_3 \cdot 10H_2O$) may be a source for sodium, while soda ash (Na_2CO_3) may be used if including boron is undesirable.

Sodium compounds are quite soluble, sometimes even after fritting, although wet grinding and filter pressing removes most of the "free" sodium. Sodium also has the highest coefficient of expansion of any of the ceramic oxides, almost always producing crazing if used in high amounts.

Potassium's action is very similar to sodium's, although potassium begins to melt at a slightly lower temperature, 1382°F (750°C), making it preferable in china paint. It is not as soluble as sodium, and its expansion is not as high. Its usual sources are potash (K_2CO_3, also known as pearl ash or lye), saltpeter (KNO_3), or feldspar.

Lithium is the lightest of the ceramic oxides, with a very low coefficient of expansion, which makes it useful in replacing sodium, as their melting temperatures are close to identical. Lithium glazes tend to have very low viscosities, making them flow and pool around raised decoration. For this reason, and because of lithium's high solubility, it was only used in very tiny amounts in china paints, and has not been used at all for the last twenty years. It was usually introduced in the form of lithium carbonate (Li_2CO_3), which is extracted from several minerals similar to feldspars.

Calcium, magnesium, barium, and strontium, the alkaline earths so beloved by potters working at higher temperatures, are of almost no use in china paints, as they do not melt at these low temperatures.

At china paint temperatures, calcium and magnesium are used mainly to modify a few colorants. In some cases, their action can be quite dramatic, as in the case of the bright pink known as Berzelius' Pink, which combines cobalt and magnesium.

Barium, when introduced into the melt in a fritted form rather than as the carbonate, is almost as powerful a flux as lead, and is sometimes used in china paint manufacture. Strontium is never even mentioned in the literature on overglazes.

Zinc is used extensively in china paints, in both colorants and bases, but it does not act as a flux. It is used sometimes as an opacifier, but its main function in base formulations is as a matting agent. The china paint variants known as matte paints contain significant amounts of zinc. Each color requires a slightly different percentage of zinc in the melt, but the average is about 30% by weight.

Zinc's other important function is as a color modifier. In combination with chrome, it makes brown shades. The presence of zinc explains why the brown shades are so often matte. Cobalt is also slightly affected by zinc, shifting to a deeper, harsher shade of blue similar to that of medicine bottle glass.

Bismuth, a very active flux, has an action much like lead's, with some notable advantages, although its cost is much higher. It has a longer firing range and is more resistant to crazing. Bismuth glazes are more durable, and completely non-toxic, although many china painters maintain that the lead-free colors are not as rich, glossy, and subtle as the leaded ones. The most intensive research in china paints today is focused on replacing lead, and bismuth has assumed a larger and larger role in recent years.

Bismuth oxide (Bi_2O_3) is usually recovered from tin, lead, or copper ore, but is more often introduced in the form of bismuth subnitrate $Bi_5O(NO_3)_4(OH)_9$. This chemical is often dissolved in resin and oil as the flux in liquid metallic lusters, and the presence of bismuth is what gives mother-of-pearl and colored lusters their distinctive iridescence.

Boron (like bismuth) is always listed in the R_2O_3 column because it contains two boron atoms for every three oxygen atoms, but its action (also like bismuth) is never that of a stabilizer. It is an anomaly in the Seger formula system, and totally unlike any other ceramic oxide. It sometimes functions as a flux, sometimes as a glassformer, and sometimes as both in the same melt. Its action is not completely understood, but it appears to

Rimas VisGarda, "Fred and the Girls," teapot, porcelain, overglaze, luster, 10½" high.

take on whichever role is needed. Boron seems to increase the durability and lower the overall coefficient of expansion when present in small amounts, but decrease durability and raise expansion values in larger amounts.

Boron is present in many lead-based frits in small amounts, but it really becomes important in the making of low-lead and lead-free frits. However, a glass made solely from boron and silica is incredibly unstable. It is even possible to make such a glass that is soluble in water! There must be at least a small amount of some other alkaline flux present to stabilize the glass, which at china paint temperatures is usually bismuth or potassium. Glazes high in boron also tend to be very soft and prone to scratching.

In the old days, most colors were made up of lead, silica, and boron only. The source for the bo-

Color	Components	Color	Components
Red	Fe CdS/CdSe Cr/Pb	Orange	Fe CdS/CdSe Cr/Fe/Zn
Pink	Au/Zr Co/Mg	White	Sn Zr
Green	Cr V/Zr/Si Ni Cr/F/Ca Cu	Blue	Co V/Zr/Si Cu/Sn Co/Al
Purple	Au/Co Au/Mg Au/Al Mn	Gray	Sb/Sn Fe/Cr Ni Ni/Co
Yellow	Sb/Pb Cr/Pb Pr V/Sn V/Zr CdS/CdSe	Brown	Fe/Ti Fe/Mg Fe/Ni Cr/Zn Cr/Fe/Zn Mn/Ti Mn/Sn
Black	Co/Cr/Mn/Fe/Ni		

Table I. Colors produced by various elements, or combinations of elements.

ron was borax, and some gold purples contained over 50% borax.

Opacifiers

As the name implies, opacifiers make glazes opaque, by remaining undissolved in the melt and scattering the light as it passes through the glaze. They also dilute and lighten colors. Some of the opacifier oxides also have dramatic reactions with certain coloring oxides.

Arsenic was the first opacifier used in overglazes, and became part of the repertoire of Chinese glaze chemists when they began using Venetian glass techniques to get the gold-based pink hues used in *famille rose* colors in the mid-18th century. Arsenic oxide (As_2O_3), though it fits chemically in the R_2O_3 amphoteric (pH neutral) column in Seger's formulas, is a glassformer. Lead arsenate ($PbAs_2O_3$), which melts at a very low temperature, was the usual source, and imparted a slightly yellow cast to glazes. It was present in china paints until the late 1950's, but it has been entirely replaced by tin, and is never used today due to its toxicity.

Tin oxide has been used as an opacifier in glazes for over 600 years, and is still preferred for its potency and for the soft, mellow whites it produces. In low-fire glazes, it was an essential ingredient in the majolica technique that was Europe's closest imitation of porcelain for hundreds of years.

Tin was introduced into Chinese *famille rose* colors as both opacifier and pale yellow colorant, in the form of lead stannate, or tin ash, but its place was taken by the oxide form by the mid-19th century.

The source for tin oxide is cassiterite ore, which is roasted at 450°F (232°C) to oxidize the impurities, and then reduced with carbon to extract the metal oxide.

In china paints, tin plays an important role in yellow stains containing vanadium. The well-known pink stains resulting from combinations of chrome and tin are not used in china paints, because the presence of lead destroys them, and because they require large proportions of calcium.

Tin oxide, one of the very few raw ceramic oxides sold by china paint suppliers, is sometimes added to raised enamels to increase the density and body of the wet material.

Zirconium is the most prevalent opacifier in china paints, since it is as effective as tin, and gives whiter whites. It is less powerful and more refractory than tin, but its much lower cost offsets the greater amounts needed. It also reduces expansion and increases abrasion resistance. Since the middle of the 20th century, it has largely replaced tin as an opacifier.

Zirconium silicate ($ZrO_2 \cdot SiO_2$ or zircon) is the usual source of zirconium. Zircon sand is milled and sold under a number of trade names. Zirconium oxide (ZrO_2) is sometimes used as well, and is refined from zircon.

Zirconium is used to make a huge variety of colors, and is the basis for most of the new colors invented in the late 20th century. Besides the attendant coloring oxide, variables that influence the color of zirconium stains are the source material for the ZrO_2, particle size, silica proportion, and calcining temperature. In conjunction with vanadium it makes yellow without silica, and blue with silica. If titanium is added as well, it makes brown. With indium (In_2O_3) or yttrium (Y_2O_3) it produces orange while, combined with silica, it makes pink with iron or gray with cobalt. It also stabilizes nickel and chrome green colors, preventing the black edges that often appear around green areas. It has been shown that almost any shade across the entire spectrum may be produced with some combination of three stains: a Zr/V/Si turquoise, a Zr/Fe coral, and a Zr/V yellow.

Titanium dioxide (TiO_2) is seldom used in china paint, as it produces a harsher white than tin, and is more expensive and refractory than zirconium. Occasionally it is used to make a blue stain with cobalt and alumina. Its mottling effect, a favorite of art potters who introduce it in the form of rutile, relies on a phase separation in the molten glass, which does not happen at the low china paint temperatures. Its one role is in the composition of lead frits, where it lessens the solubility of the lead.

Cerium oxide (CeO_2) is occasionally used as an opacifier, as its action is similar to tin oxide. Although its cost is high, it is a very powerful opacifier.

Léopold L. Foulem (Canada), "Neoclassical Vase with Bouquet of Lilacs," ceramic, decals, 11½" x 8½", 2001. *Photo: Pierre Gauvin.*

Color in China Paints

Most of the elements used in oxide form as colorants are grouped on one line (or Period) in the center of the Periodic Table of Elements, in a class known as the Transition Elements. This group also includes the fluxes calcium, zinc, and potassium, as well as titanium. The colorants within the group are vanadium (V), chrome (Cr), manganese (Mn), iron (Fe), cobalt (Co), nickel (Ni), and copper (Cu). Many of the Transition Elements have multiple valences (ionic states), and all of them readily form complexes with other elements, due to the ready exchange of ions. Other commonly used colorants that are not included in the Transition Elements are cadmium (Cd), silver (Ag), and gold (Au), which lie quite close to the Transition Elements, and antimony (Sb) and selenium (Se), which do not. The rare earth element praseodymium (Pr) is used today, and uranium (U) was heavily used in the late 19th and early 20th centuries.

Several factors influence the color produced by a ceramic oxide, or mixture of oxides, in a glaze. These include concentration, the oxide's ionic state, particle size, processing methods, chemical environment, and whether the colorant is suspended or dissolved into the base.

Colorants are usually added to china paints in much higher percentages than are normal for higher firing glazes. While most glazes show a marked shade with 1% of most colorants, and 15% would be a lot, china paints of an intense color typically contain about 25% colorant.

Many coloring oxides may exist in several ionic states, having different valences, or electrical charges. This enables them to combine with a different set of oxides, or in different proportions, often resulting in entirely different colors. This trait is what enables iron to exist in black (FeO_2) as well as red and yellow (Fe_2O_3) states.

Particle size is particularly important in the production of ceramic stains. If the grain size is too small, the colorant may dissolve completely in the melt, and the color is lost. Too large a grain size may result in loss of gloss. Very fine particle size is also important in fluxes that melt quickly at low temperatures, as is required for the production of brilliant colors with cadmium.

The processing methods used to produce ceramic stains are varied and exacting. They may include mixing the raw oxides required (sometimes with an excess of one, which will be removed later), calcining (heating) to a specific temperature for a prescribed duration, and wet grinding to a crucial size (sometimes more than once, at intervals during the process). Sometimes it is also necessary to accelerate the reaction by adding boron or other flux, which later must be leached out. Often the calcination process produces soluble salts as a byproduct, requiring thorough washing to remove them. The stain is then dried, crushed, milled again, and screened to the appropriate particle size. At every step of this process, critical parameters must be observed.

Most coloring oxides are influenced to some degree by the other oxides around them, even those that are not themselves colorants. For instance, copper in an alkaline glaze will be turquoise, while in an acidic glaze, it will be green. Chrome oxide will usually produce green except in the presence of zinc, which turns it brown.

Ceramic oxides produce color in glazes in two ways: by being suspended in them or by being dissolved in them. Most colors are suspension colors and are tiny unmelted particles floating in a clear matrix. The greater the concentration, the deeper will be the color. Chrome is a good example of a suspension color. Early in the history of overglazing, several solution colors were important, but today virtually every color is a suspension color.

Some other colors are produced by the dissolving of a tiny amount of oxide in an appropriate crystal structure, which causes the crystal to vibrate at a rate that we perceive as colored light.

Miguel Jimenez (Spain), "Floral" plate, 7" diam. A good example of iron red overglaze. Collection of World Organization of China Painters Museum. *Photo: Mary Early.*

Copper, silver, and gold are typical solution colors, with gold being the most commonly used in china paints. It has been estimated that as little as one atom of gold in 50,000 in a crystal is enough to produce a strong color.

Suspension colors work in the way that silt colors water; solution colors are more analogous to dye.

Coloring oxides are almost never used in a raw state in china paint manufacture. They are usually at least calcined and ground, for the sake of consistency. Very few of the colors have only one coloring oxide in them. They may be mixtures of several oxides, or they may be more complex and elaborately processed stains. A few colors can only be obtained by making a particular kind of crystal called a spinel.

Spinels have a very particular crystalline structure made up of one atom of element A, two atoms of element B, and four atoms of oxygen, written as AB_2O_4. They are very stable, especially those containing alumina, with very low solubility.

Some spinels occur naturally, while many others have been invented. Production of a spinel involves grinding the oxides together, adding boron to accelerate the reaction, calcining from 1652°F to 2372°F (900°C to 1300°C), depending on the desired color, for 24 hours, washing out the boron, and grinding to a very fine particle size. Some of the most commonly used spinels, with their color, are:

$$CoAl_2O_4 : \text{deep blue}$$
$$CuAl_2O_4 : \text{apple green}$$
$$MnAl_2O_4 : \text{cream}$$
$$NiAl_2O_4 : \text{sky blue}$$
$$CuCr_2O_4 : \text{dark green}$$
$$CoCr_2O_4 : \text{deep blue-green}$$
$$MgCr_2O_4 : \text{olive green}$$
$$MnCr_2O_4 : \text{dark brown}$$
$$NiCr_2O_4 : \text{leaf green}$$
$$ZnCr_2O_4 : \text{gray-green}$$

There are also a number of crystals which contain barium, calcium, or strontium in the A position. Though the configuration is the same, they are not true spinels, but some are useful as stains.

Table I lists the most common combinations of elements used to produce particular colors in china paints today. Several elements, or combinations of elements, are listed under more than one color, as differences in proportion or concentration can produce markedly different colors.

The Coloring Oxides

Iron oxide is the most widely distributed and easily available of the coloring oxides. It is used in two ionic states (Fe_2O_3, red or yellow; and FeO_2, black) and is a common component of many clays. It was one of the first colorants used in glazes. When Sòng Dynasty (960–1279 AD) Chinese potters first began working with overglaze enamels, the three colors they originally adapted from earlier T'ang Dynasty earthenware lead glazes were iron red, copper green, and a yellow that may have been based either on antimony or a form of iron.

Iron is one of the most prevalent colorants used in china paints, and may be introduced in a raw state, as a calcined prepared stain, as a spinel-like crystal, or even as hydrated iron. Small amounts of it are used to modify the shades of almost every other colorant. Iron-bearing clays, which are so heavily used as glaze colorants in the forms of ocher, umber, or crocus martis, are never used in china paint manufacture. They are too variable and impure, and contribute too much alumina.

When iron is used in the preparation of a stain, particle size and calcination temperatures are critical. Colors range from a bright nasturtium red at a calcining temperature of 1112°F (600°C), to violet at 1832°F (1000°C), while finer grain sizes tend to brighten all the colors.

The addition of calcium will make the color more gray, while magnesium will make it orange-brown. Alumina is necessary for a bright red. Zinc will make it brighter still, while silica will weaken the color. All of these variations are used to make different shades of iron reds.

Iron sulfate ($FeSO_4 \cdot 7H_2O$, also known as copperas) is usually used as a starting point in the production of ferrite crystals similar to spinels, to produce even more colors. The most common combinations are:

$$BaFe_2O_4 : \text{gray}$$
$$CaFe_2O_4 : \text{gray}$$
$$CoFe_2O_4 : \text{black}$$
$$CuFe_2O_4 : \text{dark brown}$$
$$MgFe_2O_4 : \text{orange brown}$$
$$MnFe_2O_4 : \text{dark gray}$$
$$NiFe_2O_4 : \text{black}$$
$$SrFe_2O_4 : \text{medium gray}$$
$$ZnFe_2O_4 : \text{dark gray}$$

Iron may also be used in small amounts (1–2%) to make a solution yellow color in a lead and silica base.

Iron is one of the most reactive of the colorants, and very sensitive to temperature, flux environment, and oxidation/reduction. This is what

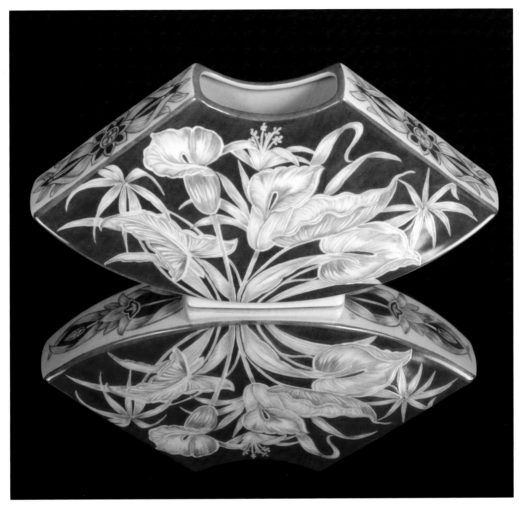

Marcia Stivelman, "Lily in Wedgwood Style" vase, 12" x 6," 2005. Iron red overglaze.
Photo: Andrew R. Goldstein.

makes it so problematic when mixing it with other colors, particularly the gold or cadmium colors. Today, china paints are usually grouped into three non-intermixable groups (gold, cadmium, and all the others) but the first manufacturer to market them to individuals in the late 19th century (Lacroix) classified them into colors containing no iron, a little iron, or a lot of iron, and said that these groups could not be intermixed.

Copper was used in the earliest overglazes to produce greens during the Sòng Dynasty. It is widely distributed in the world, and its use in metallurgy marked the transition from the Stone Age to the Bronze Age. Copper formed the basis for the *famille verte* family of colors in 18th century China.

Copper forms a strong, transparent solution color in glazes and its hue varies from turquoise in an alkaline base to a bright green in a more acidic base. Zinc and tin are sometimes added to increase its stability. Iron or manganese will modify its color.

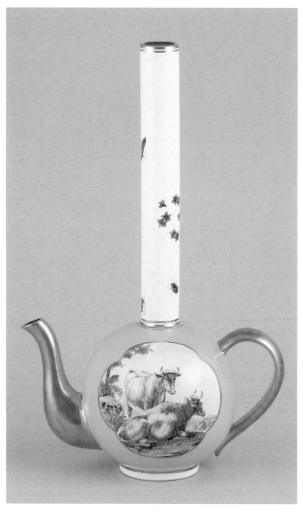

Richard Milette (Canada), "Meissen Bottle-Teapot", ceramic, 14½" high, 2003. The yellow china paint on this piece is most likely colored with antimony.

Léopold L. Foulem (Canada) "Yellow Neoclassical Vase with Bouquet of Pink Peonies," ceramic, china paint, decals, gold luster, 13¾" high, 2002. A typical antimony yellow. *Photo: Pierre Gauvin.*

The red and pink colors obtained from copper in reduction are not possible in the oxidizing china paint firing environment. Copper is little used in china paints today, due to its volatility and sensitivity to reduction. Its role has largely been taken over by colors in the chrome or vanadium/zirconium systems. Today its use is limited to metallic lusters, and additions to some blacks, in conjunction with cobalt.

Antimony may have been the first colorant introduced into overglazes after the original iron and copper colors. In fact, the first Sòng Dynasty yellow enamels were assumed to be antimony-based, until very recent scientific analysis proved them to be iron solution colors. In any case, sometime during the Ming Dynasty (1368–1644) the antimony colors replaced iron in yellows. Antimony oxide (Sb_2O_3) is refined from stibnite ore (hence the chemical abbreviation Sb) and is both a glass-former and an opacifier. Antimony is classified as a semi-metal, having only some of the characteristics of a metal.

By the late 17th century, the Chinese had developed the color known as Naples yellow, a rich mellow shade named for its use in Italian majolica decoration. This is lead antimonate ($Pb_3(SbO_4)_2$). Naples yellow is made from lime and alumina, in addition to the antimonate, and is stabilized with tin oxide. The color is made brighter by the inclusion of large quantities of soluble chlorides (usually common salt) in the melt. It is thought that this takes any iron impurities and converts them to the very volatile ferric chloride. Volatility is also a problem with the antimony colorant itself, and cerium oxide and/or alumina may be added to prevent this. The yellow color is only stable up to about 1922°F (1050°C).

The bright yellow color needs lots of lead, both in the stain production and in the flux mixture. Alkalis will destroy it, and zinc will darken it. It is occasionally mixed intentionally with iron for orange shades.

Manganese was the basis for the other of the first two overglaze colors invented after copper green and iron red and yellow. It was first noticed as a contaminant in cobalt blues, and was used as a purple/brown underglaze pigment in the same manner as cobalt. Manganese purples and browns were used to striking advantage in Ko Kutani ware in 18th century Japan.

Manganese can exist in either a divalent (Mn_2+) or trivalent (Mn_3+) ionic state, and may be introduced into the melt in the form of the oxide (MnO), the dioxide (MnO_2), or the carbonate ($MnCO_3$). The divalent form produces a weak and unstable cream or brown color, the trivalent a potent and stable purple. It is a weak flux and a solution color.

The brown form may be made more stable by including it in a spinel with alumina, preferably

Charles Krafft, "Code Blue: The Dispatched Doxie," overglaze on found china, 1993. Krafft's overglaze work in cobalt blue overglaze imitates Delft work. *Photo: Dan Walter.*

Rimas VisGirda, "Untitled Mug with Handle," thrown glazed porcelain, homemade cobalt blue decal, 6" high.

Nancy Froseth, "Swedish Stove," white earthenware, raised paste, 2½" x 4" x 8," 2002. The green color is a typical chrome green. *Photo: Hans Froseth.*

by using hydrated alumina rather than aluminum oxide. Red-brown spinels may be made with manganese and titanium, or orange spinels with tin. A strong pink stain results from mixtures with alumina, coupled with calcium or sodium.

Manganese is used most often in china paint colors to modify other colorants toward a more muted, earthy tone, particularly cobalt, iron, and chrome. It is a major component of most black stains.

Cobalt is the strongest and most consistent of the coloring oxides. Except under very specific conditions, cobalt alone always makes some shade of blue. As little as 2 parts per million in glass is enough to produce a noticeable color. Although the vanadium colors have taken over some of the role of cobalt, particularly in the lighter shades, there is still cobalt in almost every blue stain. Cobalt colors are unaffected by reduction, and vary only slightly with flux composition.

Although cobalt has been used as a glaze colorant since perhaps the 9th century AD, it was not among the first oxides to be used in overglazing. The Chinese relied on underglaze blue for hundreds of years after the invention of enamels. It first appeared in an overglaze during the Jiajing Period of the Ming Dynasty (1522–1566), but was soon abandoned for lack of a pure source of cobalt. It reappeared in the late 17th century, and Père d'Entrecolles described its use as an overglaze in his 1712 letter. He detailed its production from a mixture of quartz, white lead, and saltpeter (potassium nitrate). Later descriptions of the Chinese process indicate that the blue enamel was made by grinding a blue lead/potassium/silica glass.

Cobalt is always introduced into china paints in the form of a calcined stain. This enables it to be more finely ground and to disperse more evenly in the glaze, lessening its pronounced tendency to form specks. It also eliminates the tendency of raw cobalt oxide or carbonate to spit particles onto shelves and other ware.

The different shades of blue derived from cobalt owe their color to variations in the stain composition, in both fluxes and other colorants. Sèvres blue originally employed cobalt arsenate as the colorant, but is now made by calcining cobalt oxide with flint. Royal blue requires silica. The brightest blues usually employ zinc, alumina, and cobalt phosphate. Lighter shades of blue result from additions of tin or zirconium.

It is possible to make a few shades other than blue with cobalt. The best known is Berzelius' pink, which is made by calcining cobalt nitrate with magnesium. A green stain may result from combining cobalt with titanium and alumina.

Small amounts of cobalt are added to almost every other color system to make slightly bluer hues. You may assume that any black china paint contains some cobalt, unless it is specifically labeled "cobalt-free." Usually, some combination of manganese, chrome and/or iron is added with the cobalt.

Chrome is the most versatile and changeable of the colorants, producing a huge range of colors. Its very name, taken from the Greek word *chromos* (meaning color) reflects this. Chrome is a very strong color producer, and usually a suspension color with the lowest solubility in a silicate melt of any colorant. It also has the highest coefficient of expansion of any of the colorants, more than 15% higher than that of the next highest. This can lead to intense green colors chipping off easily after firing, especially if some of the chrome has gone into solution, thereby dramatically raising the expansion values for the base. Much depends on the source of the chrome. Introduced as the oxide or as potassium dichromate, it may be more soluble. If it's part of a spinel, it may be completely insoluble.

Green is the easiest color to make from chrome, as most flux environments will produce some shade of opaque green. Other colorants are often added to modify its color: cobalt for bluer shades,

Rain Harris, "Pinky," porcelain and mixed media, 9" x 9" x 18." The rose color in these decals is typical of gold. *Photo: John Carlano.*

antimony or vanadium for yellower, or nickel for grayer. Boron and magnesium tend to dull its color. Chrome forms a solution color most easily in lead mixtures, where it produces a yellow green.

When chrome is calcined with calcium fluoride (fluorspar), the resulting bright leaf green color is called Victoria Green. Additions of barium make it darker.

Chrome's next most common use is in brown stains, when mixed with zinc to form zinc chromate. The proportion of zinc and chrome may be varied for any shade between brown and green. Iron is frequently added to increase the warmth of these tones. Manganese may be added for yellower or grayer shades; nickel makes darker ones; alumina brightens them. The presence of zinc, which is added to china paints to produce matte paints, also makes many of the chrome/zinc browns more matte than other colors. A coat of clear "glaze" is often needed for a glossy finish.

The first color to use chrome was yellow. In 1797 a French alchemist named Vauquelin separated chrome from Siberian red lead. This lead chromate was used extensively as a colorant, but is no longer.

A red is also possible with chrome, if both lead and silica are present, alumina is completely absent, and there is no reduction. Boiling chrome yellow with caustic soda produces the coral red stain, which needs lots of lead in both the stain and the glaze. It's an unstable color, very prone to leaching, and not used presently.

Iron chromate is a valuable component of many gray colors, particularly those with a greenish tint. Chrome is also present in all blacks, except those specifically labeled as "chrome-free."

The well-known pink crystal made by firing a tiny amount of chrome with tin is of no use in china paints. For its production, the color requires plenty of calcium, which will not melt at this low a temperature. Lead will also destroy the color, as it will the less well-known chrome/ alumina pink.

Several color systems have a maximum possible temperature, but Cr/Sn pink is unique in having a minimum.

Gold has been used to produce a range of colors from pink through lilac, lavender, ruby and purple since the earliest days of porcelain production in Europe. It is also the basis for the Chinese *famille rose* palette. The gold family of colors is quite different from other colors, and do not blend easily with many of them.

In 1668 Andreus Cassius discovered the method for precipitating the purple colorant, now known as Purple of Cassius, from a mixture of colloidal gold and tin, to be used originally as a dye for cloth. It was expensive, but not nearly as expensive as dissecting tiny mollusks, which had been the only source for a purple dye previously.

To make Purple of Cassius, gold trichloride and stannous chloride are dissolved separately in aqua regia, a mixture of hydrochloric and nitric acids. The precise blend of the two acids will affect the final color of the product. The two solutions are mixed, and kaolin is added to help with precipitation. The mixture is washed to remove the acid, and a flux is added while the compound is still wet. This is then dried and ground. The flux composition, the proportion of gold to tin, and the particle size all affect the final color.

Shaw (1962) states an ideal, highly alkaline, flux composition for making Purple of Cassius as:

$$PbO\ .31 \quad B_2O_3\ 1.13 \quad SiO_2\ 2.37$$
$$K_2O\ .13$$
$$Na_2O\ .56$$

He also states that a 10:1 ratio of tin to gold produces maroon, 5:1 rose, and 4:1 light purple. Coagulants other than kaolin are sometimes used, producing even more color variations. If the final product is not ground fine enough, no color will result. With decreasing particle size, the color progresses through brown, blue and ruby, to pink. A little silver is sometimes added to make the color

redder, but too much will make it yellow. The production of Purple of Cassius is noxious, dangerous and expensive, but not difficult. I have a friend who has made it in his home microwave!

The resulting colorant is stable through cone 16. Only its expense keeps it from being a glaze colorant at higher temperatures.

Gold is the only widely used china paint colorant that is always a solution color. This is one of the characteristics that has led to its reputation as being difficult to mix with other colorants, most of which are suspension colors. Almost all the colorants may be made into solution colors, but they usually are not. Gold is also the only colorant that is used in the form of a salt (chloride).

The gold is sometimes mixed with a little cobalt to make it more purple, or with zirconium to lighten it, but these mixtures are unstable. A colorant as reactive as iron will usually mask the gold color completely.

Very little dissolved gold is necessary for a strong color. Between 0.01 and 0.1 percent by weight of gold is enough to make glass a ruby color.

The gold colors require a very alkaline flux environment, not just in the making of the colorant, but also in their glaze base. While it is possible to make the entire range of china paint colors with a few very similar frits, gold colors will need a very different one. This is the other reason for the gold colors' reputation as not mixing well with others. Appropriate fluxes for gold colors usually contain a small amount of silver as well, to brighten the color and stabilize the gold.

It is a widely held belief among china painters that the gold colors will not mix with other colors, but this is not strictly true. Though mixing with other colorants will not destroy the clear deep gold pinks, rubies, and purples, it will muddy them, and this is probably where the stricture originated.

Vanadium has assumed a greater role in colors ranging from blue to yellow since the 1960's. The usual source for vanadium is vanadium pentoxide

Sam Scott, "Porcelain vase", black matte glaze, water-based cadmium red china paint spattered on, 13" high, 2000. *Photo: Tom Holt.*

(V_2O_5), but in china paints vanadium is almost always introduced in the form of a stain. In stains, vanadium is combined with either tin or zirconium to make yellow, or with zirconium and silica to make blue. However, for all its versatility, vanadium is used surprisingly little in the production of china paints.

The V/Sn yellow stains are stronger than the V/Zr ones, but more expensive. Sometimes the two are mixed together to take advantage of their respective strengths. This yellow is made stronger and redder by adding titanium, and lightened by adding alumina. The yellow color produced is a lemon yellow, not as bright as an antimony yellow, but more stable.

The blue shades resulting from $V/Zr/SiO_2$ combinations vary from a true blue to a greenish blue. In making this stain, these three ingredients are calcined in an atmosphere free of air, and with some boron and phosphorous. Some zinc and auxiliary alkaline flux are also added. If sodium is that auxiliary flux, a bluer color results; if it's potassium, the result will be greener. Shades also vary with the source of zinc, probably due to the varying amount of hafnium, which is always present with the zinc.

All the vanadium stain colors vary with particle size, and if the grind is too fine, no color at all is produced.

Cadmium colors are, as every china painter knows, the trickiest group of colors. They are notoriously hard to mix with other colors or fluxes, and tend to disappear entirely if conditions are not exactly right. When they disappear, they usually take any other color with them, with no possibility of getting the color back in subsequent firings. Several factors in the composition of the colorant and the flux environment complicate their successful use. However, when they work, they are the brightest of the reds and oranges.

It is a misnomer to refer to these shades as cadmium colors, since they all contain some selenium as well. Some colors in the group actually contain more selenium than cadmium, and the two are quite different from each other. The actual solid suspension crystal that produces the color is a mixture of cadmium sulfide (CdS) and cadmium selenate (CdSe), known as cadmium sulfoselenate (CdS/CdSe). This is an unstable compound, and easily decomposed. Note that neither of these is an oxide; cadmium oxide has no color at all.

The range of colors produced by CdS/CdSe is determined partly by the proportions of the two crystals; the more CdS is present, the more yellow the resulting stain will be; the more selenium is present the redder the color, with the extreme being maroon. The color sold by some companies as "mixing yellow," made to blend with the other shades in this group, contains the most CdS. However, other companies sell a color billed as "mixing yellow" that is not a cadmium color at all, made to simply blend with all their other colors.

The balancing act that produces these colors begins in the formulation of the stain. Cadmium needs an oxidizing agent, such as a nitrate, to retain its yellow color. Selenium needs the opposite: a reducing agent, usually metallic silicon, to retain its red. Too much of either agent will destroy one or the other of the colors. A little zinc in the mix will brighten the reds, and a little vanadium pentoxide is sometimes added to prevent discoloration.

The flux composition is also critical. If there is too much lead, the black compound lead selenide forms. Often a little cadmium oxide is added to the flux to stabilize the color.

As stated above, a little too much oxidation or reduction in the firing will destroy one or the other colorant. This is the reason that cadmium/ selenium colors need a thicker application than other colors: it protects them from the atmosphere.

It will sometimes work to apply these colors over other fired colors, but another color or a clear flux applied over a fired cadmium/selenium color will usually destroy it, often taking the covering

color away as well. The fusion of the top coat with the underlying one destroys the precise flux balance necessary for bright reds and oranges. Many of the coloring oxides, such as iron, are very reactive, and disrupt the delicate oxidation/reduction balance needed for bright color.

A few brands of overglaze include some other colors designated as cadmium colors, particularly cadmium green, blue, black and white. These are not true cadmium colors, in the sense that the colorant is not CdS/CdSe. These colors simply contain some cadmium oxide in the flux mixture, and are made to blend with the cadmium reds and yellows.

Cadmium-inclusion stains, a recent breakthrough in ceramic color at higher temperatures, are made by encapsulating cadmium in a zircon crystal. They are never used in china paints, as they contain too little cadmium and too much zirconium.

Paul Lewing, "St. Augustine Light," china paint on ceramic tile, 8' x 8', 2004.

Paul Lewing, "St. Augustine Light," detail. The white highlight was made by mixing an iron red and a cadmium red, and letting the color disappear.

Paul Lewing, "Rain Forest", china paint on ceramic tile, 8' x 4', 1997. *Photo: Turk's Head Productions.*

Nickel is as powerful a colorant as cobalt, but has little use in china paints, although it is present as a contaminant in many other colorants. The typical greens and browns it produces are somber and variable, and its only regular use is to tone down the intensity of brighter colorants like cobalt and chrome. It is, however, possible to make a yellow stain with nickel, lithium and silica.

Nickel is interesting in the fact that it can exist in four different oxide configurations. The green (NiO) and black (Ni_2O_3) nickel oxides are both used as colorants, while the NiO_2 and Ni_3O_4 forms are not. The raw form of the oxide makes no difference in the fired color.

Nickel's main use in china paints is in grays, where it may be used alone, or in combination with cobalt, chrome, manganese, or other oxides.

Uranium was a popular colorant before its use was restricted during World War II. Those old enough to have used it remember the brilliant transparent yellows and tomato reds it gave.

The yellow color needs a flux environment high in barium and sodium, with some calcium and zinc, and no lead or boron. The oranges and reds, on the other hand, require a matrix high in lead, zinc and silica, with little alkalis or alkaline earths, and no boron, calcium, or alumina.

Bright uranium colors always need to be strongly oxidized, as any reduction will turn them black.

Silver was used early on in china paint's history to produce yellows with lead. It is a colloidal color like gold, but more stable. It has largely disappeared from the china paint chemist's repertoire today, replaced by more stable and inexpensive yellows from antimony and vanadium.

Colors labeled as "silver yellow" are still sold today by some companies, but as early as 1914, M. Louise McLaughlin was able to state that silver yellows contained no silver. Today its only roles are as a modifier in gold colors, where it moves the shade toward carmine, and as a metallic luster.

Platinum was used at one time in the production of black and gray stains, but its high cost currently precludes widespread use. Some old books mourn its loss because of the richness and depth of the colors, but today's shades have rivaled them. Platinum, like silver and copper, is used only in metallic lusters today.

Praseodymium, one of the rare earth, or lanthanide, elements has been used since the 1960's to produce a pale, but intense, yellow stain. It is produced by calcining praseodymium oxide with equal parts of zirconium oxide and silica, resulting in a zircon crystal with the praseodymium dispersed in it. One of the peculiarities of this stain is that additions of over 5% do not result in any stronger color in the melt. This stain is more expensive, but brighter, than the very similar vanadium/tin yellows. It may be added to chrome/alumina or manganese/alumina pinks to yield coral shades, or to zirconium/vanadium turquoise for light greens. Praseodymium yellows are almost completely unaffected by variations in flux blends.

Several other of the rare earth elements, such as neodymium, have been used rarely or experimentally to produce opacifiers or colorants, but they are too expensive, exacting, or unstable to be usable, or the result is too similar to other, more practical, compounds.

Many other elements have been shown to produce coloring compounds under certain conditions. These include ruthenium (purple, black, gray), rhodium (gray), palladium (gray, black), molybdenum (yellow), beryllium (green), indium (orange), tungsten (yellow), and niobium (brown,

Paul Lewing, "Rain Forest", detail. *Photo: Turk's Head Productions.*

205

Paul Lewing, "Wallace Falls", china paint on ceramic tile, 3' x 6', 1994.

yellow). None of these are used regularly in ceramics, although some have limited use as glass colorants, and palladium is used in lusters.

A Brief History of Overglaze Colors

The first overglaze enamels, concocted by Chinese potters in the late Sòng Dynasty about 1100 years ago, were adapted from earlier lead glazes. T'ang Dynasty earthenware featured three colors: green, rust, and amber, colored with copper and varying amounts of iron. These were the three colors of the first overglazes. The base fluxes were almost identical to the earlier lead glazes, with markedly less alumina. Analyses of these overglazes show that a different flux mixture was used for each of the three colors, but the proportion in all cases

was close to three parts by weight of lead oxide to one of quartz (silica), with some potassium from saltpeter.

It was assumed for many years that the yellow was colored with antimony, but modern analytical methods have shown it to be a solution color with a small amount of iron. It's not clear exactly when antimony yellow largely replaced iron yellow, but it wasn't very long after the first use of overglazes.

In the centuries between this time and the European rediscovery of porcelain making, Chinese and Japanese artists invented blues based on cobalt, and brown, black, and purple colors based on manganese.

Cobalt had been used for centuries as a glaze and underglaze colorant, but it wasn't until the 15th century that Ming Dynasty overglaze artists began using it to make blue. Its use in overglazes was soon discontinued, however, until the late 17th century, due to supply problems.

Manganese was almost always present with cobalt, and it may have been overly contaminated cobalt that provided the impetus for manganese's use as a colorant on its own. Kutani and Nabeshima wares from the 17th century make magnificent use of manganese purple.

By the beginning of the 18th century, the *famille verte* palette was highly developed, based on these few colors: iron red, copper green, manganese purple, brown and black, cobalt blue, and antimony yellow. With the exception of the iron red, these colors were all fairly transparent.

Just 41 years before Böttger solved the mystery of porcelain in Saxony in 1709, Andreus Cassius discovered the method for making a purple colorant from gold. By 1720, it had been introduced into China. Within a decade, the *famille rose* palette based on gold colors had completely replaced the *famille verte* colors. It is, however, thought that Chinese artists used gold in the form of ground ruby glass, rather than Purple of Cassius.

One other innovation was necessary for the

Jane Bowen, "Hamburger and Fries", 14" x 12", 1996. Collection of World Organization of China Painters Museum. *Photo Mary Early.*

optimum use of the gold palette. To achieve the full range from pink to purple, an opacifier was needed. This came in the form of lead arsenate for white and lead stannate for yellow. Using this opaque paint gave rise to a whole new painting style, in which the paint could be applied thickly, more like oil paint than watercolor.

In Europe, color development advanced rapidly once alchemists began applying centuries of research into gold fabrication to overglaze coloration.

Böttger is said to have invented only two colors himself, a dark red and a deep green, though his assistants came up with formulas for black, brown, and yellow grounds. However, Böttger's successor, Johann Gregorius Höroldt, became a brilliant glaze chemist. He was the first to use Purple of Cassius as a colorant, and invented sixteen new colors between 1723 and 1733, including turquoise, yellow, pea green, ultramarine, lilac, and claret red. He also invented the muffle kiln.

Once the secret of making porcelain and overglazes leaked out, it spread rapidly, and chemists with production secrets of their own and different repertoires of minerals introduced dozens of new colors. Most of the colors now in use were invented between 1750 and 1850.

Between 1751 and 1766, when Jean Hellot,

the French Director of the Academy of Sciences, catalogued the inventory and processes of the Vincennes porcelain factory for Louis XV prior to its move to Sèvres, he listed 60 different colors on hand.

The establishment of the Sèvres factory was a major milestone in the history of ceramics. No place has been more innovative, nor more generous with those innovations, than has Sèvres. The colorists there were the first to use chrome. It was first isolated in 1802, and in 1804 iron chromate was found in France, leading to a huge proliferation of green, brown, and gray colors.

Cadmium was first identified in 1817 as a byproduct of zinc refining, and its name comes from the Latin word for zinc ore, *cadmia*. However, it is rare, and there was no production of the oxide to speak of until 1840. It was not used in china paints until much later, well into the middle of the 20th century. In 1930 the Roessler & Hasslacher Chemical Co. listed in its catalogue both selenium and cadmium (as metal, sulphide orange and yellow), although it is unclear (and probably unlikely) whether any of its 340 overglaze hues are cadmium colors. Incidentally, Franz Roessler was the first to manufacture liquid bright gold in the United States, beginning in 1882 in Brooklyn, New York.

The introduction in 1875 by Lacroix in Paris of china paint packaged in small quantities for the individual artist was key to the immense popularity of the art form as a hobby and profession between then and 1920. Before that time, the material was either produced in large porcelain factories, or by small, specialized chemists, who usually knew how to produce only a few colors.

In the following decades, many artists marketed lines of colors under their own name, and some of them actually blended, or even formulated, their own colors. Franz Bischoff, for instance, is said to

have invented the famous color Ashes of Roses. The June 1899 issue of *Keramic Studio* magazine carried advertisements for ten brands of china paints, almost all with an artist's name attached.

Only one major color system has been invented since the mid-19th century: the very versatile vanadium/tin/zirconium/silica system. These and some attendant colors based on zirconium without vanadium came into widespread use in the 1960's and 1970's.

A very few hues are in general use that are based on the rare earth elements, particularly praseodymium yellow. These were also invented during the late 20th century.

One particular color system disappeared from the china paint palette in the mid-20th century. Up until 1945, uranium was the basis for bright reds, yellows, and oranges. Its being recalled by the US government is probably what led to the development and widespread use of cadmium colors. It's unclear when the first use of uranium as a colorant occurred, but the 1930 Roessler & Hasslacher Chemical Co. catalogue listed three forms of uranium oxide (black, orange, and yellow) as well as the nitrate and the acetate forms. The very bright reds and oranges they depict are probably uranium colors.

Today, research into new ceramic colorants continues, with investigations into many different elements, but these have so far proved to be too expensive, too unstable, or too unremarkable to replace any of the color systems we've known for hundreds of years. The major focus of contemporary research into china paints is on removing or lowering the lead content.

However, the Holy Grail of Ceramic Color Chemistry is still out there, eluding all of us: a brilliant, stable, cheap, non-toxic, and mixable RED.

...glaze Enamels
Russell Coates

...apan changed Russell
...l training in painting
...r and Portsmouth Art
...mith's College in south
...a teacher's certificate
...ceramics.

...ed a British Council/
...mbusho Scholarship.
...study of the Japanese
...a place at Kanazawa
...in Ishikawa Prefecture,
near the site where Kutani ware has been produced
for centuries. There, under the tutelage of Professor
Fujio Kitade, he was able to combine his skills as
both a potter and a painter in the rigorous discipline
of making overglaze enamels.

Today, in his Somerset studio, Russell makes
porcelain work, using traditional Kutani techniques,
but with his own more contemporary designs. Much
of the design is executed in underglaze blue before
the pot is clear-glazed to Orton cone 9. He fires in
reduction through much of this firing, finishing
with a neutral atmosphere. The enamels are then
painted into the spaces left in the underlying blue
design, in a similar style to the Ming Dynasty *ducai,*
or "dovetailed colors".

Preparation for overglaze painting begins with
cleaning the surface and wiping it with a solution of
gelatin made by boiling sticks of animal-bone glue
in water. This gives the shiny glaze a slightly matte
coating, which allows the brush painting to flow
across the pot, depositing an even line of color.

Russel Coates.

Old Kutani design copy dish, made
while studying in Japan.

209

Underglaze blue pigment on glass with porcelain muller, bowl of ground blue wash, teapot with painting medium (green tea), and brushes (liners, wash brush and adjustable bamboo-ferrule brush).

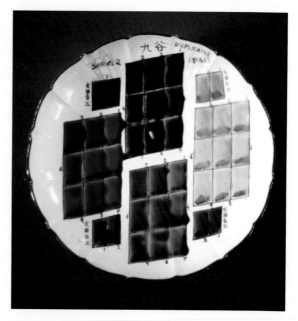

Blend of yellow, green, blue, and purple enamels.

The design is carefully brushed on in Chinese ink. Sometimes Russell will use a transfer made by tracing his design onto tissue paper. He then paints on the back of the tracing with very finely ground charcoal mixed with water. Placing the transfer right side up, he traces the design to deposit the charcoal onto the piece. The transferred outlines are then brushed over with a solution of manganese dioxide or red enamel, ground with strong green tea. The drawing is then allowed to dry for a day.

Russell has done extensive testing of enamel bases and colorants, and has settled on formulas for five colors (red, yellow, blue, green and violet). Each color requires a precise balance of flux, color, and (in some cases) silica, in order to mature at the same temperature. The colors are painstakingly ground, 500 grams at a time in a motor-driven mortar and pestle for five hours, then mixed as needed with water and a syrupy solution made by boiling seaweed in water. Prior to painting,

COATES OVERGLAZE ENAMEL RECIPES

Color	Lead Bisilicate	Lead/Borax Frit	Quartz	Colorant	
Violet	80	20		Manganese Dioxide	1
Green	75.5	20	4.5	Copper Oxide	5
Red	76	20	4	Red Iron Oxide	30
Yellow	49.2	46	4.8	Red Iron Oxide	4
Blue	78.5	20	1.5	Cobalt Oxide	0.8

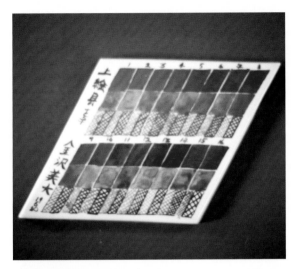

Blend of red enamel formulations.

the color is further ground on a glass sheet with a porcelain muller, 20 minutes for each 10 grams of enamel. Each color has its own set of grinding apparatus and brushes.

The paints are mixed to the consistency of heavy cream and applied with a brush. The color is allowed to flow from the brush, rather than being stroked on, in order to preserve the manganese outlines. Varying the thickness will result in different intensities of color, a characteristic that Russell uses as a decorative technique. The thickness varies from ½ mm to 1½ mm. He takes care not to touch the undecorated surface, to avoid leaving grease from his fingers.

Bowl painted with underglaze blue, ready for glazing, and tissue paper transfer pattern.

Applying the first of the enamel colors (red). Underglaze blue has been covered with clear glaze and fired.

Applying the last of the enamel colors (purple). Red, yellow, green and blue have already been applied.

The pots are then fired in an electric kiln to 1544°F (840°C). The correct melt is determined by draw trials. Small tiles are painted with each of the colors and suspended inside the peepholes on copper wire, where they may be hooked out, cooled in water, and inspected.

Russell Coates' painstaking and rigorous methods result in work that is unique and contemporary, but based on traditional techniques, materials and designs.

Bowl painted with five enamel colors, ready for firing.

He who desires nothing, hopes for nothing, and is afraid of nothing, cannot be an artist.

—*Anton Pavlovich Chekhov (1860-1904)*

Safety and Durability

The ceramic chemistry of most china paints is, and always has been, based on the use of lead oxide as a flux. There's no getting around this. If you're one of those people who refuse to have any lead-based compounds in your studio under any circumstances, china painting may not be for you. There are a couple of factors that may make the use of china paints less hazardous to the artist than higher-fired lead glazes. There are, however, other factors that may make them more hazardous to our customers.

Many china painters believe that "They" made manufacturers remove lead from china paints in the 1970's. This is not true. It is true that in the early 1970's the Food and Drug Administration (FDA) passed the first regulations pertaining to lead release from dinnerware.

In 1989 the FDA proposed tougher lead leaching standards, and the industry convinced the FDA that they would be out of business if the standards were enforced. The FDA backed off, but the State of California did not. California passed standards that were stricter than the FDA's proposed guidelines, and the industry met those standards within a couple of years. Then in 1992, FDA tightened its standards for the allowable amount of lead leaching to today's levels, which are still not as stringent as California's.

Note that these guidelines regulate the amount of lead that is leached from glazes, not the amount of lead present in glazes. How much is leached varies widely with chemical composition, fritting routine, firing temperature, and thickness of ap-

plication. In the case of china paints, the underlying glaze is also a huge factor affecting durability.

The toxicology and symptoms of lead poisoning are well documented in medical literature, and there is no need to go into them here. Suffice it to say that lead is a known toxin and carcinogen, particularly dangerous to children, and new information about its effects is being added all the time. It is, however, helpful to delineate the routes through which lead enters the human body, and what may be done to lessen or prevent the absorption of lead.

Gregory Aliberti, "Cleveland, 1910-1940", screened enameled tile on wood, 3' x 4', 1998. A collection of historic images of Cleveland, Ohio.

The major issues of concern about the artist's exposure center around lead's volatility when fired, and exposure to lead dust while working. The use of china paint on food-contact dinnerware surfaces, and its lack of resistance to acids and alkalis, is the issue for the user.

Ceramic Chemistry of China Paint

This subject is covered in great detail elsewhere in this text, but a short overview with an eye to the leaching of heavy metals from glazes is in order here.

China paints are essentially the lowest-fired form of glaze possible. Like all glazes, they are a mixture of glass-former, stabilizer, and flux. In all glazes, the most important glass-former is silica (SiO_2). However, silica melts at a temperature higher than may be achieved in even the most high-fired pottery kilns. Therefore, something must be added to make it melt at a lower temperature. This is called a flux. In china paint that flux is most commonly lead oxide, which may be added in a raw or a fritted form.

The more silica and alumina (Al_2O_3, the main stabilizer) there is in the mix, the more stable and durable the resulting glass will be. There are three problems in concocting a durable glass at china paint temperatures. The first is, in order to lower the melting point so far, such a large amount of flux must be added in proportion to the very refractory silica. The second is the extremely limited choice of fluxes. The third problem concerns the stabilizer portion. This stabilizer usually functions to make the glaze more compatible with clay, but china paint is made to be compatible with fired glaze, so little or no alumina is required.

At higher temperatures, a wide range of fluxes is available to the glaze chemist, but only a very few will melt below 1472°F (800°C). Those fluxes include the oxides of sodium, lithium, boron, bismuth, potassium, and lead. Sodium oxide (Na_2O) melts at an even lower temperature than lead, but it has the highest coefficient of expansion of any ceramic oxide, which leads to horrific crazing problems. Lithium oxide (Li_2O), with its very low coefficient of expansion, presents the glaze fit problem of shivering, which is the opposite of crazing, but just as serious. Boric oxide (B_2O_3) may act as either a flux or a glass-former (or possibly both at the same time), but boro-silicate glasses that contain enough boric oxide to get good melting at china paint temperatures are notoriously unstable. It is even possible to make a glass from nothing more than boron and silica, which will dissolve in water. Bismuth oxide (Bi_2O_3) is the predominant choice today to replace lead in china paints, but most painters agree that the lead-free colors are not as brilliant as leaded colors. Potassium is very similar to sodium in many ways, including its high coefficient of expansion, but it also has reactions to certain colorants (particularly gold) which make it useful in china paints. However, it is not a powerful enough flux to totally replace lead on its own.

This leaves us with lead, which is the perfect low-temperature flux—except for this nagging little toxicity issue. The brilliance and gloss of lead glazes are unrivalled across the entire color spectrum. Lead's ability to fit without crazing on a large variety of clay formulations, makes it seem almost elastic. And no other kind of glaze approaches a lead glaze when it comes to firing exactly the same across a wide range of temperatures.

Many artists believe that if lead is fritted it is no longer harmful, either before or after firing. This is not true. When frits came into widespread use in the ceramics industry, the incidence of lead poisoning dropped dramatically. However, it's unclear how much of the drop was caused by improved cleanup and hygiene regimens that began at the same time. Also, frits themselves are not necessarily nontoxic or insoluble. Their solubility varies with composition, manufacturing procedures, and particle size. There may also be some evidence

Keisuke Mizuno, "Red Forbidden Flower", porcelain, china paint, 9" high, 2004. Courtesy of Frank Lloyd Gallery. *Photo: Anthony Cuñha.*

that lower solubility in acid does not necessarily correlate to lower bioavailability.

There are china paints on the market sold as "low-lead", "low metal-release", and "lead-free". In all of these formulations, most, or all, of the lead has been replaced with a bismuth/boron/silica frit. The lead-free ones, most china painters agree, do not have the brilliance or color range of the lead-based paints, and some may actually contain lead, in spite of their label.

In addition to lead oxide, some china paints contain other elements which are known toxins, such as the oxides of antimony, vanadium,

manganese, selenium or cadmium. Besides these coloring oxides, there may be harmful elements, including barium oxide, that might be considered part of the base flux, added to modify shades of color. In the eighteenth century, lead arsenate (a combination of lead and arsenic) was widely used as an opacifier, although its use has been replaced with tin and zirconium compounds today.

While these compounds may be as hazardous as lead, the artist's exposure to any of them is much less. Though china paints contain a much higher percentage of coloring oxides than do higher-fired glazes, the amount of any one coloring oxide is

Andreas Knobl (Germany), "Finches," porcelain tile, 11¾" x 4¼".

quite low overall, as each of these oxides is present in only a few shades.

For more information on hazardous components of china paints, solvents, or any other material, ask your supplier for a Materials Safety Data Sheet (MSDS) on that material. They are required by law to provide an MSDS on request. While an MSDS will not give you a complete listing of all the elements in any substance, it will indicate which known ingredients might be hazardous.

Hazards to the Artist

Dust is the major health issue in the artist's studio. Lead oxide can be absorbed through the skin, but transdermal absorption of fritted lead and the colorants has not been studied. If exposure is limited to the hands, the amount of absorption is probably very small, but very cautious painters may want to use gloves, finger cots, or barrier creams.

Breathing the dust is a much more significant hazard. The danger is lessened by always working in a spray booth and wearing an appropriate facemask (professionally fitted and specifically designed to filter out dust) when using a dusty technique, such as spraying or dry grounding. Eating, smoking, licking brushes, or any other activity which brings paint-covered fingers or other objects into contact with the digestive tract, is always a bad idea. The most significant avenue of

exposure is likely from clothing and unconscious touching of the face.

Another significant exposure to any hazardous dust is simply being in a dusty environment for hours at a time. Dry vacuuming is not a good idea, as it simply stirs up the smallest, most dangerous, particles. Wet mopping and frequent sponging of work surfaces are the best preventive measures.

Two factors help to make china painting less hazardous than working with other forms of lead-based glaze. The first is that most china painters use very small amounts of the material. A potter glazing his work with lead glazes may use hundreds of pounds of lead a year, whereas most china painters will use only a few ounces. For many china painters, a teaspoonful of paint is a lot to put out at once. In spite of the fact that I may decorate as much as 700 square feet of tile with overglazes each year, I usually have less than 8 pounds of china paint in my studio at any time. When I was a production potter, I needed to keep up to 1000 pounds of dry glaze ingredients on hand.

The other factor is that, once the powder is mixed with a sticky medium, it no longer makes dust. Even water-soluble painting mediums, such as glycerin, do not dry so completely that they will become dusty. Only if the paint is mixed with water alone will it be dusty, and even then, once it has been moistened, it dries into a soft cake.

A Personal Case History

In the interest of complete investigation into the lead hazards issue, I decided it was only responsible to have my own blood level tested for lead load. I have been working with china paints for almost twenty years, and several factors might lead to my having a higher lead load than most other china painters.

First, I almost always use water as a medium. This means that, unlike stickier oils or glycerin mediums, my china paint dries to a dustier lump than most other artists' paint.

Second, as a tile muralist doing large commissions, I use a much larger quantity of china paint than most artists.

Third, I am not particularly careful about cleanliness. I try to keep my studio clean and my worktable washed down, but I do not wear gloves or use barrier creams. I get paint on my skin almost every time I work.

There are several standards in the world for actionable blood lead level, or biological exposure index (BEI), all expressed in micrograms per deciliter (µg/dL). The World Health Organization's limit is 20 µg/dL. The U.S. Occupational Safety and Health Administration (OSHA) sets an upper limit of 40 µg/dL (30 µg/dL for women of childbearing age), as do the German and French equivalents. For children, the limit is lower. A level of 10 µg/dL requires intervention by law in many states. There is mounting evidence that there is no acceptable minimum level of exposure for children. Even the smallest amount can have adverse effects on children, including children still in utero.

My blood tested at 5 µg/dL. The average level for all ages who are not exposed to lead through work or hobbies is 1.6 µg/dL.

In discussing this issue with one of my contacts at a china paint manufacturer, I learned that she had also been concerned about lead load. While the factory takes every precaution, there is still china paint dust present all the time. Her BEI was similar to mine.

Both of these instances are merely anecdotal, and the results of blood tests for lead can vary with timing, as lead leaves the blood fairly quickly, but it then deposits in bones.

Most china painters' studios are kept scrupulously clean, as even the tiniest speck of the wrong color can ruin a painting.

Fumes are of concern because red and yellow lead oxide will volatilize when fired above 752°F (400°C), and lead carbonate (white lead) will volatilize when fired above 932°F (500°C). This means that tiny lead particles may become airborne or attach themselves to dust particles and be absorbed that way. It also means that lead may deposit on the inside of the kiln and its furniture, only to re-volatilize and be deposited on other wares in later firings.

Several sources indicate that this does not happen with fritted lead compounds, such as lead bisilicate, lead sesquisilicate, and lead borosilicate. These compounds are more stable through a range of firing temperatures that extends far beyond chi-

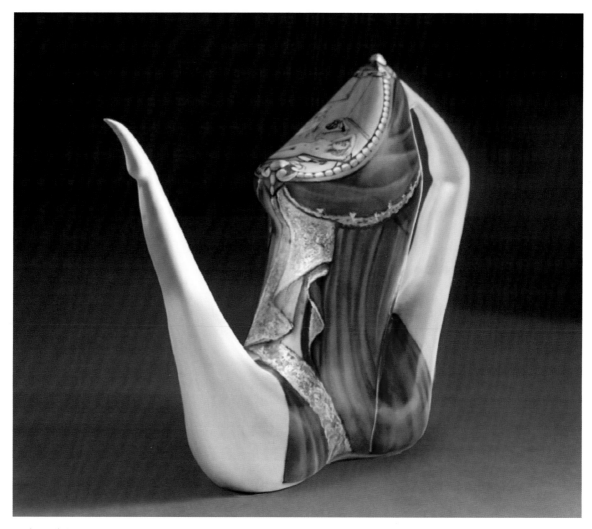

Bridget Chérie Harper, "Act I, Scene 2: The Eggplant", porcelain, 12" x 16" x 3", 2005. *Photo Tony Zeh.*

na paint temperatures, and modern china paints are always made with fritted materials. However, the slightest hint of reduction may make the fritted lead volatilize, resulting in a dull surface. This can happen when a medium rich in organic matter burns off.

I tested this in my own kiln, using a home lead-detection kit from a hardware store. I fired a pot that I knew to have a lead-free glaze, in twenty china paint firings. When the test kit indicated that no lead was present on its surface, I did the same test on a tile setter that has been fired at least a thousand times. It also tested negative.[1]

Hazards to the User

Lead may be dissolved (leached) from the surface of an unstable glass by contact with acids or alkalis. The danger then comes if the substance containing the dissolved lead is ingested.

The more prolonged the contact, and the stronger the acid or alkali, the more will be leached.

218

Keisuke Mizuno, "Forbidden Flower", porcelain, china paint, 7" x 9½", 2004. Courtesy of Frank Lloyd Gallery. *Photo: Anthony Cuñha.*

If a pitcher were to be glazed on the inside with a poorly formulated lead glaze and used to store orange juice for several days, there could be significant amounts of lead leached into the juice. There is evidence that even water or ordinary food can cause leaching in some instances.

However, decoration on the outside of the same pitcher is of less concern. Brief contact with the lips will probably release very little lead, as saliva is almost exactly pH-neutral. There are federal standards for how close to the rim of a drinking vessel lead-based color can come, and they vary widely according to the size and function of the vessel.

Acid Resistance

Acids usually interact with china paint in the form of acidic foods or liquids. In order to determine whether your work is leaching lead or other harmful substances, there are two levels of testing you may do. One is a qualitative test you can do at home, the other a quantitative professional level of testing.

To do the informal test, fire a test piece and submerge half of the decorated part in vinegar. Even though vinegar would not be considered a strong acid in chemical terms, it is as strong an acid as any your dinnerware is likely to encounter

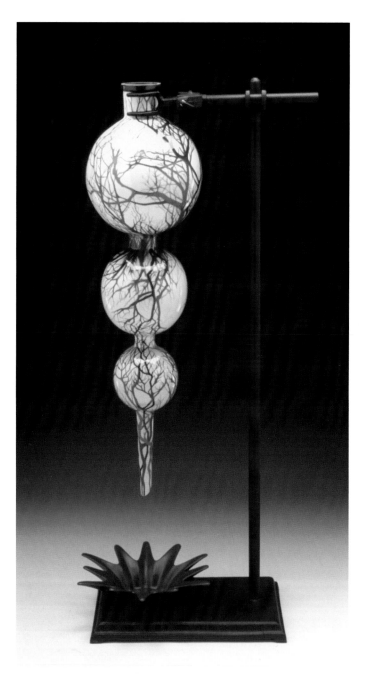

Cindy Kolodziejski "Biitersweet Chocolate Drop", earthenware and porcelain, china paint, metal support, 23½" x 5" x 9½", 2004. Courtesy of Frank Lloyd Gallery. *Photo: Anthony Cuñha.*

in daily use. After three days, take it out and compare the submerged part to the unaffected part. If there is any change in gloss or color, you may be sure that some part of the paint has dissolved in the solution. I conducted this test on a fired sample of three colors (cadmium red, gold purple, and chrome green) and could see no difference in either gloss or color.

For more information on whether your paints are leaching in acid, you need to employ a certified lab which does the FDA leach test. They will charge you a fee for the test itself, plus an additional fee for each metal you want them to test for.

I fired two layers of cadmium red china paint to the recommended cone 016 onto the inside of a small bowl glazed with a white glaze that I knew to be lead-free, and sent it off to be tested.[2] The laboratory test consists of letting an acetic acid solution (which is slightly more acidic than vinegar) sit in the pot for three days, then measuring the amount of oxide present in the leachate solution. (I made the bowls mentioned in this section solely for testing purposes, and would never sell a bowl decorated in such a way.)

I asked them to test for the presence of both lead and cadmium, because these are the only two metals for which there are definite federal standards based on toxicity. Many other chemicals are hazardous or toxic in drinking water, but the standards for these are sometimes based on what is detectable by taste, rather than on any scientific testing on toxicity levels, and the levels vary by jurisdiction.

The U.S. Food & Drug Administration has set maximum lead and cadmium release standards for several categories of ceramic shapes, as has the State of California. [3] The maximum leaching levels are much more strict for California than for the rest of the nation. The highest FDA lead release standard for any type of ware (plates) is 3.0 milligrams per liter (mg/L), which is the same scale as parts per million (p/m). The maximum for cadmium is 0.5

mg/L. My bowl released 4.06 mg/L lead and 1.03 mg/L cadmium, more than the allowable amount for any ceramic form, and far above the 0.1 mg/L lead and 0.322 mg/L cadmium limits for small bowls such as mine.

Since the regular china paint failed by such a large margin, I decided to test the same company's low-lead-release product. Again I used a cadmium red, fired two layers to cone 016 onto the same glaze as before, and sent it to the same lab. This time, the results were 2.95 mg/L lead and 0.722 mg/L cadmium leached. While this is noticeably better, the cadmium level is still above the allowable limit, and the lead level is still above the limit for all but one shape category, and then only by the slimmest of margins.

Just out of curiosity, I resubmitted the same full-lead sample bowl to the same lab for retesting. It came back as leaching 4.90-mg/L lead and 1.66 mg/L cadmium! The difference in the two results is well outside the lab's 10% margin for error, so it appears that this china paint may become less durable with use.

It should be noted, however, that these two bowls could hardly have been designed better to fail this test. The entire inner surface was covered with two thick layers (fired in between) of an intense cadmium red color. Had the surface been decorated in a more typical fashion, for instance with a small spray of flowers with a thin background wash, the results might have been quite different. The amount of metal that leaches is obviously directly related to the amount that is present.

We can only conclude that limiting oneself to low-lead colors to produce food-safe ware is a pointless exercise. And we may also conclude that continued use may make china paint less durable.

One source indicated that some cadmium migrates to the surface of the paint during firing, and is very loosely bound there. I was told that, in certain offshore dinnerware factories, some workers' only job was wiping the surface of newly fired

San Do, "Tricolor Poppy," tile, 8" x 10".
Photo: William Newberry.

ware with vinegar to remove excess cadmium. A careful painter might want to wash off freshly fired cadmium paints before handling them.

While it is possible to find china paints that are sold as "lead-free", a search through my collection of suppliers' catalogues turned up only two brands of such paints, in an extremely limited range of colors. One particular brand sells 214 regular china paint colors, but only 17 in the lead-free line. Cadmium red is not one of these 17 colors, as it is impossible to make such a color without lead, so a direct comparison with lead-based cadmium red was not possible.

I selected a dark green lead-free paint, fired it exactly as I had the others, and sent it off to the same lab. It leached 2.74 mg/L of lead! This is a significant amount, and high enough to fail to

Gisela Bylund, "Mountain Ash", porcelain plate, 12″ diam. *Photo: Steve Wilson.*

meet leaching standards for some kinds of ware. The manufacturer had no suggestions as to where the lead was coming from, but the lab suggested that, since I live in an old house and use water as a medium, that it might be the source. I had my tap water tested by my state's water lab, and found that it contains only 0.007 mg/L of lead, clearly not enough to contribute that amount.

We can only speculate about the source of the lead in this "lead-free" china paint. It may be part of the manufacturing process for the colorants, or

it may be from contaminated containers, or from poor quality control in the manufacturing of the flux. Some frit manufacturers may use the same crucibles for leaded and lead-free frits, resulting in significant contamination, even though the published formula does not reflect that.

Regardless of the lead's source, it's clear that even "lead-free" paints should be treated with respect. Also, in the case of the dark green color I had tested, there was cobalt, chrome, manganese, and vanadium present, none of which is benign.

Alkali Resistance

Alkalis are present in some foods, but the major source of contact with dinnerware is dishwashing detergents. The detergent used in home dishwashers is much more concentrated than that sold for hand washing, and the detergents used in the hospitality industry are harsher still. While leaching into wash water poses no hazard to the customer in the home, these things do not disappear, and may not be removed from the effluent by water treatment facilities. Users will, however, notice an eventual fading of color and loss of gloss, and will not be happy about it. Also, a surface that has been degraded by alkalis may then be more susceptible to further attack by acids.

A relatively easy test for stability in an alkaline environment may be done in your home dishwasher. Simply put a small sample of decorated china in the rack of your dishwasher, and leave it there for a prolonged period of time. Keep an identical unwashed sample as a control. After a significant number of wash cycles, compare the two samples for loss of color and shine.

I conducted this test on a sample that had three colors fired onto it at cone 016 (cadmium red, gold purple, and chrome green). After one hundred cycles, there was no change. This may not have been an extensive enough test to really make a difference; three hundred would probably have been more realistic.

There is also an official test procedure for tableware pattern removal by dishwasher detergents, devised by the American Standard for Testing and Materials (ASTM).[4] Essentially, the test involves boiling a sample in a strong solution of dishwasher detergent for six hours, then checking for loss of color and gloss, both visually and by vigorously rubbing with a white cloth.

I did not have all the necessary equipment to follow to the letter the very precise guidelines set forth by the ASTM, but I conducted the essential parts of the test on a commercial dinnerware plate made in China, decorated with four colors (blue, green, yellow and rose) plus gold luster, all fired to cone 016. I broke the plate into four sections and immersed three of them in a boiling solution of a popular powdered dishwashing detergent, keeping the fourth as a control. The test solution (which exceeds the detergent manufacturer's recommended concentration) was a 0.30% concentration made by dissolving 6 grams of detergent in 2 liters of water. One sample was boiled for two hours, one for four, and the other for six hours.

The results were surprising. After two hours, there was virtually no change. But after four hours, there was some change, and after six the difference was marked. All four colors of china paint and the gold luster stayed exactly the same intensity of color, but both the overglazes and the white (or clear) glaze itself were decidedly more matte. In fact, the overglazes kept more of their gloss than did the underlying glaze.

This particular plate failed the test so dramatically that I ran the same test on two more plates, from different manufacturers. These had a total of eight different china paint colors. A couple of the overglazes showed a slight diminution in gloss after six hours in the boiling solution. Most of the overglaze colors, and both of the underlying glazes, were unaffected.

These rigorous tests for acid and alkaline resistance should not be taken to be indicative of the performance of all china paints in all situations, however. The same china paint which fails one round of these tests may pass if it's fired to a different temperature, or on a different firing schedule, or on a different clay/glaze combination. My test of the first plate is a good example of this. There are, obviously, combinations of overglaze and glaze that will pass this test, but no overglaze on that particular china was ever going to come out of the test with its gloss unchanged.

An example of severe chipping in black green china paint.

Chipping

Chipping of fired china paint from the glaze constitutes another hazard to the customer. If the china paint has not been fired properly, or the coefficient of expansion of the overglaze does not match that of the glaze, it may chip off over time, usually taking a bit of the glaze, and even the clay body, with it. This usually happens when too thick a layer of overglaze has been applied in a single firing, or when the piece has been fired too many times. Black and very dark greens seem to be most susceptible to this fault. These chips are usually small, and may be easily ingested with food, although sometimes they are quite large. I saw a plate once that threw off chunks the size of a dime even before it came out of the kiln. Unfortunately, this more often happens slowly, over the course of months.

If you can see obvious cracks in the overglaze layer when it comes out of the kiln, keep the ware around for a while and watch it, particularly noting those places where the china paint is thick. If there are cracks in the surface of the china paint, chances are it will chip off eventually.

The best solution to the problem of chipping is probably prevention. Some brands of the same color are notably less prone to chipping than others. Many painters prepare the surface before they add black or dark green, by firing on a layer or two of either a clear glaze or another dark color, such as blue, iron red, or ruby.

There is a home test that will give a good indication of how a piece will hold up over time in this regard. Put the piece in your freezer for at least an hour, then take it out and immediately plunge

it into very hot water. Repeat this regimen several times, and see if any crazing has appeared. It is best to have the hot water container in a sink, and it is imperative that you wear gloves and eye protection when doing this. When pieces fail this test, they sometimes do so in a spectacularly dramatic fashion.

Safe Disposal

Inevitably, an artist will be left with some waste china paint. The two main sources are cleaning contaminated colors off the palette, and washing brushes. The amount is usually quite small, but it builds up.

Regardless of what medium your china paint has been mixed with, the most convenient disposal method is to collect it and take it to a household hazardous waste disposal site. This is allowable for hobbyists and householders, but those who sell their work, or have employees, are expected by the Environmental Protection Agency (EPA) to collect the waste and pay for proper disposal by a certified toxic waste disposal company.

Solvents

While most of the substances normally used in china painting are relatively benign, a few can cause problems for anyone, and certain people may have adverse reactions to some of them. Solvents probably cause far more problems for painters than their paints do. All of the common mediums and solvents are discussed elsewhere in this text, and the toxicology of each of them is widely publicized, in much more detail than is possible here.

Some common painting and mixing mediums, such as balsam of copaiba, are of very low toxicity, although some of the essential plant oils are actually more toxic than the petroleum distillates. A few painters like to use mineral spirits, paint thinner, lacquer thinner, and the like as solvents, but there is really no need to do so. Nontoxic alternatives do the job just as well.

Turpentine, and its derivative, fat oil, is prob-ably the substance that causes the most problems for the greatest number of people, although turpentine has a relatively low toxicity level compared to most other solvents. It is well known that turpentine is a sensitizer, which means that many people develop an allergy to it after prolonged exposure. If you begin to get headaches, dermatitis, or hay-fever-like symptoms when using it, you need to switch to another medium immediately.

The odorless versions of turpentine work as well as the traditional product for painting, are less toxic, and tend not to provoke the same allergic response. However, the market is full of "odorless" solvents and "turpentine substitutes", which may be any combination of ingredients the manufacturer chooses to include. Some are more, and some are less, toxic than turpentine. For more information than labels or advertisements provide, ask your dealer for an MSDS.

Some china painters switch to citrus-oil based solvents, believing them to be less toxic than turpentine. However, citrus oil, and its major ingredient, d-limonene, are EPA-registered pesticides, and much more toxic than most solvents.

The smartest choice is to use a water-soluble medium. Many of the water-based mediums discussed here are so benign that they are commonly added to food and cosmetics.

Even the most toxic solvents may be used occasionally with no ill effects, if precautions are taken, although children and pregnant women should have no exposure at all. Good ventilation is essential. Simply opening a window is not enough to protect you from toxic fumes, or from dust. You need a real exhaust fan and adequate airflow through your space.

If you're going to be working for any length of time with a solvent that produces noxious fumes, you need a professionally fitted respirator that's specifically designed to filter them out. A paper dust mask, or a respirator that's designed for dust, is not good enough.

Take precautions to limit your exposure, to both fumes and liquids. Keep all containers tightly closed when not in use. Keep solvents away from your eyes, mouth, and other mucous membranes. Since solvents can be absorbed through your skin, wear rubber gloves and a plastic or rubber apron.

Conclusion

Some of the materials used in china painting are undeniably hazardous. You owe it to yourself, your family, and your customers to educate yourself about them, and about any regulations pertaining to them. There is a huge, and sometimes bewildering, array of regulations, by federal, state, and local bodies, pertaining to all sorts of substances, equipment, and practices. The rules vary widely according to what types of ware you make, where you live, and whether you sell your work or not. Regulations at all governmental levels change periodically, as well. If children are present, or if you might bear children, a whole new set of considerations needs to be taken into account.

However, many things that are potentially hazardous, including sunshine, fire, and water, are part of our lives every day. We treat them with respect, and learn how to control them. The same is true for china painting.

It is up to each individual painter to decide what's an acceptable level of risk, but the decision needs to be made on the basis of sound science and hard information. There is no reason why china paint cannot be part of a long and healthy art career.

NOTES

1. The test kit I used was manufactured by Homax® Products, Inc. PO Box 5643, Bellingham, WA 98227. Phone 800-729-9029. Label states "under controlled laboratory conditions, LeadCheck® swabs will reproducibly detect 1-2 micrograms of lead", on any surface.

2. I used Brandywine Science Center Inc. 204 Line Road, Kennett Square, PA 19348, Dep. #15-301, phone 610-444-9850. Another lab that specializes in this test is Alfred Analytical Laboratory, 4964 Kenyon Road, Alfred Station, NY 14803, phone 607-478-8074. The official test regimen is available from ASTM, 100 Barr Harbor Drive, PO Box C700, West Conshohocken, PA 19428. Phone 610-832-9585, or visit their web site at *www.astm.org.* There is a fee to download the test method, which is called Designation: C 738-94.

3. For a complete chart of the standards for all kinds of dinnerware, see FDA documents CPG 7117.06 and CPG 7117.07. To get more information on US water quality standards, go to *www.epa.gov/safewater/mcl.html.* For international standards, see www.who.int/water_sanitation_health/index.html.

4. The official test regimen is available from ASTM, 100 Barr Harbor Drive, PO Box C700, West Conshohocken, PA 19428. Phone 610-832-9585, or visit their web site at *www.astm.org.* There is a fee to download the test method, which is called Designation: D 3565-89.

Glossary

A

Aufsetzweiss – A form of raised enamel for hard paste porcelain, popular in the early 20th century.

amphoteric – Capable of being either acidic or alkaline.

B

ball mill – Jar, usually porcelain in studio versions, filled with flint pebbles and a wet charge of ceramic material, rotated to grind material to fine powder.

Beleek – A thin translucent brand of ware from Ireland.

bisque – Unglazed fired ware. (See Introduction)

bloating – Blister on the surface of fired ware, caused by trapped gas in the body.

bone china – A form of porcelain popular in England, containing a significant proportion of bone ash.

burnish – To rub leatherhard clay with a smooth tool, producing a glossy surface.

C

calcine – To heat enough to drive off hydroxyls, as well as organic and volatile compounds.

cation – Positively charged ion.

ceramic – Pertaining to non-metallic, inorganic substances, fired to high temperature during manufacture. (See Introduction)

china – A vitreous ceramic whiteware. (See Introduction)

clobbering – Adding decoration to someone else's pottery, with or without permission.

closed medium – One that dries.

coefficient of expansion – Change in unit of length accompanying a unit change of temperature, important in determining glaze fit.

colloid – A non-settling suspension of a material of extremely fine particle size, dispersed in a fluid.

cone – Pyrometric cone. A small 3-sided pyramid of ceramic material, formulated to melt at a specific heat-work.

copperas – Hydrated iron sulphate. ($FeSO_4 \cdot 7H_2O$)

crawling – Separation of the glaze coat during firing, resulting in beads of glaze on exposed clay body.

crazing – A network of fine cracks in glaze, caused by improper fit of glaze and clay body. Often called crackle when produced intentionally.

creamware – White earthenware with lead glaze, decorated with overglazes.

D

decal – Colored design printed on special paper for transfer to a glazed surface.

decalcomania – The process of making decals.

downfiring – Gradually lowering kiln temperature by applying less than full power.

ducai – Five-color early Chinese overglazing style.

E

earthenware – A low-fired non-vitreous clay body.

enamel – A vitreous coating used to decorate previously fired ware, A viscous ceramic substance used to produce overglaze raised lines. (See Introduction).

end-point – Temperature at which the tip of a cone touches a horizontal surface.

eutectic – The specific proportion of two materials that melts at the lowest possible temperature.

F

faience – Earthenware with colorful decoration applied on a raw lead-tin glaze.

famille rose – A series of pink and red colors based on gold, used in 18th century China.

famille verte – A series of green colors based on copper oxide, used in 18th century China.

fat oil – Thickened turpentine.

flux – A substance which promotes fusion at a lower temperature in a fired mixture with a glass-former.

flux unity – A system of analyzing glaze formulas, in which the flux oxides add up to 1.

frit – A synthetic glaze material of specific composition, made by melting and grinding raw materials.

G

Globar – Silicon carbide rod used as a heating element in early 20th century electric kilns.

grounding – Applying a uniform deep color by adhering powdered color to a sticky surface.

H

hard paste – A form of porcelain fired to at least cone 8. (See Introduction).

heat work – The action of heat over time.

hydroxyl – Ion composed of 1 hydrogen and 1 oxygen atom; chemically combined water.

I

inglaze – Decorating technique in which color is applied over an unfired opaque glaze. Majolica, Faience. (See Introduction)

ion – A charged particle of atomic or molecular size.

J

jasperware – A vitreous, unglazed, colored ceramic ware with raised decoration, developed by Wedgwood.

jiggering – Forming a pot using a spinning plaster mold.

K

kaolin – White highfire clay; the basis for porcelain.

kiln – A refractory structure to contain ceramic pieces during firing.

kiln wash – Coating applied to kiln shelves to prevent molten glaze from sticking; usually kaolin and silica mixed with water.

KilnSitter™ – A mechanical device to shut off a kiln at a specific temperature.

L

lanthanide – One of the rare earth group of elements.

M

majolica – Decorating technique in which color is applied over an unfired opaque glaze.

medium – A liquid to be mixed with powdered color for painting.

mildew – Dark discoloration that appears on glazed ware after overglaze firing.

molecule – The smallest particle of a chemical compound capable of retaining all the properties of the compound in bulk.

muffle – Refractory lining of a kiln, to protect ware.

mullite – Interlocking needle-like crystalline alumino-silicate ($3Al_2O_3 \cdot 2SiO_2$) used to make kiln furniture.

N

nichrome – Alloy of nickel and chromium used to make kiln heating elements.

O

onglaze – Decorating technique in which color is applied over an unfired opaque glaze. Majolica, Faience. (See Introduction)

open medium – Medium that stays wet.

overglaze – Vitreous coating fired onto a previously fired glaze. (See Introduction)

oxidation firing – Kiln atmosphere in which there is an ample supply of oxygen to support complete combustion.

P

pad – To remove brush marks by blotting with foam, silk, or similar material.

Parian – A brand of soft-paste porcelain, formulated to resemble marble.

petuntse – Feldspathic mineral used to flux kaolin in making porcelain.

pinholing – Tiny craters in fired glaze, caused by escaping gases.

porcelain – White-firing high temperature clay body. (See Introduction)

pyrometer – Instrument for measuring high temperatures.

R

reduction firing – Kiln atmosphere in which there is insufficient oxygen to completely burn all the fuel.

refractory – Resistant to high temperatures.

S

saggar – Fireclay box to enclose ware during firing.

saltpeter – Potassium nitrate (KNO_3)

satsuma – A kind of Japanese soft paste porcelain.

shivering – A fault in which slivers of fired glaze chip off, caused by improper glaze fit.

sinter – To fire a ceramic material hot enough to fuse, but not hot enough to melt.

slip – Liquid or very wet clay, sometimes colored.

smalt – Blue pigment made by fusing silica, potash and cobalt oxide.

soaking – Holding a constant firing temperature.

soft paste – A form of porcelain fired to cone 04 or below. (See Introduction)

spinel – A stable colored crystal, either natural or synthetic, having the composition AB_2O_4.

stain – Stable coloring material, made by calcining, grinding, and washing ceramic oxides.

stencil – A sheet of impervious material, perforated with a design, through which color is forced.

stilt – A tripod-like refractory setter for glazed ware.

stipple – To pounce paint on with a brush which has all the bristles cut to the same length.

stoneware – A highfire vitreous clay body composed mainly of fireclay.

T

tinting – To apply an even coat of wet color, with no brush marks.

V

valence – Electrostatic charge on an atom.

vitreous – Hard, glassy, nonabsorbent.

vitrify – To make vitreous.

volatile – Having a tendency to form vapor.

Photo Credits

The following list includes credits for all the photographers whose images were used in the publication of this work. Also included are credits for contributing organizations and individuals as well as collections accessed. Unless otherwise attributed, featured artists submitted their own photographs and their names are listed in the Index.

Aquilino, Tony 1; Art Gallery of Greater Victoria BC 13, 15, 16; Bergeron, Raymonde 4, 162; Burbank, Betty 21, 37; Carlano, John 128, 129, 199; Cohn, James 104, 106; Crouch, Doug 115; Crucible Kilns 174; Cuñha, Anthony 2, 57, 215, 219, 220; Davidson, James & Joanna 15, 16; Decorative Arts Council 22; Drake, Dana 66; Early, Mary 38, 44, 45, 110, 141, 143, 193, 207; ETC Photography 154; Eugene Fuller Memorial Collection 9; Floyd A. Naramore Memorial Purchase Fund 12; Fox, Betty 76; Frank Lloyd Gallery 2, 56, 57, 58, 59, 215, 219, 220; Fremont Public Assn. Headquarters 120; Froseth, Hans 140, 198; Gauvin, Pierre 191, 196; Goldstein, Andrew R. 138, 149, 195; Gussman, John 97; Helm, Jean 37, 43; Helm, Jean & Roger 37, 42, 43; Hodgens, Miss C.F. 13; Holt, Tom 151, 157, 201; Isaacson, Martha & Henry 19, 24; Jen-Ken Kilns 175, 177; Lewing, Paul 72, 148, 172, 173; Macapia, Paul 9, 10, 12, 19, 22, 24; Martin, Ellen M. 126; Meggs, Cherryl M. 34, 39, 111; Montgomery, Walker 112; Newberry, William 103, 116, 221; Ogawa, Steven 152, 153; Olson, Keith 80; Picture Perfect Photos 92, 119; President Benjamin Harrison Home 35, 36; Schempf, E.G. 3; Scott, Sam 55; Scott, Sam & Diane 55; Seattle Art Museum 9, 10, 12, 19, 22, 24; Seattle Pottery Supply 174; Small, Mary Arlington 22; Stimson, Mrs. Thomas D. 10; Sullivan, Jospeh D. 156; Through the Flower 47, 48, 49; Turk's Head Productions 204, 205; Walter, Dan 197; Wilson, Steve 222; Woodman, Donald 47, 48; World Organization of China Painters (WOCP) 44, 45, 46, 60, 110, 116, 141, 172, 185, 193; Zeh, Tony 218.

Bibliography

Anonymous. *The Class Room #1*, Keramic Studio Publishing Co., Syracuse, NY, 1909.

Bastarache, Edouard. "Inorganic Lead and Ceramics," http://ceramicmaterials.com/cermat/education/176.html.

Berdel, E. *Einfaches Chemisches Praktikum,* Vol. 5 & 6, p. 61, Coburg, 1911.

Blair, Sheila & Bloom, Jonathon. *Art & Architecture of Islam 1250–1800.* New Haven & London, Yale University Press, 1994.

Charleston, Robert J. "World Ceramics." Secaucus, NJ, Chartwell Books, 1968.

Cline, Ann. *China Painter's Complete Guide to Kilns & Firing,* Ann Cline Studio, Inc., West Covina, CA, 2002

Denker, Ellen Paul. "The Grammar of Nature: Arts & Crafts China Painting," from *The Substance of Style: Perspectives on the American Arts & Crafts Movement*, Bert Denker, editor, Winterthur Museum, Winterthur, DE, University Press of New England, Hanover & London, 1996.

Dinsdale, Allen. *Pottery Science: Materials, Process & Products,* Halsted Press, New York, 1986.

Doat, Taxile. *Grand Feu Ceramics.* "The Manufactory of Sèvres—Its Organization." Syracuse, NY. Keramic Studio, 1905.

Emerson, Julie, Chen, Jennifer, & Gates, Mimi Gardner. *Porcelain Stories: From China to Europe*, Seattle Art Museum, University of Washington Press, Seattle, 2000.

Gleeson, Janet. *The Arcanum.* New York: Warner Books, 1998.

Hamer, Frank & Hamer, Janet. *The Potter's Dictionary of Materials & Techniques* (4th Edition), A&C Black, London & UPenn Press, Philadelphia, PA, 1997.

Hesselberth, John & Roy, Ron. *Mastering Cone 6 Glazes*, Glaze Master Press, Brighton, ON, Canada, 2002.

Jorgensen, Gunhild. *The Techniques of China Painting*, Van Nostrand Reinhold Co., New York, 1971.

Kingery, W.D. & Vandiver, P.B. "The Eighteenth Century Change in Technology and Style from the Famille-Verte Palette to the Famille-Rose Palette," in W.D. Kingery, ed., *Technology and Style, Ceramics and Civilization* Vol. 2, 1986, The American Ceramic Society, Columbus, OH, pp. 363-382.

Klimke, August. *Directions for Painting on China for Amateurs*, Müller & Hennig, Dresden, Germany, 1895.

Lee, Sherman E. *A History of Far Eastern Art.* Englewood Cliffs, NJ: Prentice-Hall, Inc.

Little, Ruth. *Painting China for Pleasure & Profit*, Brack Publications, Lubbock, TX, 1962

Mabon, Doris. *China Decoration*, Sir Isaac Pitman & Sons, Ltd., London, 1930.

McLaughlin, M. Louise *China Painting: A Practical Manual*, Stewart & Kidd Co., Cincinnati, OH, 1914

Mikami, Tsugoy. *The Art of Japanese Ceramics.* New York: Weatherhill/Tokyo: Heibonsha, 1972.

Monachesi, Nicola di Rienzi. *The Techniques of China Painting,* New York, Van Nostrand Reinhold Co. 1907.

Munsterburg, Hugo & Marjorie. *World Ceramics from Prehistoric to Modern Times.* New York: Penguin Studio Books, 1998.

Nelson, Gladys Burbank. *The Anthology of a Porcelain Artist,* Pasadena, CA, 1981.

Nelson, Glenn C. *Ceramics; A Potter's Handbook,* Holt, Rinehart & Winston, New York, 3rd Edition, 1971.

Norton, Frederick. *Elements of Ceramics,* Addison-Wesley Press, Cambridge, MA, 1952.

Parmelee, Cullen & Harman, Cameron. *Ceramic Glazes,* (3rd Edition), Cahners Books, Boston, 1973.

Patterson, Gene & Wiersema, Ricki. *Porcelain Painting: A Book for the Curious Painter,* Patterson Studio, Ft. Worth, TX, 2004.

Perkins, Walter W. Editor. *Ceramic Glossary 1984,* The American Ceramic Society, Westerville, OH, 1984.

Peterson, Susan. *Shoji Hamada: A Potter's Way,* 3rd Edition, The American Ceramic Society and A&C Black, Columbus, OH/London, 2004.

Riley, Noël. *A History of Decorative Tiles,* Grange Books, Kent, 1987

Rossol, Monona. *Ceramic Ware Hazards,* Arts, Crafts & Theater Safety, Inc., New York, 1993.

Rossol, Monona. *Keeping Clay Work Safe & Legal,* 2nd Edition, National Council on Education for the Ceramic Arts, Bandon, OR, 1996.

Scott, Paul. *Ceramics & Print,* A&C Black, London/UPenn Press, Philadelphia, 1994.

Shaw, Kenneth. *Ceramic Colours & Pottery Decoration,* MacLaren & Sons Ltd. London, 1962.

Shiritsu, Osaka & Bijutsukan, Toyo Toji. *Masterpieces of Oriental Ceramics.* Museum of Oriental Ceramics, Osaka: Nissha Printing Co., 1999.

Southwell, Sheila, *Painting China & Porcelain,* David & Charles, Newton Abbot, Devon, UK, 1995.

Tailor, Heather. *Easy Onglaze Techniques for China Painters & Potters,* Kangaroo Press, Kenthurst, NSW, Australia, 1992.

Taylor, Doris W. & Hart, Anne Button. *China Painting Step by Step,* D. Van Nostrand Co. Inc. Princeton, NJ, 1962.

Vandiver, P. B. & Bouquillon-Mossman, Anne & Scott, Rosemary & Kerr, Rose. "The Technology of Early Chinese Overglaze Enamels from the Chinese Imperial and Popular Kilns," *Techne,* Vol. 6, Winter 1997, pp. 25-34.

Wood, Nigel. *Chinese Glazes,* A&C Black, London/UPenn Press, Philadelphia, 1999.

Zakin, Richard. *Electric Kiln Ceramics,* 3rd Edition, Krause Publications, Iola, WI, 2004

Resources

Suppliers

Willoughby's Colors & Supplies
PO Box 574
Shingle Springs, CA 95682
Phone or Fax: 530-677-1071

Rynne China Co.
222 W. 8 Mile Rd.
Hazel Park, MI 48030
Phone: 800-468-1987,
248-542-9400
Fax: 248-542-0047
www.rynnechina.com

Ann Cline Studio Inc.
1318 Workman Ave.
West Covina, CA 91790
Phone: 626-339-0555
Fax: 626-339-6676
www.anncline.com

Jayne Houston Products
1708 E. Lincoln Ave. Ste. #6
Ft. Collins, CO 80524
Phone: 970-490-6175,
877-349-3768
Fax: 970-490-8950
www.jaynehoustonproducts.com

Reusche & Company
1299 H Street
Greeley, CO 80631
Phone: 970-346-8577
www.reuscheco.com

Seeley's China Paint
118 Commerce Road
Oneonta, NY 13820
Phone: 800-433-1191
www.seeleys.com

Andreas Knobl Porcelain Paints
Gilgenhöfe 5
D-83661 Lenggries, Germany
Phone: (+49) 08042 / 501565
Fax: (+49) 08042 / 501979
www.andreasknobl.de

The House of China
PO Box 6835
Louisville, KY 40602
Phone: 502-491-4628
Fax: 502-491-9688

**American Art Clay Co. Inc.
(AMACO)**
6060 Guion Road
Indianapolis, IN 46254
Phone: 800-374-1600
Fax: 317-248-9300
www.amaco.com

Standard Ceramic Supply Co.
PO Box 4435
Pittsburgh, PA 15205
Phone: 412-276-6333
Fax: 412-276-7124
www.standardceramic.com

Scharff Brushes, Inc.
PO Box 746
Fayetteville, GA 30214
Phone: 888-724-2733,
770-461-2200
Fax: 770-461-2472
www.artbrush.com

Kathy Peterson's "The Good Stuff"
4919 E. 38th Ave.
Denver, CO 80207
Phone: 303-377-0762,
888-590-6628
Fax: 303-377-0954, 800-377-6009
www.thegoodstuff.com

Maryland China Company
54 Main St.
Reisterstown, MD 21136
Phone: 888-632-4462
Fax: 410-833-1851
www.marylandchina.com

Dallas China
8428 Highway 121 N
Melissa, TX, 75454
Phone: 972-837-2600
Fax: 972-837-4104
www.mrandmrsofdallas.com

Westfield House China
British Porcelain Artist
Westfield House, North Avenue
Wakefield, West Yorkshire, WF1
3RX, England
www.westfieldhouse.co.uk

Brittains Tullis Russel, Inc.
55 Walls Drive
Fairfield, CT 06824
Phone: 203-256-9522
Fax: 203-256-8306
www.tullis-russell.co.uk/brittains
Decal supplies

Wise Screenprint, Inc.
1011 Valley St.
Dayton, OH 45404
Phone: 888-660-9473
Fax: 937-223-1115
www.wisescreenprint.com
Decals and supplies

**Seattle Pottery Supply/
Crucible Kilns**
35 South Hanford St.
Seattle, WA 98134
Phone: 800-522-1975
Fax: 888-587-0373
www.seattlepotterysupply.com
Kilns, clay, supplies

Paragon Kilns
2011 South Town East Blvd.
Mesquite, TX 75149
Phone: 800-876-4328
Fax: 888-222-6450
www.paragonweb.com

L&L Kilns
PO Box 1898, 8 Creek Parkway
Boothwyn, PA 19061
Phone: 877-468-5456
Fax: 610-485-4665
www.hotkilns.com

Jen-Ken Kilns
3615 Ventura Drive West
Lakeland, FL 33811
Phone: 863-648-0585
Fax: 863-701-9867
www.jenkenkilns.com

Freddi's China Closet
3573 Hayden Ave.
Culver City, CA 90232
Phone: 310-836-2660
Fax: 310-836-3421

Royal Brush Manufacturing
6707 Broadway
Merrillville, IN 46410
Phone: 219-660-4170
www.royalbrush.com

**Royal Brush
Manufacturing (U.K.) LTD.**
Block 3 Unit 3
Wednesbury Trading Estate
Bilston Road, Wednesbury,
West Midlands WS10 7JN

Skutt Ceramic Products
6441 S.E. Johnson Creek Blvd.
Portland, OR 97206
Phone: 503-774-6000
Fax: 503-774-7833 kilns
www.skutt.com

Magazines, Mailing Lists & Organizations

Porcelain Painters International Online
www.porcelainpainters.com or
www.ppio.com

The China Decorator
PO Box 575
Shingle Springs, CA 95682
Phone: 530-677-1455
Fax: 530-677-1408

**World Organization of China Painters
The China Painter & WOCP Museum**
2641 NW 10th
Oklahoma City, OK 73107
Phone: 405-521-1234
Fax: 405-521-1265
www.theshop.net/wocporg

**International Porcelain Artists &
Teachers, Inc.**
Porcelain Artist & IPAT Museum
PO Box 1807, 204 E. Franklin St.
Grapevine, TX 76099
Phone: 817-421-7643
Fax: 817-421-7643
www.ipat.org

Australian Porcelain Decorator
PO Box 156
Walkerville, 5081, South Australia
www.porcelaindecorator.com.au

Backachers Books
PO Box 402
Osyka, MS 39657
Phone: 601-542-3548
Fax: 601-542-3269
www.ppio.com/backachers.htm

Index

CHINA PAINT & OVERGLAZE

CHINA PAINT & OVERGLAZE